Advance Praise for
Still Standing...

"This is the life story of a street kid who turned the hard times into funny monologues on national television and stages across the country. Whether onstage or just sitting around with him after a round of golf, he never fails to make me laugh. I guarantee you will too."

—CLINT EASTWOOD

"Tom Dreesen is one of the greats. His entertaining and moving new book will take you on an amazing journey from his youth on the South Side of Chicago, through his days in the military, and on into his remarkable career in show business, including his teaming with Tim Reid to become America's first black and white comedy team, and his fourteen years touring the nation with the 'Chairman of the Board,' Frank Sinatra. He is a great American patriot and friend who has entertained our troops around the world. I know you are going to love this book!"

—GARY SINISE

STILL STANDING...

MY JOURNEY FROM STREETS AND SALOONS TO THE STAGE, AND

Sinatra

TOM DREESEN

WITH DARREN GRUBB & JOHNNY RUSSO

Post Hill
PRESS

A POST HILL PRESS BOOK

Still Standing…
My Journey from Streets and Saloons to the Stage, and Sinatra
© 2020 by Tom Dreesen
All Rights Reserved

ISBN: 978-1-64293-360-4
ISBN (eBook): 978-1-64293-362-8

Cover design by Cody Corcoran
Interior design and composition by Greg Johnson, Textbook Perfect

This is a work of nonfiction. All people, locations, events, and situations are portrayed to the best of the author's memory.

Post Hill Press
New York • Nashville
posthillpress.com

Published in the United States of America

Foreword

Tom Dreesen is not my oldest friend, but he may be my best. I met him in 1975 in the driveway at The Comedy Store on Sunset Boulevard. I had just arrived from Indiana. I came to Los Angeles to become famous and wealthy. I soon learned there was a very long line of men and women in Los Angeles for the same reason. One was Tom. He was the first comic I got to know at The Comedy Store. It was like meeting the president of the Chamber of Commerce. He introduced himself, asked where I was from (Indiana), and then began talking about himself and, as of this printing, has not stopped.

Tom really is Mr. Show Business. He has worked with Sammy Davis Jr., Frank Sinatra, Elvis Presley, Johnny Carson, Madonna, Barbra Streisand, Drake, Justin Bieber, Jesus, Kim Kardashian, Frankie Avalon, Cardi B, Janet Jackson, Lady Gaga, and others. He has entertained every president from Trump to Oprah. Tom is not only a great entertainer but a true humanitarian. Fifty years ago, Tom launched *FFMAWWCST* (Foundation for Men and Women Who Can't Stop Talking). Ask anyone touched by Tom's foundation (if you can get a word in) and they'll tell you he's changed their lives.

Tom lives to love and loves to live. I don't know what that means. But Tom has always been my friend. I stole his car. I set fire to his house. I pissed away his kids' college fund on keno and prostitutes. After he finished the Death Valley one hundred-mile run, I drank his last Gatorade. And still, with all this and more, we are friends.

For thirty years, I hosted a mildly successful late-night talk show and Tom was graciously a guest dozens of times, always well groomed, personable, and eager to perform. As we have grown older, Tom and I are still best friends, and of course, he is still talking. And oh, the stories! I haven't read it yet. I'm sure I will, maybe this summer. You, however, should read this book immediately, and tell your friends. Like me, you will love Tom."

—*David Letterman*

Introduction

Riverbend Music Center, Cincinnati, Ohio
September 7, 1986

The evening was getting late. Frank Sinatra was into his closing number, "New York, New York," and the crowd was going wild. It was a vintage Sinatra performance, full of verve, swagger, and showmanship, and Frank was really swinging that night.

The Riverbend Center was one of those outdoor arenas with a roof above the audience, but with all the sides open. Because it was a warm and humid night, Frank's voice was in top form. He once explained to me that on these kinds of nights, his throat (or "reed," in his words) responded better. "Yah, da humidity loosens up my troat muscles," he would laughingly say in his best New Jersey tough-guy accent.

In all the years I toured as an opening act with world-class entertainers—Sammy Davis Jr., Natalie Cole, Smokey Robinson, Frankie Avalon, Gladys Knight & The Pips, Tony Orlando and Dawn, and Liza Minnelli, to name a few—one of my favorite things to do was to watch the headliner perform during the closing number. I always wanted to see how the audience reacted in the crescendo of the evening before rendering a final judgment on the show.

On this night in Cincinnati, Frank warbled that final note on "New York, New York" and held it for what seemed like an eternity. The audience jumped to its feet, honoring him with a resounding, almost deafening roar. The orchestra continued to play while Frank took a brief bow and headed toward the wings. I was standing there, waiting for him as I always did.

His legendary blue eyes flashed in my direction after scanning the crowd as he walked off the stage. As he approached, he gave me a satisfied half-smile and simply said, "Let's go, Tommy."

Frank breezed right past me into the well-lit caverns of the arena toward the waiting limousine, with me a few steps behind. We jumped in, and the limo immediately began to move, climbing a ramp and emerging onto a street that was blocked off from pedestrian traffic. Seconds later, we were joined by a police escort of squad cars and motorcycles, lights flashing, as we sped to the airport, through the gates, and onto the private tarmac. Frank's idling private jet was waiting for us, all revved up and ready to go the moment he stepped aboard, which was always the custom.

Within a span of maybe seven minutes since Frank clipped the vibrato of his final note onstage, we were airborne, flying high over the arena where we had just performed. Most people in the audience had not even reached their cars in the parking lot. Next stop: Chicago, my hometown.

I had been traveling as Frank Sinatra's opening act since April 1983. No matter how many times we made these incredible exits, I never got over how quickly we vanished from the scene and headed for the next destination. But this night was special. For some reason, this night, I realized the extent of my good fortune: I was on tour and performing with the one and only Francis Albert Sinatra. There had to be thousands of entertainers who would kill for this opportunity—and here I was, the one guy who had overcome perhaps the longest odds, sitting aboard Sinatra's private jet as we climbed north into the late-summer night.

As the plane leveled off for the short hop to Chicago, Frank unbuckled his seat belt nonchalantly. "Great show tonight, Tommy. I heard some of your new material from backstage. Good stuff."

"Thanks, Boss. That means a lot," I replied.

He then began talking about Chicago and how much he enjoyed going there during his long career. You can hear that enthusiasm any time you hear "My Kind of Town" or "Chicago," the classic standards celebrating the city that was beginning to appear over the dark horizon.

Frank and "that toddlin' town" were certainly kindred, metaphoric spirits, meant to coexist with one another—both vibrant, full of life, and always teeming with adventure and controlled, happy chaos. Frank's eyes sparkled as he imagined out loud how much fun we were going to have. The city of Chicago had recently spent eight million dollars to renovate the old Chicago Theatre, and we were going to be the first performers to inaugurate the new digs. "We'll knock 'em dead, Tommy," he said.

At that moment, the strangest thing happened. My head began to spin and a lump rose in my throat. Appearing around the country with this living legend and enjoying all the wonderful perks of that life had not really hit me. This night, I got knocked square in the jaw.

Frank continued talking in his big, boisterous way, but I was barely listening. All I could think was, "Oh my God. I'm in Frank Sinatra's jet. We're flying to my hometown. My name is going to be in lights on the marquee of the Chicago Theatre with the 'Chairman of the Board.'"

My mind flashed back to my years in taverns on the South Side of Chicago after working as a laborer on construction sites. Frank's voice percolated out of the jukebox for a mere nickel, singing songs like "Come Fly with Me." Now, here I was, flying with him in the most literal sense, and he's telling me how we're gonna knock 'em dead in Chicago.

I looked out the window of the plane and locked my gaze on the rising moon in the night sky. Tears began to form in my eyes. I bit the inside of my cheek to keep the moisture at bay and attempted to focus on his words. I'm glad Frank kept talking, because I would have blubbered had I tried to speak.

I go back a long way with Frank Sinatra and jukeboxes. The first time I remember hearing his voice was as a young boy in those same taverns in the blue-collar neighborhood of Harvey, Illinois. If America is indeed a melting pot of cultures and backgrounds, then Harvey represented the stew inside. The town was a wonderful mix of people from all races and creeds, churches of all denominations, and patrons of all taverns. Man alive, did we have taverns. Thirty-six in all—serving a population of about thirty thousand.

When I was in second grade, I started shining shoes at night in all the saloons around the factories that dotted my neighborhood. At that time, as it seems to be now, Frank Sinatra's songs were a staple of the magical music boxes that orchestrated an evening at hand. Whenever one of his songs came on, rising gently over the familiar din of tavern talk, laughter, and the clink of glasses or thud of bottles on the bar, you could almost feel the reverence of the patrons rise too.

Frank's music served as an aspirational anthem for the working class, a soundtrack of the emotions and experiences of what could be in life, even if it wasn't possible in your own. As a kid who'd made good from the similar streets of Hoboken, New Jersey, Frank had earned the praise and respect of his tavern brethren in Harvey, and of those in thousands of saloons across the country.

I am a born and bred product of Harvey. I'm proud of this. No matter where my life takes me, I feel like I've never strayed too far from my old neighborhood. I can close my eyes and, in a heartbeat, summon up the image of a little boy wearing raggedy clothes, hauling a worn wooden shoeshine box from bar to bar in the bitter cold.

That job, along with selling newspapers, setting pins in bowling alleys in the winter, and caddying for golfers in the summer, is how I earned money to help feed my brothers and sisters at home. Those jobs kept me busy and mostly out of trouble, but they also kept me from Little League baseball fields and other childhood activities I would have preferred—although most of my childhood pals didn't have eight kids in the family or two parents who enjoyed alcohol and barhopping and arguing loudly into the wee hours of the morning. That was my childhood, and the funny thing is, I'm not bitter. I am what I am, and I am grateful for what I have.

However, I don't think you can grow up the way I did and completely wash the experience away. If you were ever hungry as a child, really hungry, that feeling in your stomach is never far removed; it defines how you face the world when the world is finally yours to face on your own terms. I'm not championing or making excuses for how others handled similar circumstances. My only point is that every individual can decide to make a better life. Some of us were blessed to finally catch a real break, and looking back, I am aware of my fortune.

I am a big baseball fan, the greatest game America ever invented. Those who know and love baseball will tell you that it's a game of inches. A ball hit one inch this way or that way, or a pitch thrown here rather than there, can be the difference between victory and defeat. I believe life is the same way, but rather than inches, a life can be defined by the metric of a few key moments. There were many days I wasn't sure things would turn out for me at all, but I worked my ass off to make sure I was ready to take advantage of my moments when they appeared.

I've been in show business now for more than fifty years—since September of 1969, when I went onstage for the first time alongside Tim Reid. We were "Tim and Tom," America's first black and white comedy team. Sadly, we turned out to be the last. My career has taken me many places and afforded me the opportunity to perform on the same bill as some of the greatest performers this world has ever known. But nothing could compare to my time performing with Frank Sinatra.

By the time our jet landed, Riverbend Music Center seemed like it was a million miles behind us. The wistful narrator in my head perhaps made it feel that way. This I know for sure: I was glad to be back home and on the other side of the mountain, and I finally acknowledged how deeply fortunate I was at that moment in my life.

Sinatra and I went on to enjoy a very successful week at the Chicago Theatre. I continued to travel with Frank for thirteen years, doing as many as fifty cities a year from coast to coast, including all the great venues in gambling towns like Las Vegas, Atlantic City, Reno, and Lake Tahoe. While New York City may be known as the "city that never sleeps," these towns get maybe a few hours of shut-eye a night, and I've got vivid memories of each place.

The feeling of pride and nostalgia that overwhelmed me that night as we flew to Chicago never happened to me again. I can't explain why it happened at all, but it's a moment I'll never forget. Life is funny—and cruel. My life has brought me to tears, in equal parts sorrow and joy. I'm a composite figure of the happy and sad times I've experienced over the years, and I'm better for having gone through it all.

I'd like to share some of those moments with you now.

1

I never gave it much thought that we didn't have a car. The Dreesen kids, eight of us in all, were accustomed to walking everywhere in our hometown of Harvey, Illinois, a small suburb on the South Side of Chicago.

It was Thursday, October 28, 1948. I had just turned nine years old, and the town was abuzz with excitement. People lined the streets and spoke among themselves with delight as they looked intently up the road. In the distance, car horns began to honk repeatedly, signaling the advent of...something.

Then the cars appeared, all in a line, a motorcade moving slowly, parade-style, up 154th Street. The procession grew closer, and a handsome young man came into sight, sitting in the back seat of a fancy red convertible, waving to the throngs of people who had gathered to see him. The motorcade turned south on Center Avenue and headed toward the Elks Club on 155th Street.

I watched the scene unfold from a street corner where I was selling copies of the *Harvey Tribune*, our local newspaper. "Hey, what's going on?" I asked a man who had just traded me a nickel for a newspaper.

"It's Lou Boudreau Day!" the man answered, looking at me as if I should know. "He's a famous ballplayer from Harvey who plays shortstop for the Cleveland Indians and also manages the team. They just won the World Series, for Chrissake!"

"WOW!" I said as the man walked away, newspaper tucked under his arm while giving me one last bewildered look. I didn't know who Lou Boudreau was, but I felt a burst of euphoria that made me want to be part of this. I sold as many papers as I could before the excitement of the festivities overtook me and I began to follow the trailing throng. I reached the Elks Club just as a luncheon of local dignitaries honoring Lou Boudreau was finishing. Boudreau was standing on the front steps of the club, saying a few words to the admiring crowd.

I watched in awe as people cheered for our hometown hero. He received thunderous applause at the conclusion of his speech and then got into his waiting convertible for the ride to the football field at Thornton Township High School, Boudreau's alma mater, where he and other celebrities would gather for a brief ceremony.

The procession of cars roared to life once more and followed the convertible. The sound of blaring car horns again filled the air, adding to the sense of jubilation. I began to follow the procession on foot, but soon the line of cars moved out of sight. As I hurried my pace and my breath quickened, I thought to myself, "Gee, if Dad had a car, we could ride together and blow the horn like everyone else." My next thought disabused me of that notion. The Dreesens didn't have enough money for a car, and even if we did, it was probably safer for everyone that Dad didn't drive, since he often drank a lot.

After another long walk, I arrived at the high school to see that the ceremony was over. Everyone seemed to be gone, except for one lady who was surrounded by little children waiting for her autograph. Her name was Fran Allison, a television star on a show called *Kukla, Fran and Ollie*. I didn't know anything about her or the TV show. We had no money for a television set either, but that didn't stop me from wanting her autograph. What the hell, I had just walked all that way trying to find Mr. Lou Boudreau. I might as well say hello to Ms. Fran Allison, whoever she was.

I took my place behind a line of kids who had notebooks and little cards for her to sign. I didn't have anything, so I picked up a discarded ice cream wrapper from the ground as I got to the front.

"You want me to sign this?" she said, not sounding flattered.

"Yes, ma'am, please."

"Do you have something to write with?"

I didn't. She looked around and borrowed a pencil from another child standing nearby.

"Here you go, sweetie," she said, handing back the ice cream wrapper with her signature scrawled across it—the first autograph I had ever received.

As I walked home, I kept thinking about what I had witnessed that day. I thought about how excited everyone was that someone from Harvey was famous. I thought about how famous Lou Boudreau must be to have such a special day planned in his honor. And as little boys often do, I began to daydream about a scene where I was driven down the main street of Harvey, waving at a crowd who had come out to cheer for me.

It certainly didn't seem likely to happen—but what good is a boy without his dreams to keep him occupied?

2

Harvey, Illinois, was founded in 1891 as a "temperance town," the manifestation of a social movement that shunned the consumption of alcohol—a groundswell force of Puritanism that helped usher in the Prohibition Era in the United States. Harvey became a municipal laboratory of sorts, although I'm not sure the lesson of the experiment resonated or took hold among the citizenry, and certainly not after the end of Prohibition.

It was 1943, the height of World War II, and I was nearly four years old. If I reach deep into the furthest corners of my mind, I can still see clearly our apartment on 147th Street. The front room overlooked a tavern across the street—a view that quickly gave way to the sight of the railroad line behind the tavern that separated the neighborhood from the steel mill, which was situated just beyond the tracks. The mill was called Ingalls-Shepard, and most of the neighborhood men worked there during one of three shifts, doing their part to help equip the military boys halfway across the world in the Pacific theater.

Off the front room was the bedroom where Mom and Dad slept, then a small living room in the center of the apartment. We had a small kitchen, with a bedroom off to the side that I shared with my older sister, Darlene, and our older brother, Glenn. I was the third of eight eventual kids.

Our apartment was located directly above Polizzi's Tavern, which was owned by my Uncle Frank and Aunt Marge, my mother's sister. Situated directly behind the bar was a small apartment where they lived and raised their two sons.

I remember many nights being in my bedroom and hearing the music coming from the tavern's jukebox during the lulls between passing trains. My mom sometimes helped Uncle Frank by tending bar late into the night. Occasionally, the sound of her voice would waft into my consciousness, rising above the clinking of mugs and mumble of drunken voices. I remember hearing her sing along with the jukebox, or in a spontaneous duet with Uncle Frank to harmonize on "Galway Bay" or another Irish dirge—a vocal skill she later taught me and my siblings.

I recall other sounds too, like the loud, bass-like thumps coming from the hammer shop down the street, which pounded through the night to manufacture crankshafts destined for military vehicles around the world. In between that rhythmic beating of hot, sparking metal, I heard the screaming sounds of the Grand Trunk Railway, where locomotives would whoosh through once an hour at high speeds, punctuated by the creaky whine of the intersection gates moving up and down in sync with the symphony of flashing red lights and clanging signal bells. These sounds of the night, familiar to us since birth, simply served as soothing white noise, the native backdrop to our subconscious. Somehow, we slept through it all.

My mother was born Glenore Algoe in Pontiac, Illinois, the youngest daughter of Irish Catholic parents who emigrated to New York's harbor in the 1870s. Pontiac was a small town on the banks of the Vermilion River, a meager dot of human activity otherwise surrounded by farmland. In addition to fertile soil, the town was known for its proximity to the Pontiac Correctional Center, a gated community for many who didn't find honest farming to be an interesting enough pursuit.

Mom had three older sisters: Marge, Gladys, and Mabel. They all lived under the shadow of their brother, Joe, who was tragically killed in a car accident when my mom was a young girl. When Marge moved from Pontiac to Harvey, Illinois, and married Frank Polizzi, my grandmother went to live with them and brought along my mom, who was eleven at the time. Mom attended Ascension Catholic School, which I would one day attend myself.

As was typical in those days, when my Mom turned sixteen, she joined the workforce and took a job at the Chicago Stove Works factory in Harvey, which made stoves and other household appliances. Mom was very close to her sister Marge and, by extension, her husband, Frank. In fact, it was Frank who was responsible for introducing Mom to the man she would marry.

Walter Dreesen's parents emigrated from Germany and set down roots in Riverdale, Illinois, a small town next to Harvey. He was also the baby of his family, with an older sister and brother. Dad was musically inclined and learned how to play the trumpet at an early age, a skill he excelled at enough to land him first chair at Thornton Township High School. After graduation, he took off for a life in vaudeville, playing the trumpet and performing around the country before returning to Riverdale when he was in his early thirties.

Frank Polizzi was also a musician, fronting a band called The Venetianaires. Frank was looking for additional members to join his band and drove to Riverdale to scout a young trumpet player he'd heard about who had just returned from the vaudeville circuit. He found young Walter Dreesen playing pinochle in the back of a tavern and recruited him to become a Venetianaire. Walter told him that he was planning to return soon to New York City but agreed to play a few gigs until then. Later that night, Frank introduced Walter to several friends and family members, including his sister-in-law, Glenore.

Dad joined the band and quickly began a relationship with Glenore, which soon led to them getting married and her becoming pregnant, although the exact chronology is a matter of debate. Walter Dreesen never returned to New York City or vaudeville after that chance encounter. Instead, he set off to build a life in Harvey.

STILL STANDING...

* * *

We didn't have a lot growing up, but Mom and Dad both had steady jobs to help make ends meet. Dad spent his days in Blue Island, another town close to Harvey, working at a factory called Libby, McNeil and Libby that made canned goods. Mom worked nights in Polizzi's Tavern. I'd jostle awake in my bed sometime when I heard her come through the front door in the middle of the night, after closing out the register and cleaning the bar. Since Mom worked nights, it meant that I had her all to myself during the day while the older kids were in school, even though she would often take long afternoon naps.

It's hard to believe how much freedom kids had in those days, but I certainly had a lot of latitude in my comings and goings. Even at a tender age, I would wander out in front of the apartment and play on the sidewalk and talk to everyone passing by, or walk around the neighborhood and talk to the woman named Marie, who owned a little grocery store, or visit with Leo, who owned the hardware store.

Sparrow's Tavern was on the corner, owned by Mr. and Mrs. Sparrow, as we called them (their actual surname was Wroblewski). I would often mosey into Sparrow's and talk to Virgil, the bartender, and any customers drinking during the day shift.

Little did I know that one day I would be a bartender in that same tavern after I returned from serving in the Navy. If little kids had come in during the middle of the day and talked to me, I would have silently wondered, "Don't these kids have parents?" But in my day, it was commonplace.

When I think back on those very early years and the adults in my world, they all had a couple of things in common—mainly alcohol and cigarettes, which they enjoyed to excess. There were thirty-six taverns in the town of Harvey back then, including six within two blocks of our apartment. Rarely were any of them empty, no matter the hour.

Harvey provided a classic midwestern American backdrop, where hard work fell in love with hard living. It was common for men to get off work at the factories and immediately head for one of those more inviting establishments to blow off some steam over a few beers or shots before going home for dinner. It was also not uncommon for some of those fellas to have a shot and beer before they went to work.

To some, taverns were as important to Harvey's community fabric as churches, and each had its tribe of loyal followers. Children were always welcome inside the taverns, especially on "fish fry" Friday nights for the Catholics who didn't eat meat that day. Protestants and Jews were always welcome to join, and many did.

Our parents would stroll into the tavern, children in tow, and seat us all at a table in the back. They'd order sodas for us kids while they went and sat at the bar to drink, occasionally looking over to make sure we were all still on the premises and not misbehaving too much.

In those days, foul language was never permitted in the taverns and considered highly inappropriate and disrespectful—especially when women or children were in the place. If some guy swore while telling a story or a joke, or after stubbing his toe on the jukebox, the other patrons or the owner would quickly reprimand him for the infraction. And if the off-color language continued, he was quickly thrown out, often physically, and sometimes banned entirely.

There were tavern bowling leagues in the winter and softball leagues in the summer. After the games, everyone went back to the tavern to verbally replay their athletic exploits over drinks and smokes. Some of them stayed for a drink or two and then headed home, while others stuck around until the place closed at 2:00 a.m.

Every fall, there was a big community picnic where all the taverns set up booths serving hot dogs and hamburgers, and, of course, beer, with tables nearby where families could sit and eat and mingle with other families and stragglers. The organizers set up an area with games for the children to play, with prizes for the winners. The adults played horseshoes and gambled on the outcome, and no matter who won or lost, they celebrated or brooded by drinking.

Tavern owners in Harvey were unquestionably the celebrities of the neighborhood because their names were on the signs outside. When you went inside a place, more likely than not the owners were behind the bar, holding court and regaling customers with stories and jokes for hours on end, as if on a stage.

Most people in those days would tell you that the reason they frequented one bar rather than another was because they felt a connection to the owner or the bartender. Alcohol is alcohol after all, and in Harvey, it flowed fast and freely. Often it was the name on the sign outside the tavern that drew patrons in to see the personality behind the bar.

There was no one in Harvey more accomplished in the art of alcohol-anchored entertainment than Uncle Frank. My earliest childhood memories are of going into that tavern and seeing him behind the bar. I admired him greatly, and looking back, it was my first exposure to the life of a performance artist—someone whose entire existence was to entertain a captive audience.

I loved watching him at his best, behind the bar—his bar—telling jokes and laughing along with the patrons. It meant something to him, a responsibility to honor those who chose his bar over the dozens of others in the vicinity. Sometimes when the mood struck him right, he'd begin to sing songs—or pull out his saxophone from behind the bar and play between slinging drinks or making wisecracks. The customers always enjoyed the spontaneous performances. Lord knows they were searching for something to take their minds off their crummy jobs or bad luck or lousy situations in life. Uncle Frank supplied the tonic and balm, providing them with a personal, if temporary, vacation close to home. The next night, they'd likely be back for more.

I always felt a sense of warmth and comfort to know Uncle Frank was so close, just beneath our apartment, perpetually holding court. He was truly my favorite uncle. I had a strong affection for him, and he reciprocated by doing nice little things for me, like slipping me a quarter when no one was looking. For my fifth birthday, he bought me a brand-new cowboy outfit. It was a classic western costume, replete with a vest and chaps and a belt that holstered a toy six-shooter, which I loved.

My older brother, Glenn, was eight and a little jealous; he didn't understand why Uncle Frank had gone out of his way for me. But Uncle Frank downplayed it, saying that he saw the outfit on sale in a store and just had to get it for me, little Tommy.

When tavern owners wandered outside their establishments during daytime hours, they were often recognized and treated as stars, like when elementary students spot a favorite teacher doing normal, everyday things outside of school. Everyone knew who they were and identified them with proper reverence: "Look, it's Al!" (Al's Corner Club); "Hey, there goes Ed!" (Ed's Curve Inn); "Wait, is that Fuzzy?" (Fuzzy's Tap). "Hiya, Mrs. Sparrow." (Sparrow's Tavern).

We even had a bar called Johnny's Gay Club. Back in those days, the word "gay" was universally recognized as a synonym for "happy." And Johnny was happy—how could he not be? After all, he owned his own tavern with his name on the sign outside, which made him a resident celebrity.

In my case, the sightings were even more personal. "Hiya, Uncle Frank!" I'd say, when I saw my mom's brother-in-law on the street. He would wave or come over and give me a hug, his celebrity passing to me through an anointing embrace. Uncle Frank was so popular that he decided to run for elected office several times. He never won, but his prominence in the community never diminished. He continued his own brand of public service in a full room of constituents every night.

I always felt an affinity when I was around Uncle Frank and his family. Aunt Margie, my mom's oldest sister, had jet-black hair and kind eyes. A lady if there ever was one, she was well mannered, well groomed, soft spoken, and eternally kind. I never heard her raise her voice, except when she was singing in church. She was a true

Catholic, attending church every Sunday and Benediction on Tuesdays. She adored Uncle Frank and took pride in raising their sons, Don and Richard, who was better known as "Buzz."

She'd often whisper to me as an aside, "Tommy, you know that you're my favorite nephew," and I'd reciprocate by assuring her she was my favorite aunt, which she was. I was also real close to my cousins, Buzz especially. He was five years older than I and taught me a lot about living, including how to impress girls. For Buzz, this came naturally. He was an extremely handsome guy, and one day, as we were walking on the street, a girl was eyeballing him so intently that she walked straight into a parking meter.

When he was in eighth grade and I was in third, Buzz taught altar boys how to serve Mass by taking the "priest part," which meant that he played the role of the priest and showed us what to do as we practiced the protocols of a Mass ceremony. He was a very intelligent guy who later became bipolar and experienced a lot of tragedy in life.

The Dreesens and Polizzis functioned as one big family. For years, we lived in such proximity that it felt like we were all brothers and sisters, and in many ways, we were. The Dreesen siblings, however, were connected in a more intangible way.

As glib and joyous as tavern life seemed, there was a distinctive underside, which I learned firsthand from the lifelong habits of my dad. When the whistle blew and his workday was done, his evenings began and often lasted well into the following day.

Dad never drank wine or whiskey, only beer, and Lord knows, he could put it away. No one was ever considered an alcoholic when I was growing up. Although Dad was unquestionably an alcoholic, most people would say, "Nah, he only drinks beer," as if there were no alcohol in beer. Mom would never call him or anyone else an alcoholic. To pacify us after some fatherly transgression, whether it was missing a ball game or forgetting a birthday, she was quick to say, with a forced smile on her face, "Well, you know, your father likes his beer." She'd leave it at that, and we learned to as well.

At some point, I realized that, while he certainly liked his beer, he also liked your beer, and the neighbors' beer. I often joked that Daddy would rather hear that he had six months to live than to hear that we were out of Schlitz. Everyone gave his alcoholism a pass, employing a convenience of choice to look the other way. For my mom and his family at home, it was impossible to miss the ramifications of his own national pastime.

3

There are two days that I remember most growing up. The first is August 20, 1944, the day my sister Judi was born. My venerated distinction as the baby of the family was taken away in one fell swoop by this tiny little intruder. Years later, I read that when you're no longer the baby of the family, you become resentful, envious, and sometimes downright mean to the sibling who dethroned you. I was shocked to read that, because I adored that cute little girl. I love her even more today.

My brother Glenn was three years older than I, with blond hair and blue eyes. He was a bigger guy, but quiet and reserved until provoked. Glenn would pick on me like all big brothers do, but he wouldn't let anyone else do so. Everyone knew that to mess with me was to mess with Glenn, and that wasn't a good idea.

Darlene was eighteen months older than I. She had a real Irish beauty about her—mahogany hair, crystal blue eyes, and freckles, a feature that she resented but that also defined her. Like Glenn, she was quiet by nature and possessed a strong instinct to care for her family, especially me. I can't remember a day when she wasn't holding my hand to cross the street, lifting my spirits when I was down, or just making sure I knew how much she loved me. She was my second mother in every regard for her entire life.

The other day that I recall is September 2, 1945, which was just nine days before my sixth birthday. I was playing on the sidewalk when the steel mills' hammers suddenly stopped and the shift signal whistles began to blow loudly, again and again. Cars horns were blaring, and people were rushing out from the factories and into streets before streaming into the bars. They were hugging one another, laughing and crying and shouting, "The war is over! The war is over!"

I was playing with friends in the street when this abnormal commotion began. Confused, I quickly ran upstairs to tell my mom and dad. They excitedly shared the significance of the moment, and Dad immediately pulled a quart of beer out of a bag, ready to take part in this worldwide celebration. I ran back down the stairs and stood out in front of the tavern, waiting patiently to see the soldiers I was so sure were going to march over the railroad tracks at any moment.

I waited until dark, when Mom finally called me to come back upstairs. The soldiers didn't come home that night, but they slowly came home in the weeks that followed, one at a time, from all branches of the service. Harvey was well represented by young individuals serving in our armed forces, and as was the case for so many other towns across America, many hometown boys did not return home.

Those who did return home soon populated all the taverns in Harvey. The two things they had in common were that they liked drinking, and none of them liked talking about their exploits. They would acknowledge each other with a firm nod of the head or a knowing glance, quietly honoring the fact they had shared experiences witnessing the ugliest of humanity before turning their attention back to the drink in front of them.

Times were lean and things weren't always pleasant for my family, yet I still have fond, romanticized memories of that neighborhood. I remember being sad when we moved from our apartment above Polizzi's Tavern at the end of my second-grade year to a place about a mile and a half away.

Our new address was 15040 Vail Avenue, a small house that my parents rented. It was smaller than our old place, and there were no taverns in sight. After one day in the new place, I became wide-eyed with wonder and inquisitiveness because most of our neighbors were "colored." Much like the term "gay," this is another word imbued with a definition that has evolved over time—in fact, it seems so strange and inappropriate to even type that word, but that was considered proper terminology in those days.

My new surroundings placed me squarely in a world that was both white and black, and I didn't distinguish any difference. The day after we moved in, I began to wander around, exploring the new neighborhood, and happened upon a place that would change my life.

I was walking along 151st Street when I looked to my right and saw that there was a little nine-hole public golf course called the Dixie Hi. I was passing what I later learned was the fourth hole, and to my left stood five black boys who were all a little older than me. They were on the street, staring at a tee box about two hundred yards away where a foursome of golfers was teeing off. I have never really been shy, and curious to know what the object of their interest was, I walked right up to them and said, "Hey, what are you guys doing?"

They all kept their eyes on the tee, but one of them glanced my way and said out of the side of his mouth, "We're ball hawking, man."

"What is ball hawking?" I curiously replied.

The answer came almost immediately when one of the golfers got ahold of his drive shot and hit a ball over the fence and into the field about fifty yards to our left. All five of the boys bolted across the street and into the field and spread out like hawks, looking for prey. It only took maybe twenty seconds for one of them to claim victory and yell, "I got it!"

The other boys walked back slowly, heads a bit hung, as their triumphant buddy came running back toward the fence with the stray ball and yelled out to the approaching player, "Sir, I found your ball!" The player came over to the fence and said thank you and asked if he could have it back. The boy looked him straight in the eye and said, "Fifteen cents." "I'll give you ten cents," the player said, to which the kid agreed and exchanged the ball for the dime in a swift, smooth transaction.

I was immediately hooked by the erratic sport of it all—plus the chance to make a little money doing something as ingenious and entrepreneurial as ball hawking. Competition was fierce. There was always a group of kids assembled along that fence line, mostly regulars but occasionally some other newbies, all waiting for the next round of misfired shots to clear the fence.

There was a certain athleticism required to be any good at the rogue sport of ball hawking—a mix between being an agile center fielder and a lightning-fast track sprinter. First, you had to locate the ball as it was hit off the tee against the backdrop of the sky, keeping an eye on its trajectory as it sailed over the fence for parts unknown. At the same time, you had to already be in a dead sprint toward the spot you calculated the ball would land in the field, battling the waist-high grass along the way with a high step and a swinging of the arms to help clear a path for your feet. And you certainly had to be as fast as or faster than the other guys who were practicing the same techniques. When the ball bounced into the field and you saw it, you swooped in like a hawk to claim your prize, an almost guaranteed winning ticket for which loose change was immediately paid.

There was another way to make money outside of the golf course, and that was to separate from the pack of ball hawks along the fence and walk solo around the perimeter of the course, where golfers might hit a stray ball and never give it a second thought. Some balls were shanked so badly and so far out of bounds and difficult to spot from the sanctuary of the fairway that it wasn't worth the golfer's time to traipse around for five minutes, holding up the game for the other fellas. Thank God for terrible golfers, because finding those balls was like finding dimpled spheres of gold. Once secured and wiped clean with a little spit and a pocket rag, you could then sell the balls back to the players for more money. The general condition and brand of the ball helped to determine the sale price, anywhere from ten cents to a quarter (Spaldings and Titleists fetched more than a "Po-Do," Walgreens' private-label ball for the budget-conscious duffer).

A dime went pretty far in those days, and a successful day of chasing down five or six balls meant that I could walk away at sundown with enough money to bring a smile to my mom's face when I plunked down a handful of change on the kitchen table. "Well look at this," she'd say, taking fifty cents and then handing me back a dime for my efforts. It made me proud that I was able to help our family, even a little bit.

I continued to ball hawk for several years, and I cannot remember a happier time as I scraped together a small income to bring home. The skills I acquired in that noble pursuit also helped me a few years later when I "graduated" to the other side of the fence and became a caddy.

There was one man I caddied for named Leo Sample, who owned a drugstore in Harvey. He was my regular, and whenever he played, he asked for me. It was rare when I could not track down a ball hit by a player for whom I was caddying, and I never lost a ball for Leo all year.

Leo once got ahold of a ball and hit a monster 200-yard line drive. The shot looked beautiful for about three seconds, until the spin began to slice it hard right, straight into the bank of a creek. I saw mud fly up and immediately "marked it" as I went tearing off toward it, only to hear Leo shout, "Leave it alone, son. It's lost." I disobeyed and kept sprinting, making my way along the bank, where I plucked the ball out of the mud and cleaned it off before triumphantly handing it back to him. Leo was stunned. In front of all the other players and caddies, he chortled, "Will you look at this kid? He's a goddamned bird dog!" From that time on, the caddies called me "Bird Dog," which I took as a great compliment. Looking back, it defined what I would have to do to succeed in life.

4

The Dreesens weren't the only white family in the neighborhood. There were several others, and I became friends with some of the white kids my age, but they didn't mingle or play with the black kids like I did. I never understood why, but I did know that I was learning a lot of life lessons from my new friends of a different color.

For one thing, they taught me a game called "mumble the peg" that was played with a pocket-knife. The goal was to complete a course of stunts with the knife, ideally without slicing your digits in the process. At the end of the game, you would take a small branch and whittle it down to a peg, and then each boy would get three whacks on the peg with the heavy end of the knife to pound it into the ground. The loser of the game was supposed to put his face in the ground and dig the peg out with his teeth, bobbing for wood as it were.

That's the way the white boys played the game anyway. The black boys played a little differently. On those rules, whoever lost had to go through a gauntlet of pain called "the paddle machine." The players would spread their legs wide while the loser crawled as fast as possible through those arcs of flesh, leather belt straps cracking the loser hard across the ass the entire way. It took me a while to learn the intricacies of the game, so I often lost a couple of games a day, which was about all I could handle—my ass was sore. But my competitive nature kept me going back for more.

I spent a lot of time scrambling through that paddle machine before I learned to play the game. But I also learned that, like baseball, there was no crying in mumble the peg. You took your whupping, cringed from the pain, and held back the tears however you could. It hurt like hell, but I earned respect because I kept at the game until I became good enough to compete with the best of them, even though I took some beatings along the way.

As often happens when young boys spend a lot of time together in the years when testosterone tends to swirl at a crazy rate, a fight would occasionally break out. When it did, and if it involved you, it was important to stand up to anyone you believed was taking advantage of you. You didn't always have to fight, but if you didn't, you lost the respect of the others. I learned early on that even if you lost but put up a good fight, it earned you some "cred."

There was one boy in the neighborhood that no one messed with. His name was Everett Nicholson, and for whatever reason, his nickname was "Goochie." He was about five years older than I and never spoke directly to any of us boys. He would just quietly walk by all of us and maybe offer an authoritative nod. All the other guys would whisper, "Are you crazy? Don't screw with Goochie. You don't want to be on the wrong side of Goochie."

Goochie was the epitome of "walk softly but carry a big stick." He never started trouble and, in fact, viewed fighting as a means of last resort. When trouble brewed, Goochie used his brawn and presence to try and talk people out of confrontations so they could sort things out civilly. But if you got in his face, all bets were off, because Goochie was an undisputed badass.

Goochie's father was also a man of respect, but in a different way. We called him "Mr. Nicholson," because he had worked hard to earn the respect of everyone in the neighborhood. He was the first black businessman in Harvey and founded a plumbing company called Nicholson Plumbing. Goochie worked for his dad after school and on weekends. One day, Goochie was walking home after work when he really saved my ass—a moment that would become the foundation for a long-lasting friendship.

The biggest problem I had in the fight scene those days was in the form of two brothers, Curtis and Damon. If I got sideways with one brother and we ended up sparring, the other brother would knock me down, so that the first brother could pivot and get on top to pummel me. This was going on when Goochie happened to be walking by and saw Damon and me in a scrap.

After observing the scene for about a minute, Goochie intervened and pulled Damon off me, threw him back into a standing position, and then got right in his face. Speaking with an unmistakable sternness, Goochie looked at the brothers and said, "From now on, if you fight that white boy, you do it one at a time. You hear?"

They heard all right, and it never happened again. Word began to spread around that I was "Goochie's boy." I wasn't under his protection per se, but I sure didn't say anything to dispel that notion, and from that time on, I would strike up a conversation with Goochie every time I saw him. He was always cordial to me, but over time, we began to converse more, and one day, I made him laugh while doing an impression of his younger brother, Leroy.

Goochie and I built a friendship that lasted until his death fifty-five years later. He was a part of my early comedy routines, and I talked about him numerous times on national television and on stages all over America. Years later, when I released my comedy album, *That White Boy's Crazy*, Goochie was in the cover photo. He enjoyed that, and we remained friends to his dying day.

5

My family seemed to get poorer and poorer. Dad continued to drink heavily, and Mom was working off and on as a bartender. There was never enough money, and we were always way behind in the rent. Our landlord was named Mr. Burrell, a kind man who truly seemed to like us and gave my folks as much leeway as possible. He was constantly apologizing to my mom around the middle of every month.

"Mrs. Dreesen, I'm so sorry to bother you, but you still owe the rent from last month, and you're two weeks late on this month," he'd say. Mom would drop her head a little and ramble on about how sorry she was, saying that some unexpected tragedy had happened and assure him it would all get straightened out soon.

In the meantime, it was my little sister Judi's turn to lose her status as the baby of the family after two years; our baby sister was born in the home on a cold and snowy December night in 1946. My parents named her Margie, after my favorite aunt.

Once again, I dropped down a notch in the family hierarchy, but I was not at all unhappy with this because we all adored Margie, just as we had adored Judi before. Darlene and Judi fussed over Margie constantly. Glenn and I were outnumbered now, three girls to us two boys.

21

I always had a great relationship with Glenn and the girls, even when they were just toddlers. Our parents were gone most of the time, either working or drinking, so we quickly learned to look out for one another.

Children of alcoholics bond in a different way. Over time, a silent code began to define the relationship among the Dreesen siblings. Darlene literally helped raise the rest of us. As the oldest girl, she was our proxy mother and took on all the heavy responsibilities: cooking, cleaning, and looking after our general welfare. Glenn served the role of protector for his sibling brood.

I lived up to expectations as a stereotypical middle child and did my part to keep the mood light and irreverent. My mom came down with a serious case of pneumonia one time that landed her in the hospital. When she returned home, she was on bed rest, and I decided to cheer her up. I dressed up in an old coat and fedora hat I found in Dad's closet and accessorized with a pipe and walked into her room, pretending I was Bing Crosby. Doing my best Crosby impersonation, I sang her a song, which caused her to begin laughing hysterically. Encouraged, I swooped out of the room and returned as Bob Hope, singing another little song and cracking one-liners, which again brought on peals of laughter—probably not the quiet rest her doctor had ordered, but it was a fun moment, and I remember feeling glad for my impromptu performance for my audience of one.

I found other ways to make my younger siblings smile and laugh, entertaining them to provide a momentary distraction from the harsh realities of our surroundings. It was my defense mechanism in some way, one small area of my life I could possibly control.

I'd tease them or play little games to pass the time or come up with silly ways to get them in trouble. My dad would be reading the newspaper in our small living room, and he might be half shit-faced or sober, it didn't matter, and I would say, "Here's a little game we're gonna play.... You guys have to copy everything I do, got it?" The girls would smile and nod their heads.

I'd go into the living room first and say, "Hey, Dad, reading the newspaper, eh?" He'd look up and say, "Yeah." And then I'd go in the other room and Judy would have to walk in and do the same thing. "Hey, Dad, reading the paper, huh?" He'd look up and say yes, sensing something. Finally, little Margie would walk in on the third pass and sing, "Hey, Da—"

Dad cut her off, pissed, "Now what in the HELL is going on?"

He was wise to the con—and we were strangely gratified by the attention Dad paid to us, even if it was out of annoyance.

We leaned on each other in good times and bad. The older kids were expected to contribute to the family's financial health. It's not that our dad didn't work hard or love us. Truth be told, he was probably overwhelmed by what was expected of him to adequately provide for a young and growing family. He coped with it all by drinking heavily, which resulted in placing a burden on other able bodies in the family, including Mom, Darlene, Glenn—and me.

Glenn showed us the way to help the family make ends meet. He was a hardworking guy with an entrepreneurial spirit and a keen sense at a young age of the responsibility to care for a family, something our father seemed to be neglecting. He'd buy bottles of pop for five cents, put them in a squeaky-wheeled wagon full of ice and then sell them for ten cents to workers during lunch breaks outside the factories. After school, he had a paper route and would deliver the *Chicago Tribune*, *Chicago Sun-Times*, and *Chicago Herald-American*, back when papers had both morning and afternoon editions.

Glenn instilled the same work ethic in me, and I when I was seven, I joined him in selling newspapers. We'd wake up at 4:30 in the morning and head to the *Harvey Tribune* in the bitter cold to get our newspapers. Harvey was a thriving metropolis in those days, driven by steel mills and factories and where people intersected in a swarm to commute to jobs beyond town. We would set up outside the train station to catch the flow of riders catching the train and those getting off for jobs. We'd also go across the street by the bus station, walking up and down selling the day's news for five cents a paper.

People would occasionally give me a dime and tell me to keep the change, which I gladly did. Glenn used to tease me and say, "Tommy gets more tips because people think he's cute."

I attended Ascension Catholic School, which started at 8:00 a.m. sharp, beginning with Mass every morning. I was an altar boy, so my punctuality was not optional. Around 7:00 a.m., I'd head back to the newspaper office to drop off any leftover papers. Then I would trudge a mile through the snow to school, with holes in my shoes and wet socks, a sensation no child ever gets used to.

During lunchtime, I would walk back to the newspaper office to collect my unsold papers and sell them for an hour before hustling back to school for the afternoon. I would have preferred to be playing with my friends.

6

It was during this season of life that Glenn also made the business case for shining shoes to generate family income. We had the most success by working the taverns in Harvey, and on a good evening, we would each take home two or three dollars. Some nights, if we did exceptionally well, we'd stop at the bakery on the way home and buy day-old éclairs for our siblings. I can still see and smell those wonderful éclairs, with chocolate on the top and the center filled with a sweet, golden custard. This didn't happen often, but when it did and we walked through that door with those éclairs, our siblings thought we were national heroes.

Shining shoes is tedious, backbreaking work. There isn't much heroic about it because it is a humbling task. Of all the days when Glenn and I worked to support our family, there is one that stands out: the day when Little League baseball came to Harvey, Illinois.

I was ten years old, and every young boy who loved baseball was as excited as if it were the night before Christmas. Tryouts were at 4:00 p.m. right after school let out, and I was nervous. Hell, I could hit, I could field, I could run and throw, but what if I had a bad day? It could happen, you know.

What made me even more nervous was that I had to be out of there by 5:30 p.m. Glenn had two passions in life in those days. One was shining shoes to make some money so our mom could buy some groceries to feed us, and the second was kicking my ass when I was late for shining shoes.

I showed up on time, and I hit the ball hard, threw the ball straight, fielded well, ran fast, and I made the team. Mr. Turngren read my name and assigned me to a team. Then he announced that, on opening day, there would be a parade in downtown Harvey, with a band leading us to the new Little League Field for the first game. Holy cow!

Then he said something that made my heart sink: every player had to bring twenty dollars to be on the team. The uniforms were free, of course, but we'd have to buy our own spikes, gloves, and insurance. The local sporting goods store would give us a discount, but the total would come to twenty dollars. He might as well have said twenty thousand, because there was no way I was going to be able to come up with twenty bucks.

I kind of just drifted away from the field and headed home to get my shoeshine box. I met my brother and we headed out to the taverns to get our evening started. The first tavern we came to was Sparrow's, which had a long, straight bar where about thirty guys just off the clock at the steel mill would sit or stand and talk loudly about whatever was on their minds.

I started at one end of the bar and my brother started at the other. I remember hearing Frank Sinatra on the jukebox singing "All the Way" in those early minutes. The first two guys we approached declined, somewhat politely, but the third guy turned around and said, "Hell yeah, I want a shine." He was a big, fat red-faced guy who was obviously quite drunk. He said, "Not only do I want a shine, but I'm also going to give you two dollars."

We only asked for fifteen cents a shine and usually got a quarter. He held up two crisp dollar bills in his hand and said, "Do you want that job?" My brother looked at me with that look in his eyes that said, "This could be éclair time..."

"Yes sir," I said, and I started to get down to shine his shoes.

"Oh no. I'm not going to give you the two dollars just for the shine. You have to sing 'Chattanoogie Shoe Shine Boy' while you shine my shoes."

I knew the song; it was on every jukebox in town. But I was shy and scared. "I don't know the song, sir," I said. My brother looked at me with cold eyes that said, "It's not only éclair time; it could be ass-whippin' time too."

Glenn said, "He knows the song, sir." The big guy said, "Well, sing it while you shine my shoes and these two dollars are yours."

I got down on my knees and I started to mutter, "Have you ever passed the corner of Fourth and Grand, where a little ball of rhythm has a shoeshine stand..."

"Oh no, no, no. I can't hear you," the big guy chortled. "You have to sing loud so we can all hear you. Right, fellas?" All the guys in the bar yelled, "Yeah! Louder! Louder!"

At that moment, I hated this big, fat, red-faced, drunken son of a bitch...and I hated my father for having me down on my knees in this smelly bar, shining shoes when I should be over at the playground, practicing baseball with the other little boys and getting ready for opening day.

I felt a rage inside me as I started to sing that song with all the anger a ten-year-old boy could muster up.

And as I sang every line of the song, I popped that rag loudly, just like the shoeshine man did in the song.

I popped the rag again. *Pow! Pow! Pow! Pow!* Then I stood up, glaring at this man with my hand stretched out for the two dollars. It was silent for a second—and then everyone started to applaud.

The big guy handed me the two dollars. "Great job, son," he said as he started to applaud. Suddenly, this big, fat, red-faced, drunken son of a bitch looked like Santa Claus to me. The applause felt so warm. No one had ever applauded me before.... "Hell," I thought, "I could get used to this!"

From that day on, whenever I passed a ballpark and saw a little boy with holes in his shoes and raggedy clothes on his back, peeking through a fence, watching other little boys playing baseball in their new shiny uniforms, I knew just how he felt. And to this day, when I see someone onstage, getting applause and cheers for their very first time, I know just how he feels too.

7

Dad began working at a new factory called Acme Steel in River-dale, the town where he was from. He would get paid on Friday and take the train to the Park Avenue station in Harvey, then immediately cash his check in one of the eight taverns near the station.

Trouble was, he often wouldn't get home until three in the morning, penniless after a night of lost poker games and bottomless drinking. That meant the family had no money for rent or food—much less any indulgences like new clothes or toys for the babies. Mom finally had enough and gave Dad the classic ultimatum for a marriage in turmoil: shape up or ship out. He chose to ship out.

Mom began to work in a place called the Rubber Factory that made rubber products, from toys to tires. She also continued to tend bar at nights. That's when her mom, our Grandma Algoe came up from Pontiac to live with us and watch us kids while Mom worked.

Grandma Algoe was a strong Irish woman who didn't take a lot of lip from adults and certainly didn't take any backtalk from children. It was like we had a stern Catholic nun living with us, which wasn't a hard transition for me because I was going to Catholic school, where the nuns were very strict disciplinarians. I didn't give Grandma any more lip than I gave to the actual nuns, which is to say none. In fact, I really liked her. I think she got a kick out of me, as I could make her laugh with my antics and behavior. She called these my "shenani-gans" and claimed that my gift of gab had to be the product of me kissing the Blarney Stone at some point.

After about six months, my dad's sister, our Aunt Ella, arranged for Mom and Dad to meet and discuss reconciliation. Mom took me with her downtown to a place called Scott's Five and Dime, where there was a lunch counter. I was just a little boy, and I hadn't seen Dad for a long time, so I hid behind one of the counters. When he finally arrived, I jumped out to surprise him. Seemingly puzzled, he saw me and flatly stated, "Oh, look at you." My parents had a long lunch over sandwiches and fountain drinks as I continued to play around the lunch counter. A couple of days later, Dad returned home.

Things seemed to be going smoothly for a while, but it wasn't long before the thirst that controlled his brain and darkest impulses returned. He went back to his perfected routine of getting off the train after work, cashing his check with his personal banker behind a mahogany wood bar, and blowing a week's worth of wages in a few short hours.

It got to the point that Mom began to meet his train at the sta-tion on Fridays, cajoling the check from him so that she could cash it herself in the traditional sense. She would stash enough money in her purse for the upcoming rent payment and then take him to the local store to purchase a week's supply of groceries. At first, she would also buy beer at the store to try and entice him to come home with the groceries, but he didn't go for that. Friday night was his night to "bar hop," and he was committed to the ritual.

Mr. Burrell, our landlord, finally had enough of the rent always being several months behind. One day he told Mom that he was going to rent our place to his brother and his family. As evictions go, it was as polite as possible, but we had to move once again.

This time we moved about two miles away, which was good news for Dad because it was closer to the taverns. He could easily stroll to them when he felt like it, and he always felt like it.

We were poor. Raggedy. Ass. Poor. The shack we lived in was home, but it was also a haven for cockroaches and rats, which came to visit quite often. The rats would burrow under the house, and Glenn would take me around the neighborhood to find bottles that we would break and put the glass into the rat holes. Rats are intuitive little creatures, and they would just burrow holes in another spot.

There was never enough heat in that place during the cold Illinois winters. We had an old coal stove that would only warm you if you stood right in front of it, and we often couldn't afford coal. Taking matters into his own hands, Glenn would drag me out, and we'd go behind the grocery stores to find wooden crates in the garbage pile. We'd take them home and break up the wood to put in the stove with old newspapers to start a fire.

Other times we'd go to the railroad yards a few blocks away, where I would quickly climb up on a coal car and toss coal down to Glenn one brick at a time. Glenn would stuff the coal in a burlap sack, and when it was full, we'd be on our way. We had to act fast because there was a watchman who patrolled that area, although he never caught on to us, or so I thought.

Years later, when I returned from the Navy, I worked as a bartender in a local tavern. One night, the same watchman walked into the bar and sat on a stool right in front of me. It was the first time I'd ever been that close to him. He ordered a shot and beer and started to put money on the bar to pay me.

"No, sir, these drinks are on me tonight," I told him.

He looked up and said, "Now why are these drinks on you?"

"You don't know who I am, but—"

"I know who you are."

"You do?"

"Yes, I do, you little shit. You and your brother used to steal coal off the train cars when they'd come in. One of the other cops knew you were stealing coal to heat the shack you lived in. He asked me to turn a blind eye so you kids could have coal, so that's what I did. Every night I said a prayer that you wouldn't fall off and kill yourself when that goddamned train lurched forward or I'd have it on my conscience the rest of my life. And that's what I did. No, you ain't buying me nothin'. Get the fuck outta here."

Not only were the Dreesens habitually late on making rent, we were always tardy paying tuition at Ascension Catholic School, which didn't sit too well with the nuns. The nuns had a subtle way of reminding us that we were basically freeloading on our Catholic education, saying things like, "There will be a field trip to the local library followed by cupcakes and milk for all those students who have their tuition paid. Those who don't will remain in Sister Bertilda's class until we return."

Glenn was a talented artist by the time he was in eighth grade, but because our tuition was always months behind, he wasn't allowed to display his artwork with the other art students in his class. I know he was hurt but shrugged it off, like so many things one had to accept when your father's priority was cold beer.

In my heart, I don't believe that my father was really a bad guy, but I never had a close relationship with him. None of my siblings did. He just wasn't cut out to be a father except in the most literal sense of the word—there were eventually eight of us after all.

For the most part, he seemed indifferent to what his children were doing. Dad spent very little of the "quality" time with us that so many other kids desired. He never took me out for a walk or an ice cream, never took me aside to talk one-on-one. We never played catch. He wasn't even remotely interested in anything that I was doing. I honestly never really felt bad about that, but maybe it's because his aloofness was so familiar. It was all I ever knew.

When Glenn graduated from Ascension, Darlene and I were told that we would also be leaving the school to attend Bryant Elementary, a public school, where the teachers wouldn't be hounding Dad for tuition money.

In eighth grade, I was named captain of the Bryant School lightweight basketball team. We had a good team and made it to the league championship tournament. In the first game, I scored twenty-eight points and helped us win and advance to the semifinal game. Darlene, forever my fan and supporter, came home and told Mom and Dad how she wished they could have seen it. I had been playing soccer and basketball on the school's teams for three years at this point, and they had never attended a single game.

Playing competitive sports is such a rite of passage for most kids. Someone once told me that when you're a parent, kids don't look up in the stands and notice if you're there, but they notice when you're not. If you played sports growing up, you understand this, and you probably remember if your parents were in regular attendance on game days. Sure, things come up from time to time that prevent parents from seeing every game, whether it's an illness, a new baby at home, or the need to work late to make ends meet.

Still, I recall how most of my teammates had one or both parents in the crowd. Win or lose, those games were chronicled in an official scorebook somewhere, but more importantly, they were memorialized in a family record through a shared experience. My parents' habitual absence meant that I didn't know any different, but I knew the loneliness I felt wasn't how it was supposed to be.

The next night, Mom cajoled Dad out of a bar and brought him to Thornton Township High School for the game. We lost by twenty-five points, and I only scored two points, which happened on one glorious shot. I threw up a long Hail Mary shot that swished through the net to end the third quarter. Knowing my Dad was there, I immediately looked up into the stands to see if he was watching, and to my delight, he was. He had the biggest grin. I remember how great it made me feel. For such a nominal expression of pride and affection that my Dad was showing, to see his face made me feel like I had won the lottery for my family. My Dad was proud of me. I don't remember ever experiencing that feeling from him again. To this day, the image of his big smile is emblazoned in my mind.

It was around this time that I really began to understand the lengths Dad would go to secure a drink. When I graduated from eighth grade, my brother Glenn gave me a present. I had never owned a watch before, and Glenn gave me a Crawford 17 Jewel watch. It was beautiful, and I wore it everywhere. One day, I couldn't find it.

Looking for it in the living room, I said to my parents, "Did anyone see my watch?" My mom put her head down and looked over at my dad. I turned and looked at him and realized what had happened: he had pawned my watch.

I saw the sad, embarrassed look on his face, and I stifled what I was about to say, taking weird solace in knowing that he probably got a few beers for it. Instead, I downplayed the whole thing. "You know, I didn't wear that watch that much anyhow. I was just wondering where it was. Don't worry about it." I truly felt sorry for him.

My childhood experience provided me with a mix of disappointment and somehow finding the grace to forgive, and as a result, I've always had a sort of sympathy for drinkers. I never thought of my dad as worthless or a bum; I knew the disease of alcoholism had a stranglehold on him, and it washed over me that the sickness had cost me my only watch.

The one Dreesen kid who escaped Dad's indifference was Glenn, on whom he was really rough. We often witnessed the two of them going at it, which was heartbreaking. The violent outbursts usually happened when Dad was drinking and got angry over something and hit Glenn, repeatedly. He lived to regret it.

On a hot summer night, when Glenn was sixteen years old, Dad came home after a long night in the taverns and started in on Glenn. "Here we go again," I thought. My older brother was considered a tough guy in the neighborhood, someone who would throw a punch in a heartbeat just to make a point.

There's an old saying that if you beat a puppy long enough, it will grow up to become a mean dog. Glenn wasn't a puppy anymore, and that night, he decided the beatings were never going to happen again. Full of rage and emotions bursting forth after years of abuse, Glenn told Dad to step outside because he was ready to stand toe-to-toe and offer payback for what Dad had been doing to him for years.

There was a conviction in that sixteen-year-old's voice that was not to be mistaken.

He meant every word, and Dad must have felt it, because he stayed parked in his chair. I'm glad the two of them didn't go outside, because I know how it would have turned out and believe my brother would still be in prison.

Glenn had made his stand against our old man that night, and now it was time to make his exit—a lifetime of maturing and growth condensed into a single moment. Glenn left home that night and went to live at the YMCA for a year, then enlisted in the Navy.

I remember that night so vividly and marvel to this day how that sixteen-year-old boy challenged a grown man and then went out to challenge the world. He was my big brother in every regard, and he taught me a work ethic that would stay with me all my life. I missed him deeply, and there was a strange emptiness in the home that I couldn't quite understand after he left. Looking back now, I understand. That boy was the only man in the house.

8

After Glenn left, things didn't change; in fact, they got worse. Mom seemed to give up and began to embrace her reality—a sad personal twist on the old saying, "If you can't beat 'em, drink with him." Mom always drank with Dad, but only occasionally to excess like he did. Now, however, on some days, she was matching him drink for drink. He would go to work every day, hangover in tow, and she would struggle through the day before leaving to tend bar at night.

By this time, my newest baby sister, Alice, was born, and Dennis came along a couple of years later. As the oldest, Darlene absorbed the responsibility of watching over the rest of the kids, and by the age of sixteen, she was working after school at a small grocery store, making a meager seventy-five cents an hour. She never really got paid, because each night she'd spend her earnings to bring home a loaf of bread, bologna, or milk. She would get home around the time Mom left for work, from where she often met up with Dad and closed down the bars, not returning until after 2:00 a.m.

That's when the arguments would start. It didn't happen every night, but it was often enough that we came to expect it, and some nights it got real rowdy. The kids would wake up to our parents swearing horrible things at one another. We'd trudge sadly out of the bedroom into the living area and beg them to stop fighting. The girls would start crying, pleading with them to calm down. There were many mornings when we went to school short of sleep and long on despair.

As horrible as it was, this became the norm, and I learned to accept it. I began to hit the streets as often as I could, where at least I felt like I had a little control over my life. One place I considered a personal harbor was a downtown bowling alley called Bowl Center, where I got a job setting bowling pins during my eighth-grade school year. Setting pins night after night was really hard work for a skinny, malnourished thirteen-year-old. But the physical labor of shining shoes in saloons for so many years, playing sports, and walking everywhere had conditioned me well, and I found peace in the task. At least I wasn't at home, a helpless witness to another ugly parental spat.

Some evenings at Bowl Center, we'd set pins for three different leagues: the five o'clock league, the seven o'clock and the nine o'clock late league. There might also be a "pot game" after the nine o'clock league finished, when a group of bowlers turned gamblers would put money in a pot, maybe five bucks each. Bowlers who made a strike or spare during each frame took money out of the pot—usually a dime for a spare and a quarter for a strike. If someone blew the frame and knocked down anything short of a strike or a spare, they had to put money back in. At the end of the night, the bowler with the highest score took home the remaining pot money.

The best part about this quasi-league was that the players, heavily inebriated by this time, would always tip the pinboys after the games. The problem for me was that the games would often last well past midnight and the last bus departed at midnight sharp, so I would often have to trek three miles home. I'd get to bed about around 1:30 a.m. only to awake at 7:00 a.m. to go to school.

The shack we lived in didn't have a bathtub or shower, so after setting pins all night, I'd get up in the morning and take a quick "dog bath" at the kitchen sink, using a rag and diminished bar of soap before rinsing myself off with cold water.

All the other kids at school would arrive rested, clean, and dressed in the current fashion. I was lucky to have any clothes at all, mostly hand-me-downs or secondhand-store duds. On top of that, we had to walk two miles to school, so I often didn't smell of jasmine or lavender when I got to my first class. I was tired all the time and often dozed off, especially in study hall. It should have been called nap hall as far as I was concerned.

When I wasn't setting pins, I spent a lot of time in the poolroom below the bowling alley. The poolroom had eighteen tables, including two billiard tables and one snooker table. The last pool table in the far corner was for the pinboys, where we could play for free. We hung out there a lot, which the owner preferred because he knew where to find us if needed. If the owner had to search for you, you were fired on the spot when found.

I played a lot of pool and got very good at it. I began to play in some nine-ball money games that I really couldn't afford. There were times when I would get in a money game and didn't have any money at all, which was called "playing on your guts," and if I lost, I found myself at the mercy of some of the meanest sons of bitches I ever met in that den of iniquity.

Harvey attracted a lot of guys who came from the South looking for work, mostly from Tennessee, Kentucky, and Alabama. We called them "hillbillies," which they sometimes embraced and other times resented. They called us "damyankees," which I got a kick out of, because I had never heard that phrase before.

There was a word that came extremely natural to hillbillies back then—two syllables that captured the worst kind of bigoted talk and ingrained racism one can imagine. My experience growing up on the streets and in a mixed neighborhood gave me a certain bravado that intersected with my core belief that all people are God's creation, no matter their color or creed.

A lot of my friends were black, and when I heard this kind of vulgar, inhumane talk from the ignorant kind, I would correct them—politely at first—and say it wasn't right to speak that way.

This led to overheated encounters and loud barbs that I was nothing but a "nigger lover." I didn't give a fuck. Right is right.

I must have seen a hundred fights in that poolroom and in the alley out back, and I participated in my share of scraps. My knowledge of life on the streets informed and prepared me well for what was to come.

9

By the time I was fourteen years old, I was pretty much on my own. Dad never cared about what I was doing. Mom would occasionally inquire where I was going or what I was up to. She was a good woman, especially when she was sober. When she was drinking, she became a different person but kept half an eye out for us. In between sporadic attendance at school, I lived my life on the streets, bouncing between Bowl Center and the saloons and anywhere else I damn well pleased.

One day, a couple of buddies of mine had an idea to run away from home and hitchhike down south. It was a summertime getaway, and I was always game for adventure. The romanticized ideas we had about hitchhiking the countryside and meeting interesting people were quickly diminished by the realization that we were not very good at a critical element of the venture: finding a ride.

It was hard to get a ride with three guys, as we'd likely outnumber any driver with capacity in the car, making it an uneasy and risky gamble for them. We soon learned that our luck improved if we split up, with one guy standing on the side of the road with thumb pointing north, while the other two hid behind some bushes just off the highway. If a driver stopped and agreed to pick up the solo, the other two would dash out from the hiding place to help plead our case.

Once the driver sized us up and got comfortable with the idea, more often than not, we were all invited to hop in.

The irony of this cloak and dagger approach was that it wasn't always clear what the driver's intentions might be. On two different occasions, we were propositioned by guys who offered to pay us to perform a certain lewd act on all three of us. Now we may have been poor street kids in need of money and looking to explore new horizons, but there was no way in hell we were going down that road, if you know what I mean.

Most of the time during our journey, we met friendly people who enjoyed the company of three adventurous teenagers or tried to appeal to our better angels. One time a driver who picked us up had a Bible on the front seat of his car and wanted to quote Scriptures to us, which was far preferable to deflecting blow jobs. My two buddies were not very religious, but as a former altar boy, I carried that classic Catholic guilt, so I would listen dutifully as he quoted from the Bible while driving us mile after mile.

Other times, I witnessed the despicable underbelly of the South in those days in the open display of extreme racism. As a white boy from a predominantly black neighborhood, I had never imagined that there could be such hatred towards other human beings.

Whenever we got into a redneck's car and were subjected to vile diatribes against blacks, I would wince and clench my teeth as my anger boiled up inside. But we also needed that ride, so I had to suppress my natural desires and instead fantasized about beating the shit out of the ignorant racist bastard. Viktor Frankl, a famous author and Holocaust survivor, once said, "There are two races of men in this world...the 'race' of the decent man and the 'race' of the indecent man." During our trip, we encountered both.

Our plan was to hitch along Route 41 straight to Miami, but at some point, we got crisscrossed and found ourselves well off course. We ended up in Biloxi, Mississippi, which was still a world away from Harvey. I got a job as a bellman's helper at the Edgewater Beach Hotel in Biloxi when I fibbed that I was sixteen years old, the minimum age for being on staff. I'd get a share of the bellmen's tip pool at the end of each day, and then I'd meet up with my other buddies and we'd explore the town or just relax.

I was gone three days when I decided to drop a handful of dimes into a pay phone inside the hotel to call home and check in with my mom. My parents never had a phone in the house, so if I ever wanted to call home, I would tell the operator to ring our neighbor, Mrs. Worley, and say "person-to-person call for Mrs. Glenore Dreesen," which cost a little more.

Mrs. Worley would have to run next door to fetch my mom, who would come over and state her name to take the call before the operator would say "Okay, Mrs. Dreesen is on the line. Go ahead."

"Hi, Ma," I said, and it was obvious that she had no clue that I had left town and been gone for days. I've never forgotten that feeling. Biloxi may have seemed like a world away from Harvey, but in one phone call, I realized how tethered I was to my lonely childhood back home.

My summer excursion ended a few days later when I decided it was time to head back north. This time, there would be no hitchhiking for me; I used the tip money I had earned and bought a one-way Greyhound bus ticket and was afforded another unvarnished portrayal of how brutal racial tensions were in the South.

Early in the return trip, exhausted, I fell asleep, using my jacket as a pillow against a cold window, and slumbered until I was awakened by the bus pulling into a rest stop. People filed off the bus toward the small restaurant illuminated by a neon sign and the light from the rising moon. As I made my way off the bus, I heard a voice behind me, a black sergeant in the U.S. Army who was sitting in the very back of the bus, because that's where blacks had to sit.

"Son, would you do me a favor?" he asked.

"Yes sir, what can I do for you?"

"Would you ask the driver to please turn down the air conditioning? It's really cold back here in the bus."

"You got it, sir."

As I got off the bus, I passed by the big redneck bus driver and told him of the simple request. He craned his fat neck towards me and said, "Is he a white man or a nigger?"

"He's colored, sir," I replied, taken aback, "and he's an Army man."

"Listen, you little shit. You tell him to mind his own fucking business and keep his black mouth shut."

I was stunned. When I got back on the bus, the sergeant asked if I spoke to the bus driver. I said, "Yeah, but since some people want it warm and others want it cool, he doesn't know what to do. He's just going to leave it alone."

"Okay, son. Thank you."

I didn't have the heart to tell him that I had failed the chance to stand up for him. I was far from my home turf and knew the score. The white racist rednecks ruled the South and wouldn't give a thought to beating the hell out of—or maybe even killing—a white man who stood up for a black man. The racists lurked in plain sight for the world to see. Sometimes they even drove the bus. That's just the way it was in the South, and I knew there wasn't much I could do to change it. Sadly, it wouldn't be the only time I was witness to blatant racism that was running rampant in the South—and across America.

When I returned and settled back into my routines on the streets of Harvey, I realized that my worldview had expanded, especially when it came to issues of race. My excursion down south didn't change how I interacted with my black friends, but it impacted how I dealt with my white friends who harbored years of ingrained racism.

Years later, I was interviewed by LaTanya Junior. She was the daughter of Marvin Junior, the lead singer in a popular group called the Dells that had won ten gold records. She asked me how it was that I had grown up in an era marked by racial intolerance and strife and managed to bridge the divide between black and white through my array of friendships.

As cliché as it sounds, I told her that I just never saw color. I just respected people for who they were. I admired the deeds and character of an individual, not the stereotypes associated with any race or religion. Looking back, I'm not entirely sure why I calculated life and friendships this way, but I'm glad I did. I would soon learn that I belonged to a minority of my own in this regard.

10

The school bell rang one day during my sophomore year at Thornton Township High School, and I walked out the door for good and never looked back. Mom was a little perturbed that I'd dropped out, but it didn't last long. Dad didn't care either way.

I was running with a pretty tough crowd and found my way into a street gang. We called ourselves "the Jokers," which I always found ironic since I later became a comedian. One of the gang members was a good artist and painted the face of the villain from the Batman comics on the back of each of our black leather jackets. At the time, there was nothing funny about roaming the streets.

My gang buddies became my "other" family. We often got into street fights because that's the way you ended disputes in Harvey in those days. Tough guys were respected in our circle, and the more fights you got into, the more "rep" you had that you didn't take any shit from anyone.

The unwritten code was that you always backed your fellow gang members whomever they fought, and we lived by that code. I had several fights that, even to this day when I think of them, I'm ashamed of. We got in trouble with the law on several occasions, and I was finally placed on probation, along with eleven other guys.

My probation officer was John T. Lane, a mean son of a bitch who told me on day one that he oversaw more than one hundred boys and if I fucked up just once, he would have me put away until I was twenty-one years old. The day I was assigned to him, Lane told the judge these exact words: "Your honor, Dreesen is of no credit to his family or community, and if I had my way, he'd be committed to confinement in a state institution." A cold chill went through me, and I felt a deep fear like I had never known before. Street kids tended to admire guys who had done time in the "joint," as prisons were called. I wasn't cut out to be one of those guys.

I was wandering aimlessly through life. Deep down, I knew that I needed to get straight and find my path. If I didn't, there was a good chance I'd end up in a daily commute between the factories and the taverns, with a few stops in between, like maybe jail. I began to realize I wanted more.

I didn't know what "more" was, but all it took was looking around Harvey to find a clue. Young men in town at some point either went to work, went to college, or joined the military. Harvey was loaded with former GIs who had earned their stripes serving the country: in World War I, World War II, Korea, and Vietnam. There are more than twenty names of boys from Harvey on the wall of the Vietnam Veterans Memorial in Washington, DC.

I met a lot of veterans when I was a kid shining shoes in the bars. There was also a pizzeria we hung around called Tony's, where Darlene was a waitress for a while. If you walked into Tony's and saw ten guys hanging out, it was a good bet that nine of them had served in the military. Harvey was that kind of town.

I always respected those guys and told them so. I had also seen how the service could help a man to mature and grow, including Glenn, who, of course, ran off and joined the Navy.

Glenn didn't take shit from anyone, and he kept me out of a lot of fights when we were kids. While he was gone, an older guy from around town began giving me a bad time. He was much bigger than I, and I couldn't take him on my own. I figured that as soon as Glenn came home on leave, he'd take care of this clown. Always the protector, Glenn only had to take a quick cue from one of his siblings to deliver hell upon whoever was giving us trouble.

When Glenn came home from boot camp, I told him what had happened and asked him to confront the guy. To my surprise, Glenn said, "Tommy, I don't do that anymore. No more fights."

I was shocked. Not only did I feel exposed to a certain beating from a bigger guy, but Glenn had informed me that his days as the muscle behind Tommy Dreesen were done. He had hung 'em up. I was more intrigued by the military than ever before, and I felt pulled to learn whatever lessons had helped Glenn escape the lure of the streets.

On my seventeenth birthday, I enlisted in the Navy, determined to once again find my way in the steady footprints of my brother. I was still on probation and figured it wouldn't be a problem, since John T. Lane had made it clear he had too many punks on his docket anyway. When the recruiter called to ask Lane if he would be willing to release me to Navy custody so I could enlist, Lane scoffed, "Hell no, Dreesen serves out his probation," which was another six months.

The recruiter had taken a liking to me and had a quota to fill, and since I had two guys willing to join up with me on the "Buddy Plan," he kept pleading with Lane, who finally agreed, telling the recruiter I wouldn't last the four years. I decided to prove him wrong.

It was a life-changing decision that expanded my worldview. For one, the Navy provided certain luxuries that I had never experienced before. Growing up with no bathtub or shower, I could now let as much hot water flow over me as I wanted. I had my own bed that I could slide into between two clean sheets every night. They shaved our heads, everyone received the same clothes, and I finally had more than one pair of shoes.

We also received three meals a day; I had never had three meals a day in my life! The days of being a raggedy kid with tattered clothes, holes in my shoes, and a hungry stomach were now a memory, although a deeply ingrained one.

Growing up, the greatest delicacy we had would be chicken occasionally. We didn't have regular meals where the whole family would sit down, except on those rare nights when a chicken found its way into our pot.

The first time I ever saw a steak was at the Blackhawk Restaurant in downtown Chicago. I remember getting off the train at the Randolph Street station and walking by the restaurant. Through the front window you could see the grill, where butchers and chefs prepared cut after cut of beautiful beef. Each time I was down there, I'd stand in front of the restaurant as people entered and left, just to get a whiff of those sizzling steaks wafting out of that place. I never had a steak like that until I visited New York City on shore leave from the Navy. I was out with a buddy of mine and we found a steakhouse near Times Square. I didn't know a filet mignon from a New York strip. I didn't know medium rare from Medusa, but I was damn sure going to finally have a good steak. For a meal that I'd never had before, it tasted just like I had imagined for so many years.

I was sent to boot camp at Great Lakes, Illinois, where I was surrounded by a company of sixty men from Charlotte, North Carolina, to Des Moines, Iowa, and from Birmingham, Alabama, to Detroit, Michigan, all dressed the same, heads shaved, and bellies full. For the first time in my life, I was on the same level as everyone else. I had a sense of belonging that I didn't feel when I was running around with the Jokers.

After three months of boot camp, I came home on leave for the first time. I didn't have many civilian clothes. It was chilly one night when I was getting ready to go see some friends, and my mom said, "Well, here's your Jokers jacket." She had hung it in a closet for me, a keepsake reminder of my nights on the street. I took one look at it and told her I didn't want to wear it anymore, because now I had a new uniform. I saw her eyes get misty as she told me it was one of her proudest moments. I was becoming a man, she said. After three short months in boot camp, I was ready to endure the cold night in shirtsleeves rather than wearing a punk street jacket.

I soon learned that the feeling of equality I experienced in the Navy didn't extend to everyone in my company. Even as members of an elite group of young men wearing the uniform of service to our country, the scourge of racism managed to penetrate the rigid walls of the Navy bubble.

After boot camp, I was sent to Quonset Point, Rhode Island, where I was stationed with a squadron called NATU (Naval Air Torpedo Unit). I became fast friends with a light-skinned black guy named Jack Smith, who was from the South Side of Chicago and grew up around 63rd and Halsted Avenue, a sweetheart of a guy. We had Chicago in common, but one thing we didn't share was a proficiency in swimming.

As part of the certification to fly with a Navy squadron, which I sometimes did as a non-crew member on many training missions, you had to pass the "Dilbert Dunker" exam, featuring a big machine that was originally called the Underwater Cockpit Escape Device. The exercise was used to train pilots and crew on how to escape a submerged plane in a simulated underwater evacuation.

If you've ever seen the classic movie *An Officer and a Gentleman*, there is a scene that vividly and accurately depicts the exam. The trainee straps into the "cockpit" on the edge of the pool, and then the Dunker lurches into the water and sinks to the bottom. You'd have to unhook your safety straps, escape the cockpit, swim around an imaginary wing, pull the strap on your "Mae West" (life jacket) and emerge on the surface of the water—all timed on a stopwatch.

I was a terrible swimmer. On the other hand, Jack was a great swimmer—which was unusual, because inner-city blacks normally weren't comfortable around water. The reason had to do with the sad history of race in our country: blacks weren't allowed to swim or play in pools. Growing up in Harvey, I never saw black kids in any of the public swimming pools, because they were prohibited. Jack was very athletic and had become an excellent swimmer. He helped me through the whole course, and I passed the Dilbert Dunker exam, which bonded me to him even more.

Many months later, we were both assigned to the USS *Tarawa* (CVS-40) aircraft carrier, Jack in a squadron and me as a member of the ship's company. One night, after a month at sea, we pulled into port at Norfolk, Virginia, and I reunited with my childhood friend stationed there, Roy Charleston, who had joined the Navy with me on the Buddy Plan. I introduced him to Jack, and the three of us went out for drinks on East Main Street in Norfolk, six blocks of nothing but bars on both sides of the street. We walked past about three bars before we ducked into one, found a booth, and ordered three beers. On our third round, the waitress came over and said, "Boys, please don't get mad at me, but I'm going to get into all kinds of trouble. We ain't supposed to serve niggas in here."

"What are you talking about?" I said, puzzled.

"I thought your friend was a Cuban or something because he is so light-skinned," she said, looking at Jack. "Please don't be mad. One of my dearest friends in the world is a nigga gal. She lives by me, and we're the best of friends. But we just can't serve them in here. I'll get in trouble."

Just then, a skinny, beady-eyed bouncer came up and said, "Boys, you heard what the woman said. Get your nigger friend out of here. Now."

Roy and I were stunned, but Jack wasn't angry and didn't protest. He just put his head down and quietly said we should leave. "Bullshit," I thought, as I stood up to confront the bouncer.

"I want to ask you a question. She thought he was from a foreign country and served him. Then she found out that he's an American in the US military and she can't serve him?" I raised my voice a little and said, "Explain that to me."

As my reasonable question trailed off, the prick bouncer reached into his pocket and pulled out a metal sap wrapped with leather. He cracked me hard across the left side of my face, and I went down hard, as if a lightning bolt had shot through my eyes. I wasn't knocked out, but he rang my bell good. I had boxed a bit in the Navy and had taken my share of punches in street fights. I had my nose broken twice, but I was never knocked out and never felt a blow as when this skinny redneck smacked me. To this day, my left ear rings with tinnitus because of that whack.

We made it outside, and I was wobbly. A couple of Navy shore patrol officers were passing by, and I told them what had happened, figuring they'd be pissed and go drag the guy out of the bar. I was wrong. The shore patrol guy said we should have known better, that they don't serve "coloreds" down here. To magnify the indignity of the evening, the officers put Jack, Roy, and me in lockup. We were finally released just before midnight, the time we had to report in, so we ran to catch the last bus back to base and reported to our ship just in time. As much physical pain I felt, when I looked in Jack's eyes as we said goodnight, I knew he was in far more pain emotionally.

A few days later, Jack and I took the bus back into town for dinner. Exiting the bus stop, we saw a restaurant that was obviously segregated, because it had separate entrances for whites and coloreds. Jack looked at me, and I nodded as if to say, "Why not?" and we walked toward the colored door, which was tucked behind the back of the restaurant. The black waitress who greeted us could not have been more pleasant and took us right to a booth, then took our order. It wasn't two minutes before a black guy in the back started in on me.

"Sheeeyet. Hey, white boy. What, you doin' us a favor in here? You gracin' us with your presence? Don't you wanna sit with your white folks 'round the corner?"

The guy had clearly had too much to drink, and seeing a white guy in his space caused him to bubble over. Before I could even contemplate a response, the waitress jumped all over his ass. "You shut up. I don't want hear another word out of you. Shut up and mind your own business," she bellowed. The guy mumbled something before returning to his drink. I thought to myself that if it's difficult for a white man to have a black friend in the South, apparently it was no easier for a black man to have a white friend.

* * *

Spending significant time aboard Navy ships taught me many new things, including the concept of "intellectual combat." In Harvey, if people began to argue in a bar, things would quickly escalate until someone simply said, "Outside!" and that's where they went to settle their differences, as mundane as they may be. Two guys would be arguing about the Cubs and the White Sox when one of them would say, "I'm tired of your bullshit. Outside!" and to the back alley they went.

On a Navy ship, however, I would see a black guy from Detroit, a redneck from Arkansas, a Jewish guy from New York, and a Polish guy from Chicago get into heated debates about all kinds of issues. Yet they all abided by a central rule: no "skylarking," which meant no pushing or shoving because you could get hurt joking around when the next thing you know, someone has fallen down a gangway or even over the side. If anyone was ever caught "skylarking," you were written up and faced court martial.

Watching these conversations often turn into heated debates, there were times I was convinced things were about to boil over into a full-blown fistfight, but they rarely did. At the end of the verbal joust, someone would concede, "You know what, that's a good point. I never thought about it that way." And they'd all shake hands and walk away, perhaps respecting each other a little more. I had never seen that before, and it was fascinating to me. Of course, on a ship hundreds of miles from shore, it helps when the taunt of "Outside!" isn't really an option.

I did get into one serious altercation off the ship—one that stayed with me for years. We had just returned from sixty-six days at sea in the Antarctic, with a stop in Rio De Janeiro on the way back. It was a memorable tour, and on one of the first nights back stateside, my buddies and I went into town on a tour of our own, sampling the cultural offerings of a bunch of bars. At the end of the night, well lubricated, we jumped onto the "Blue Goose" naval shuttle bus that picked us up at the main gate at Quonset Point and would drive us across the base to the pier where our ship was docked. There was another guy from our ship on that bus who apparently didn't like me, although I didn't realize it at the time.

All my guys were being rowdy and talking loudly, continuing the party. When we arrived back at the pier, the other guy got off the bus first. As I stepped onto the pavement, he hit me square in the face and knocked me down, my two front teeth retreating with force into the back of my mouth, and he kept pummeling me.

I realized that I was losing consciousness because I didn't feel the pain, but I heard the punches land, one shot to my head after another. My buddies finally pulled him off me, and the guy scampered up the gangway onto the ship.

I was helped aboard ship and immediately taken to sick bay, where it was confirmed that my nose was broken. I also had to have my teeth wired because of the initial blow that had knocked my front teeth toward the roof of my mouth. I had two black eyes and bruises all over my chest. On a ship of more than 2,500 men, I didn't know who had done that to me and I certainly didn't understand what had brought on this beating. My pummeling was still a hot topic within my division and among my pals when I was released from sick bay three days later. Nobody knew who had done it.

About a month later, I was mustering a crew in Norfolk, Virginia, to bring aboard supplies when a guy came up to me and said with a smirk, "I'm the guy who did that to you," pointing to my face, which by this time had gone from black and blue to yellow.

"Are you now?" I said, somewhat shocked that my assailant would present himself so boldly. Minding the rules of no skylarking, I contained the urge to kill the guy and instead said, "Well, two things: First, I want to know what the fuck that was about. And second, I want to know when you and I are going to meet—only this time I'm not going to be drunk and have my head down. We're going to finish this."

"That's fair," he said, like a fucking wiseguy. Then he told me that he had once served on a working party with me and when someone mentioned Chicago, I made a joke and said, "Hey, smile when you say Chicago. That's my hometown."

Of all the flippant things I had said in my naval career, this was what got my ass kicked? Rather than seeing the self-deprecating humor in my remark, the guy had taken it like I was a smart-ass.

Seething, I called him out "You ambushed me, you fucking prick. You hit me when my head was down, and I had no fucking chance at all. Let's do this like men some other time."

He said, "Yeah, that's okay with me. We'll do it." And he walked away, but now I knew who the guy was.

The irony is that I never saw him again as an enlisted naval member. Shortly after our encounter, that guy, whose name I finally discovered was Denardo, and four other guys had beat the hell out of a second-class petty officer at an enlisted men's club, putting him into a coma. All four of the goons were arrested, sent to the brig, and dishonorably discharged.

A year or so later, I was traveling with my buddy, Dennis "Pikey" Pietz. We were hitchhiking to Long Island, where we both had girlfriends at the time, and had stopped in Brooklyn for lunch. We were on the street when Pikey said, "Hey, isn't that your friend?"

I spotted Denardo leaning up against a street sign in front of a candy store with four of his Italian buddies.

"Yeah, that's him all right."

In a pure gift from heaven, the other guys walked inside the candy store, leaving Denardo outside by himself with his back turned to us.

"Do you want to do this?" Pikey said.

"I don't know. What do you think?'

"Let's do it. Let's get that son of a bitch."

"Well, if we do, we gotta do it fast because I know those greaseballs inside will be here the second we make a move."

We went in between two parked cars, and I summoned the memories just from the Blue Goose ambush and said, "Hey, Denardo…" And as he turned around, I nailed him as hard as I could and so did Pikey, who thumped his ass with a boom, boom, boom.

Denardo hit the ground hard and we took off running...and kept running for about three miles.

My revenge realized, every time my ship pulled into port after that, I would peer over the railing and scan the gathered crowd of friends and family, looking for any sign of Denardo, because I was sure he was going to come at me again. However, I soon was honorably discharged, proud of my service to country and excited for my return into civilian life and a new beginning. While in the Antarctic, I received a letter from my mom saying that I had a new baby brother, Wally. I was ready to get home and see my family.

11

I was discharged from the Navy in July 1960 and returned home to Harvey after four years of military service. I had proved John T. Lane wrong, but I also had more respect for him because he had woken me up. The town hadn't changed much, and I soon realized that perhaps I hadn't either. I still had some growing up to do.

The first thing I did was borrow my brother's car and head to Tony's Pizza, where my sister Darlene worked. We hugged, and she immediately started bringing me food. Italian beef, some sausage, and slices of pizza. Sitting in a booth on the other side was a young, pretty girl with her hair up in curls. I nodded at her and turned away, talking to Darlene. The girl headed for the bathroom and came out five minutes later with her hair all made up and fresh lipstick applied, cute as a button. I nodded again and finished my meal and tried to pay the check, but Darlene told me she'd already paid for it with her tip money. "Welcome home," she said.

Meanwhile, the girl walked out the door as I was saying goodbye to my sis, and by the time I got in my car, Miss Cute as a Button was walking on the sidewalk about fifty yards ahead of me. I pulled up alongside her and said, "Would you like a ride home?" She said yes, and we hit it off right away—and married a short time after.

Now the story I always told our kids years later was that I rolled the window down and said, "Would you like a ri—" and before I could finish, their mom dove through the window and said, "YES!!" Her name was Maryellen Sebock, and she was indeed cute and very quiet—until after we married, that is. She remained cute, always, but not so quiet.

My first order of business was to find a job. There was one problem: I had no real skills. The Navy had taught me valuable lessons of discipline, structure, and camaraderie. However, none of the trade skills I had learned were easily transferable to the job options in Harvey. My first job was as a shoe salesman at Thom McCann, which I didn't enjoy and made very little money doing. I only lasted about four months.

I became a laborer for almost every construction job imaginable: hanging drywall, wheeling concrete, erecting scaffolding, and hauling brick and mortar up and down that scaffolding before tearing it all down at the end of the day. I cleaned sewers and got to know the city commissioner, who gave me a job as a city inspector of streets and alleys. I also worked construction on the road for ARS Construction, which contracted with McDonald's franchises around the country to install these huge beef machines. And since construction work was basically nonexistent during the Chicago winters, I always kept a bartending gig to help make ends meet. I tended bar in places I had shined shoes as a kid, Sparrow's Tap and Frank Polizzi's old bar, which had been bought by Joe Falica and renamed Joe and Mary's Dugout.

I got fired from several of the labor jobs, but most of the time, I quit because I hated what I was doing. I would sit in bars until the wee hours of the morning and say to myself, "What the hell am I doing with myself?" I still didn't know where I belonged, and with no other options, I continued the slog in construction.

I worked hard to compensate for the fact that, unlike most of the workers, I'm not a big guy. I was a scrawny five-foot-nine and weighed 145 pounds. I was on a crew for a company called Fuller

Construction that employed twenty-four laborers—twenty-three big, strapping black guys and me. On jobs where a new building was being erected, we'd haul these big, heavy concrete forms across the site to the exact spot where they were to be put into the building's framework. You had to put these huge forms on your right shoulder to balance the weight, which in short order produced a series of knots on your shoulder, the pain radiating up your neck and down the sides of the body. The work was grueling.

A buddy of mine named Mike Yoniles was looking for work around the time our crew needed a laborer. Mike came by one day, and I introduced him to the foreman, who liked what he saw. Mike was a big, strong guy, and the foreman said the job "interview" would be for Mike to carry one of those concrete forms to a spot maybe fifty yards way. Without blinking, Mike strapped the form on his back and started out. He struggled a bit to find his balance at first but successfully made it to the spot and set the form down, no worse for wear.

The foreman said, "Yeah, okay, you're hired." Mike said, "Fuck this, I quit. I ain't doing this shit." And that was the end of Mike's construction career.

Construction work was steady, and the pay was decent, but I'd hop from one laborer job to another and still find myself dissatisfied. I got bored easily, especially after I learned the nature of the job and what you had to do time after time after time.

I went to work as an inspector for the City of Harvey. My job was to inspect the conditions of streets and the alleys and report back. The job was so mundane that I quit after eight months. I went to a trucking firm called Jones Motor to a job loading trucks, just to keep my mind active. After thirty days, I was automatically made a member of the Teamsters Union. I'd read the manifests like they were Proust, reviewing them twice and taking a sharp eye to understand the hundred or so different items I had to load and unloaded from the semis. This kept me alert during the day and helped me sleep better at night, but still, there was no real challenge.

The terminal manager from the company called one day and said, "Look, you're too smart to be doing hard labor. We're going to make you a foreman," which was okay by me.

Becoming a foreman meant that I could be a leader—my true instinct—rather than a follower. In order to be a good leader, you must know what the followers' jobs were and how to earn their respect or admiration on a personal level so that they'd work for you. Keeping with my nature, I always tried to keep the mood light and would tell jokes and cut up with the workers.

One of the early mistakes I made was that I'd go to the bars where they hung out, like I did when we were all dock hands. Now, as their boss, I realized things had changed. If I got too friendly with the crew, they didn't give as much as I needed from them during the day.

As a foreman, I had to learn all the cities across the U.S. where our company trucks went and the logistics it took to coordinate all of them. The real task, though, was managing the forty-eight Teamsters who reported to me. There were some decent guys who believed in a good day's work for honest pay. Then there were others who intentionally worked slowly so they could get overtime. And, of course, there were the lazy asses who didn't do either because they felt protected by their real bosses in the union halls.

The unions were loaded with mob guys, and the Teamster workers adored them. Most of the dock workers were full-blooded Polish, Irish, and Italian guys from the streets. When I became foreman, half of the workers said, "Good for you, kid. You got too much smarts to be hauling shit. Leave it to us." The other twenty-four guys adopted an attitude more along the lines of, "Fuck off, you piece of shit. I ain't doin' nothin' for you."

They were tough—but not so tough that they'd handle things themselves. Instead, they would call the union hall on me in a heartbeat just to disrupt my day or break an order I had given.

There was a big guy working the dock named Lombardo, who always brought a book with him on the job. He'd read a novel a week while on the clock, instead of working. I'd have to drag him out of the bathroom every hour. "Come on. We've got work to do. Get your ass out here," I'd say.

Lombardo got off his ass long enough to call the union hall to say I was harassing him. The next day, when the crew was on break out front, two big black Buicks came flying in, brakes slamming. All the doors swung open and a swarm of mob guys popped out, all tough like. "Where's this fucking punk piece of shit Dreesen? Where is he?"

Well, Dreesen was up in the dock shack, going over paperwork. They quickly found me and started in with the noise.

"What's this we hear about you harassing our men?" the head goon said.

"Who the fuck said I was harassing them?"

"Lombardo, you lousy piece of shit."

I looked the goon straight in the eye and said, "Look, Lombardo weighs about two hundred and fifty-eight pounds. Look at me. I'd be embarrassed to admit I was being harassed by a skinny little shit like that. If you mean that asking Lombardo to get off his fat fucking ass and do some work is harassment, then yeah, I'm harassing him. A fair day's work for a fair day's pay is all I'm asking."

They didn't give a shit and kept trying to rattle my cage. Because I'm a street guy, I knew it was mostly bullshit. They finally stormed out of the office and went to the terminal manager, who put a couple of hundred bucks in an envelope and gave it to them and said, "Fellas, have a few drinks on the way home on me," which I'm sure they did—but not before finding fatso Lombardo on the way out to say, "Yeah, we took care of that little punk, and if he gives you any more shit, you let us know." It was all a fucking scam, and I continued to tell Lombardo to get up off his lazy ass and do his job. I also was chomping a lot of Rolaids at the time to help with all the indigestion caused by stress.

No matter what unforeseen adventures my days as a foreman sometimes brought, my nights remained predictable. I always ended up in the taverns, on one side of the bar or the other. I was drinking a lot, morphing into a caricature of what I didn't want to become.

I had begun to adopt the tavern mentality of my dad, which instructed that if a man wants to stop and have a few beers after work, then dammit, it was his right.

When Maryellen sometimes chided me for being out too late, I'd get pissed and say, "Dammit, I worked all week long and brought home the check!"

She'd say, "Why do you make that sound like it's something unusual? That's what you're supposed to do!" She grew up with a father who'd started working in a foundry when he was sixteen years old with the lowest job and worked his way up to become the plant manager. He worked eighteen years without missing a day, took a day off to play golf, then worked another seventeen years straight. He brought a check home every Friday. The bills were always paid. There was always food on the table. He also was very quiet and wasn't very fond of me in the beginning, honestly.

That was the stable environment Maryellen had grown up in, and quite frankly, it was what she expected when she married me. She couldn't understand why I was making a big deal out of putting in a full workweek. In retrospect, she was right. But that was her father figure, not mine.

Maryellen gave me a lot of leeway, but always with a raised eyebrow. On Friday nights, I'd go out with my buddies. She accepted that it was my night to howl, and I'd walk in at three or four in the morning after going from bar to bar, sometimes getting into fights.

As I said earlier, we had this neighborhood code that always prioritized your buddies above anything else. If you were at a tavern and one of your buddies was drunk and obnoxious and did something stupid, you stood by him no matter what—even if you knew he was out of line or dead wrong. The next day, you could tell him his behavior was unacceptable, but in the heat of the moment, you never left your buddy's side. This was a lingering lesson many of us learned while in military service.

One night, I was sitting at home when several buddies came to the front door. With alcohol on their breath, they reported that a group of guys in Blue Island had jumped a friend of ours in a restaurant called the Grand Grill. Without thinking twice, I went to the bedroom and started changing into my clothes to go help.

My wife looked up and said, "What are you doing? You're a married father of two children. What the hell is wrong with you?"

"You don't understand," I told her as I zoomed out of the house to once again join the fray, which turned out to be a large fight in the alley behind the restaurant. Again, looking back, I realize my wife was right. What the hell was I thinking? It was a stupid, immature thing to do.

12

For seven years, from 1960 through 1967, I had every job known to man, and not one of them was I very good at doing, and I certainly didn't enjoy the work. I was still wandering, without a clue of what I was put on Earth to accomplish, other than to drink a lot of beer. Ironically, it was over a beer one night when I was presented with a new opportunity to get off construction sites and back into the streets, but in a different way.

I ran into an old friend at the bar named Dennis LaValley who worked for Columbus Mutual, a large insurance company. Always the salesman, after a few pleasantries and catching up, he began to pitch me on why I needed to buy a policy from him, particularly since I had a wife and young family. I wasn't biting, but we continued to talk, and he continued to sell.

After another beer, he stopped selling and, suddenly, started recruiting. "Have you ever thought of selling insurance? You're an outgoing guy. You like making new friends. I think you'd be good at it," he said.

"Let me get this straight," I said. "All I have to do is talk to people, and if they like me enough and buy something from me, then I make money?"

"You could make a lot of money. I think you'd be really good at this," he replied.

I was sold.

I joined Columbus Mutual at a time of incredible growth for the company—and really, the entire insurance industry. The company had recently hit the billion-dollar mark for life insurance policies in action and was looking to continue the momentum by growing their sales force. I was happy to hit the streets in pursuit of world domination.

As my friend had predicted, I was really good. I've never had a problem striking up a conversation—or just talking in general. Years later, my manager Dan Wiley was talking to a guy who was going to interview me for a radio show. The guy wanted to know what to ask that would lead me to tell some energetic stories. Dan said, "Easy. Just say, 'Tom, how's your day?' and then get the fuck out of his way."

I sold the hell out of insurance and had a lot of fun doing it. It was a competitive industry, and I was always looking for an edge, any way to meet and win over new prospects. I had this unique approach to selling young newlyweds. The woman was usually the easy sell, so I would focus on the guy. "Look, I'm not here to sell you death insurance. I'm here to sell you *life* insurance. I like to call it *optional retirement income*. Are we going to insure you in case you don't make it to retirement? Of course, because, God forbid, if something happens to you, we're going to take good care of your family. But we want you to make it, and here's how much money you're going to get when you do make it."

I'd then pull out a sheet showing how much he was going to put into the company and a projection of how much money he would get in retirement by taking out a policy with me. Under the pestering spell of his wife's gaze, the guy normally signed up on the spot. I was damn good at this gig. The first year, I was given all kinds of awards for record-breaking sales. The second year, I quit. I'll tell you why.

A few years earlier I had joined the Jaycees, a civic group that trained young men to become leaders through projects and volunteer efforts that benefit the community. In addition to serving the common good, this turned out to be a prime target audience of young men who didn't realize they were in the market for new insurance policies, and I set out to educate them on the opportunities.

I was about to discover an opportunity of my own.

13

Let me now share an American fairy tale that happens to be true. *Once upon a time in America, there was a young black man and a young white man who were so idealistic and so naïve that they honestly believed that if they could get people to sit down and laugh together, then maybe, just maybe, everyone could live together too.*

The year was 1969. The New York Jets were Super Bowl champions. *Sesame Street* made its television debut. *Midnight Cowboy* won the Oscar for Best Picture, and John Wayne won for Best Actor in a movie called *True Grit*. Paul Newman and Robert Redford were doing big box office in *Butch Cassidy and the Sundance Kid*. Richard Nixon was president, and he vowed that the Vietnam War would be over soon. It ended four years later, but not before 58,318 young Americans sacrificed all to have their names etched on a wall in Washington, DC.

The 1960s was a rough and divisive decade, politically and socially. President John Kennedy was assassinated in 1963; Robert Kennedy was murdered in 1968 while seeking to pick up the torch of Camelot from his fallen brother. Only a few months earlier, the Reverend Martin Luther King Jr., the preacher of nonviolent resistance to end racial segregation and inequality, was felled by a most violent bullet, ending his life but not his dream.

African Americans believed that the system was leaving them out. The events of the previous year lit a long, dry match, and 1969 was a year marked by protests and riots that sometimes burned up square blocks in cities like Detroit; Columbus, Ohio; New York; Los Angeles; Chicago; and Harvey, Illinois.

Harvey's crime rate was slowly moving up the ladder in the United States for a community of its size. I used to joke that being rated number one really made townspeople feel good because they had been number two for so long. However, it wasn't a laughing matter. There were a lot of directionless kids roaming the streets of Harvey, looking for something to fill the void in their lives. The fact was not lost on me that, only a few years earlier, one of those kids was me. Luckily, I had found a new path, thanks to my budding career with Columbus Mutual, and belonging to the Jaycees opened my eyes to how an organization could have a real, positive impact on the community. I was proud to be a member of the Jaycees and found purpose in the chance to help others.

I began to raise my hand for volunteer opportunities to help young kids from the kind of impoverished neighborhoods that I came from. One of the things that I realized early was that nearly 75 percent of all teenager crimes were drug- or alcohol-related. Of course, this was something I knew about firsthand from my child-hood, so I wrote an education program to teach grade-schoolers the ills of drug abuse.

The program was based on getting the kids laughing and in a good frame of mind to build credibility and trust—much like my early approach to gaining acceptance with dock workers during my construction days. Once the kids bought in on you as a person, you could begin planting seeds in their minds on how to resist the temp-tations of drugs and alcohol.

The night I proposed the adoption of this drug prevention pro-gram to the general membership of the Jaycees, a young black man named Tim Reid was introduced to me after my presentation. Tim had just graduated from Norfolk State College and E.I. Dupont had recruited him into Chicago to work for them. Tim's banker happened to be a Harvey Jaycee and brought him to the meeting.

Tim was impressed by what he heard and wanted to work with me to implement it across the community. I was glad I had won him over, but I told him I'd already found a partner to help launch the program. The very next day, the guy who was supposed to work with me got a new job and backed out. Immediately, I called Tim Reid, who, after some persuasion, agreed to be my partner. Little did we know where it would take us.

We began to speak to students and work with administrators in the school system. The program became an instant success—in no small part because of the adage "People hear what they see." Instead of a racially mixed classroom of students hearing from two white guys on the dangers of drug use, they saw a white guy and a black guy who clearly liked each other, both delivering the same message—a powerful visual given the backdrop of discord in America at the time.

We received great feedback, and the popularity of our empowerment message began to grow, which kept our schedules full. One day, after a particularly good session with an eighth-grade class at St. John's School in Harvey, a young girl named Vicki Surufka said, "You guys are funny. You ought to become a comedy team."

We both laughed it off, but that little girl managed to plant a seed of her own. The following day, we were sitting around telling each other jokes when Tim asked me, "Are you thinking about what that little girl said?"

"Yes."

"Would you do it?" Tim asked, hoping for a certain answer.

I said, "Yeah, I'll do it if you will."

And just like that, we became America's first black and white comedy team.

Neither one of us had any idea how to write a routine or come up with material, so Tim and I listened to comedy albums and developed concepts with the help of my good buddy, Dick Owings. The three of us worked on material for months. We camped out mostly at Tim's house, where we damn near drove his wife Rita crazy, asking her every five minutes, "Is this funny?" Finally, one night she said to us, "Guys, please get out and try this on an audience of more than one."

There were no comedy clubs in those days, so we went to a night club on Chicago's South Side called the Party Mart Supper Club, which drew a young, progressive audience. I started selling our act to the club owner like I sold Columbus Mutual insurance, and after some initial resistance, the owner agreed to let us go on after the jazz band he had booked finished their set that night.

We were scared to death, pacing back and forth in the kitchen, running lines to each other and trying to swallow the adrenaline bubbling up in our throats. When the guy finally introduced us onstage, we were off to the races. We wanted so badly to remember our lines that we were talking a hundred miles an hour, never giving the audience a chance to catch up. "Hi, we're the comedy team of Tim and Tom. He's Tim, I'm Tom and..." Rather than the smooth, practiced delivery of Martin and Lewis, whom we imagined ourselves to be, we sounded like two guys off the street on speed who happened to find a stage.

I can't remember if we got any laughs because we were both in such a hurry to get off. After our last line, we bolted off the stage and said to the owner, "What didja think? HUH? Did we do good?" We were still talking very fast. The owner said, "Calm down, fellas. I don't know if you're funny. You never gave me a chance to laugh. Come back here tomorrow night and try it again. Maybe a little slower?"

We returned the next night and slowed down enough to let the act breathe and keep the audience engaged. We got a few laughs onstage with some of the things we had written, which was more than enough validation for me. There is nothing like the feeling when an audience of strangers reacts and laughs at a line or a joke you've written from scratch. It is the most gratifying feeling I've ever experienced as a performer. And like a scene from a corny cult movie where the dark clouds open up and the sun comes bursting through, it hit me: "This is what I'm supposed to do," I told myself. I wanted to be in show business doing comedy.

We went around the neighborhoods trying to find places to work. In Chicago Heights, there was a place called the Golden Horseshoe that had live shows on weekends. The owner was a guy named Eddie Warner, who also performed at his club, playing the Hammond organ. We walked into his club one afternoon while he was rehearsing and introduced ourselves as a new comedy team. Without even auditioning us he said, "That's a good idea, a black and white comedy team."

He scheduled us for the following weekend and said he'd pay us thirty dollars for two shows on Friday and two shows on Saturday. Fifteen dollars apiece. We were going to be paid entertainers. The big time.

We went onstage at the Golden Horseshoe the very first night, which was almost our last. After our set, where we received a warm reception from the crowd, we went to celebrate at a table in the back of the room. One of the performers that evening, a pretty female singer, came up to say she enjoyed our show and began to linger. At some point, in the middle of her obvious flirtations, she showed off her diamond engagement ring, somewhat dampening our moods. "Oh, congratulations!" we feigned, and both Tim and I gave her a quick kiss on the cheek and returned to our drinks.

Apparently, the girl's boyfriend had witnessed his beloved cutting up with the two cut-ups basking in the glory of their successful performance. He was a big, burly guy (who we later found out had played on the practice squad for the Chicago Bears). After the show, Tim and I were still at the table when the Bears reject walked by, took a lit cigarette, and smashed it in Tim's face.

Stunned, Tim got up and fell back against the wall. I went up and over the table and threw a punch at the guy. He grabbed my arm and pulled me over the table and began crushing me to his chest. I could hardly breathe. My mind flashed back to Norfolk, Virginia, with Jack Smith when that prick bouncer had whacked me upside the head unexpectedly.

The next thing I knew, this guy flipped me up in the air, and my body came down hard and broke the table like a damned wrestling act, except nothing was pretend; my legs were sore and bruised for months afterward.

Two bartenders rushed over to help break up the fight. I caught my breath and searched for my bearings as they pulled the guy off me, but he wiggled out of their grip. The owner came out of his office upon hearing all the commotion, and it turned into a real donnybrook. A lot of punches were thrown. We finally got the guy down and, with the help of the bartenders, ushered him outside. An auspicious beginning? Our first legitimate job had turned into a bar-clearing brawl.

"Welcome to show business!" we joked much later.

We returned to the Golden Horseshoe the next night to do our shows. This time, I strategically invited a few guys from the neighborhood, just in case this clown showed up again. Lucky for him, he stayed away, because our built-in audience of muscle was ready to show him what happens to fourth-squad football players who get out of line. Still, we did our sets and got the hell out of there.

14

Tim and I both knew we needed more stage time to hone our act, so we worked anyplace we could, even volunteer gigs for charities. We met a guy named Steve Sperry, who was working for Dick Marx, an orchestra leader who also owned a studio and wrote jingles for commercials. His young son, Richard, used to wander around the studio with his dad and, of course, went on to become a popular recording artist and sought-after producer in his own right.

Dick Marx had decided to branch out even further and go into management. Chicago has always had a lot of talent, but performers knew that to make it on the national scene, they had to leave Chicago to get the representation that could make that happen on one of the coasts. Dick hoped to change that.

Like Marx, Sperry was a talented writer of songs and jingles for artists to record, including himself. He later won gold and platinum records for his work on the popular NBC show *Fame*.

Dick had put Steve in charge of finding new talent to bring under contract. At the time, he was managing a comedy team called Edmonds and Curly, who were working the college circuit and had a few national TV appearances to their credit. Steve connected us with an agency called Projects IV out of Minnesota that booked college tours, and we started doing small-college dates in Minnesota, Missouri, Indiana, and Illinois.

As all performers know, the more gigs you do, the better your act becomes. The college tours gave us a chance to really refine our act, which gave us more confidence each time we walked onstage.

One cold, snowy night in the winter of 1971 during this period of growing confidence, we were doing a show at the University of Illinois. We had the audience right where we wanted them. There were certain nights when Tim and I were both really "on" and the audience would get caught up in our rhythm and it was joyous to be up there. This was one of those nights.

Until it wasn't. Some punk college kid thought it would be funny to disrupt the show. He went outside and returned with an ice ball made from the wet snow. He packed it good and hard and then came inside and fired it like a dart at us. It hit me squarely in the face. The stage lights were in my eyes, and I didn't see it coming, so I was completely fazed, and it hurt like hell. It happened so fast, Tim didn't realize something was amiss and kept going on with the act.

As soon as I realized what had happened, I went ballistic. I grabbed the microphone and screamed, "Turn on the lights! I want to see the face of the chickenshit motherfucker who threw that ice ball. Turn on the lights. Where are you, you cowardly piece of shit?"

Tim was staring at me like I had totally lost my mind. Half the audience was laughing, thinking this was part of our act. The other half was looking at Tim to step in and do something about his deranged partner. The only two people who knew what was going on were me and the punk kid.

I began to slowly realize that I had fucked up by reacting the way I did, giving the prick the pleasure of disrupting the show, and now had to resume our show. The momentum was gone, and we tanked.

After the show, Tim began to lecture me about "professionalism" onstage regardless of blinding ice balls screaming towards my face. "It's not like it was a squishy tomato," I protested, before noting that he always worked to my right and that the ice ball had come from the right and he would have been the target, had he not moved upstage for a second at the moment of impact. Tim understood now, imagining what he would have done if he'd gotten zinged with an ice ball, and he was pissed. Still, his point was taken: the show must always go on.

We were basically self-taught comedians, and it was an interesting process to learn how to write material and figure out what was funny and what was not. Regardless of the material, we learned that timing in the delivery is the obvious and most important ingredient in comedy.

The trick is to know exactly where the laugh is and how long to surf on the audience's reaction before continuing, to find the next wave. It's also pausing at the right moment—what's referred to as a "take"—just before delivering the punch line. The takes are different every show, because the audience is different every night. To me, it's an instinct that simply can't be taught. Either you have it or you don't. Tim and I discussed these concepts at length because if you're onstage alone, timing is important. But if you're a comedy team, timing is everything.

Another topic we liked to discuss was how to deal with any hecklers we might encounter in the audience. In addition to doing college dates, we were also working all-black clubs, affectionately known as the "Chitlin' Circuit." Within show business, these were regarded as prestigious venues to play: the Twenty Grand in Detroit, the High Chaparral and the Burning Spear in Chicago, the Sugar Shack in Boston, and the number-one club in all the "Chitlin Circuit," the Club Harlem in Atlantic City.

Tim and I were working the Twenty Grand in Detroit and getting ready for a show and working on material when I came up with an idea to neutralize a heckler in his tracks. I said, "Tim, if we ever get a white heckler who starts heckling you, I'll jump up in front of you and I'll say, 'Hey, buddy, leave him alone. Go get your own. He's mine and, after all, you know how hard they are to train.'"

Tim looked at me sideways and said, "Aw, Tom, I know you didn't mean it, but that's kind of a racist remark."

"I'm sorry. That wasn't my intention," I said.

"I know it wasn't, but it was kind of racist."

"Tim, I'm truly sorry..."

He said, "You don't need to apologize. We're brainstorming material here. It was a good effort on your part. But I think it's kind of racist."

I said, "I'm sorry." And Tim said, "Don't worry about it."

That very night, during the second show at the Twenty Grand, a black guy jumped up and yelled at me, "Hey, honky. Hey, white boy, what the hell are you doing down here?"

Within one beat Tim jumped up and said, "Hey, hold it, brother. He's mine. Go get your own. After all, you know how hard they are to train." And the whole room burst into laughter.

Later, Tim said, "Hey, man. That was some funny shit you wrote."

"How come it wasn't funny when I wrote it?" I asked.

Perfectly on cue, Tim said, "Timing, my brother. Timing."

One of the greatest things that ever happened to Tim and Tom was Hugh Hefner, the creator of the Playboy empire. Hefner was the founder and editor-in-chief of *Playboy* magazine, and he extended his lifestyle brand to a series of "private key" clubs in major cities, including Chicago, Atlanta, Detroit, Philadelphia, New York, Boston, Baltimore, Kansas City, Phoenix, Los Angeles, Miami, New Orleans, Des Moines, Cincinnati, Denver, Dallas, Buffalo, St. Petersburg, San Diego, Columbus, Lansing, and St. Louis. Playboy also had two destination resorts in Great Gorge, New Jersey, and Lake Geneva, Wisconsin, which hosted business conferences and conventions.

The guy who first booked us in the clubs was named Billy Rizzo, then shortly thereafter Irving Arthur, and later Sam di Stefano, who became a good friend. The Playboy Circuit was the closest experience we had to the days of vaudeville, when performers could work regularly around the country and hone their acts to perfection. Rather than doing one gig here and another gig there, when Arthur lined us up on the Playboy Circuit, we got to do five or six shows a night in one location, and for good money too—$750 a week as headliners. Then we'd move on to the next city.

Now since Tim and I split our proceeds fifty-fifty, we were each making $375 a week, which wasn't a lot, considering we had to pay our own way everywhere. To save money, Tim and I would usually share a room at a nearby hotel where the club had negotiated a cheap rate. In Cincinnati, we stayed at the Milner Hotel, where the rooms didn't have private bathrooms. If you had to use the facilities in the middle of the night, you had to walk down the hall to the community bathroom. Not exactly the Waldorf Astoria.

We also had to pay for food and travel costs and everything else. So that $375 didn't stretch too far, and there certainly wasn't much left over to send home to our families. However, our stage act was getting better, since we were doing six shows in about six hours every night. And walking inside the Playboy Club every night was sure hard to beat.

Upon entering the club's mahogany doors, you had to flash a silver metallic membership card—a highly treasured wallet accessory for men of a certain ego. (In the early years, access was granted by showing your personalized engraved key, which featured the iconic Playboy logo.)

From city to city, the layout and architecture of most clubs were similar, and nearly all the clubs had multiple levels, featuring various bars, lounges, and showrooms. Unsurprisingly, the clubs tended to be larger in the bigger cities like New York and Chicago, but all the clubs were decorated as if modeled on Hef's ideal bachelor pad: elegant mid-century modern design, with dark wood furnishings, leather chairs and sofas, chandeliers, and lots of chrome and gold accents throughout. Like my future boss, Frank Sinatra, Heffner also had a strong affinity for orange, which dominated the color schemes of the rugs that warmed the floor.

The Hefner formula for success was simple: get as many people into the club as possible and find ways to keep them there. And the "ways" began with lots of beautiful women, all wearing the iconic Playboy costume: a tight-fitting, shiny, corset-style one-piece dress, with see-through pantyhose and, of course, bunny ears and a bushy tail.

Heffner was a pioneer of the sexual-freedom revolution and a strong advocate for equality and civil rights. He did not discriminate when employing Bunnies and went out of his way to hire women from all races and ethnicities, so it was a very diverse group of Playboy Bunnies working the clubs.

The first room you came to off the lobby in most Playboy Clubs was the Pool Room, where several Bunnies would be playing a game of bumper pool. Guests were invited to join and take on one of the Bunnies, whom you were encouraged to tip if she beat you—although most of the guys tipped a few bucks regardless, because it's not every day you get the chance to mingle with and hand over money to a Hefner-approved Playboy Bunny. Two of the best hailed from Harvey, Nancy Perry and Kim Forbes, who worked in the Chicago club. (Nancy and I became an item after I later got divorced—and we're still together.)

Even though Playboy Clubs catered to an "all-male" clientele, many patrons brought their wives or girlfriends along on occasion, probably to ease some obvious fears. I always thought that, in terms of fidelity concerns, it was far safer for a husband to be inside a rarified Playboy Club rather than at the corner tavern—because at a tavern he could probably meet somebody and get laid. The Playboy Club had strict rules prohibiting Bunnies from dating customers. If a big spender was working his ways with a Bunny and asked her out on a date, she could say, "Oh, you know I'd love to go out with you, John, but I'll lose my job." This was a Hefner rule that protected his girls and kept the egos of his top clients intact. Guys could tell themselves, "Yeah, I know she wants me, but rules are rules."

In addition to a colony of Bunnies, each club also featured top entertainment acts to keep customers around all night. Some of the best comedians in the country worked the Playboy Circuit at some point, including George Carlin, Richard Pryor, Professor Irwin

Corey, Kelly Monteith, Dick Gregory, and a slew of others. What is remarkable is that they all worked "clean," meaning they couldn't use excessively crude language in their acts—another Heffner rule to keep the club experience elegant and refined.

Every Playboy Club had a "Penthouse" and a "Playroom" venue, where comedians and musical groups or singers performed on a well-executed rotation. Customers might start by having dinner in the Penthouse room as they watched a female singer, followed by Tim and me—the headliners. Each room had seating for one or two hundred customers, and when the Penthouse was at capacity, the managers would begin filling up the Playroom downstairs from the line of people waiting to get in.

The timing worked like this: The female singer would perform for twenty minutes. Then we'd take the stage, and she'd wait backstage as we did the first part of our show. When we had about five minutes left, she would make her way to the Playroom and begin her set downstairs. We'd finish upstairs and wait in the wings of the Playroom for her to conclude so that we could then take that stage for our second performance of the evening. In the meantime, the patrons in the Penthouse upstairs were ushered out and a new crowd was welcomed inside, food and drinks flowing again. Soon, the female singer would be back upstairs in the Penthouse for her third show, and we'd follow when we concluded in the Playroom.

Given the frequency of doing shows five or six times a night, our act was as tight and sharp as we'd ever been. Later, when we booked Mr. Kelly's in Chicago, one of the critics for the *Chicago Daily News* said, *"[T]o watch the comedy team of Tim and Tom is like watching two master ping pong players. Their timing is impeccable."* That came from working those Playboy Clubs. Thank you, Hugh Hefner.

15

An entertainer once told me that, as a performer, the worst thing that can happen is if your audience walks out after a show and they don't feel anything, one way or another. If you've performed and an audience walks out emotionless, you've not done your job.

That's kind of how I felt when Walter Dreesen died. I didn't feel any real sense of loss, but I was sad that he didn't realize what he had. When I wept at his funeral, it was for what he missed out on as a father to eight great kids. Perhaps except for Glenn, his kids loved him despite his many and deep flaws. Children are a gift from God, which is how I consider my own children today. And the responsibility of a parent is to take care of your children. That's it.

Lying in that coffin as eight children wept over him was a guy who would often blow his hard-earned paycheck on beer instead of groceries for his family, which meant we had to go out and shine shoes or sell newspapers or bus tables in a tavern or pizza joint to help make family ends meet. And then we had to chip in to pay for his burial. We had a small icon in the shape of a trumpet molded onto his tombstone, because that's the one thing he exhibited his love for, playing that trumpet, in his day.

After he passed away, I never missed him, because we never had a real relationship. To me, that is the sign of a wasted life, one that is not missed by those who should miss you the most.

16

Tim and I finally made it to the Club Harlem in Atlantic City—a feat to be celebrated if you're working the Chitlin' Circuit. The week didn't begin on a happy note: Tim had taken some time off before our gig started to return to Norfolk for his own father's funeral. I knew it was a tough time for my friend, and when we reunited in Atlantic City, the world was squarely on his shoulders.

At the Club Harlem, you opened on a Saturday night and closed on the following Friday—a full six-day run, with plenty of advertising and word-of-mouth to propel you to the next level of venues if you did well.

There were five acts on the bill each night. There was Mama Lou Parks and her dancers, a big heavyset black woman with all these young black boys and girls who would dance to the music of the 1920s through the 1960s. Mama kicked off the show with a bang before turning the stage over to the Sons of Robin Stone, a singing group, followed by the Quiet Elegance, a trio of black girls who sang and harmonized. Then it was time for a comedy act—our slot—and then finally Ronny Dyson, Smokey Robinson, the Dells, the O'Jays, or the Temptations, whoever the headliner was that week.

On Saturday opening nights, your first show started at 10:00 p.m. Your second show was at 2:00 a.m., and your third show, called the Breakfast Show, competed with the sunrise at 6:00 a.m. This was the show that all the waiters and waitresses, bartenders, and anyone else who worked at clubs around town came to, in addition to all-night patrons.

All the pimps from Newark, Philadelphia, and New York City brought their "hos" down for the Breakfast Show, and it was a quite a scene to behold, knowing that most Americans were only looking at newspapers and empty coffee cups on the breakfast table.

The pimps would pull up in front in their Cadillacs and their Rolls-Royces and limousines. They'd stroll in the front door and tip the owner, Pop Williams, then tip the maître d' and then be seated down front, where many of them would snort cocaine off the tables. The capacity of the place was about 1,300 and the Breakfast Show was always jammed tight.

When it was our turn to go on, the emcee would say to the audience, "Are you ready for some comedy?" And they'd go, "Yeah." And he'd say, "No, are you ready for some comedy? Lemme know, are you ready for some comedy?" And, of course, the audience would cheer and say, "Yeah!"

And he'd say, "Well, we got us a comedy team here (not mentioning one of us was white). They come from Chicago. Ladies and gentlemen, please welcome the comedy team of Tim and Tom."

Then Tim would walk out there by himself, step up to the microphone and say, "We're really happy to be here. See, we just got in town from Chicago, and we've never been to Atlantic City…"

But by this time, some of the brothers and sisters in the audience would be going, "We? This motherfucka keeps saying something about we… I only see he, what's he talkin' about we?"

Sensing the moment build from behind the curtain, I'd slowly enter at stage left. As I entered, the spotlight would hit me and the audience would see this white face looking out at the all-black audience, slowly trying to make his way onto the stage. That's when the laughter would start. I worked my way from down stage left, peeking into the audience, and slowly make my way toward Tim, but always looking into the audience.

When I hit my mark next to Tim, he would say, "Where you been, man? And what are you looking for?" And I'd say, "I don't see any of my people out there." Another huge score. Tim would look in the crowd and say, "No, I don't see any of your people out there, either." Then I'd move closer to Tim, "Well, then, we'd better be funny." And he'd say, "What do you mean *we*, white man?" And the whole room would burst into laughter.

At that point, we'd go into our routine. One of our standards was, "Who is Tim and who is Tom?" We'd point out how Tim was taller, with a moustache, while I was shorter and clean shaven. Obviously, we were of different races, and Tim would say, "...And you never call a black man 'Tom,' so he's gotta' be the Tom." Another peal of laughter.

One morning at the Breakfast Show during this routine, a black dude in the very back stood up and screamed as loud as he could, "Hey, Honky! I'm talkin' to you, white boy! Listen to me, goddammit, I'm talkin' to you!" And the whole room was startled quiet. "Why don't you call him a nigga? 'Cause that's what you'd call him in Mississippi."

Without hesitating, I said, "Hell, I've called him a nigga in Chicago!"

Silence. For several seconds. Absolute silence.

And then, mercifully, the room erupted in laughter. Everybody in the room was pounding the tables and laughing. I suddenly realized what I had said, it just came out of me without thinking.

Tim said later, "Wow, that was really a funny line, Tommy, but damn, it was risky." My heart was pounding afterward when I realized that I had taken some liberties. Being raised in an all-black neighborhood and hearing that word used repeatedly as an affectionate term caused me to blurt it out in that vein, honestly, as if I was back on the streets of Harvey, hanging out with my friends. Had I stood up there in denial and said, "Oh, I've never used that word, sir. I don't use the N- word," it would have come off as phony.

I've always found that being honest with an audience, and letting the cards fall where they may, works far better than trying to be something you're not. This was particularly true when joking about the racial reality of life in America.

Even the black guy who heckled me understood that. After my retort brought on the stony silence of Club Harlem, probably the quietest that place had ever been, that guy just stared at me for a second and then pointed his finger at me and began laughing and nodding and shouted, "That's *real*, brother!" Because it was an honest response.

We scored heavy that night and at the Breakfast Show at the Club Harlem. Our audience left feeling something, standing and cheering us as we left the stage. We had done our job as entertainers. Tim and I walked outside the club onto Kentucky Avenue at 8:30 a.m., and it's difficult to describe how we felt.

Comedy soars and dives, from the highest of highs to the lowest of lows. That night, it felt like we were flying high above Atlantic City's world-famous boardwalk. We felt that we had arrived. And not only had we arrived, but we survived. We had taken insults and physical abuse from black racists all over the country who had attacked Tim. We took abuse from white racists who had attacked me. And sometimes they all got together in weird unison and attacked us both.

What we found out was that, if there was a black person who hated white people when Tim and I appeared, he wasn't mad at me, he was mad at Tim for being with me. You see, Tim would be considered an "Uncle Tom."

If there was a white redneck who hated black people at our performance, he wasn't mad at Tim. He was mad at me because I was with Tim. In the warped racist mindset, by merely standing next to Tim, I gave him validity that they believed he didn't deserve.

As we walked back to our motel, dawn light breaking above us, I felt a brotherly bond with Tim Reid that exists to this day. We were spontaneous pioneers—a fortunate result of a chance meeting. We were different from any comedy team that had come before or since, not because we were of different races, but for the dues we had to pay because of that simple fact.

I thought to myself, "Ain't no stopping us now."

Once upon a time in America, there was a young black man and a young white man who were so idealistic and so naïve that they honestly believed that if they could only get people to sit down and laugh together, then maybe, just maybe, they could live together too.

17

The ending came almost as suddenly as the origin.

Working the Chitlin' Circuit and touring Playboy Clubs were gratifying detours on the long and lonely road to going our separate ways. For six years, Tim and I struggled to break into show business, and we sure as hell struggled to stay there. We traveled the country doing gigs from jazz clubs to prisons to retirement homes, all the while sharing small motel rooms and splitting our earnings fifty-fifty. This was nothing like the brochure that "show business" advertised, but we soldiered on—although it was clear that Tim was becoming restless and less confident in our prospects for success.

As an act, we never reached a point of feeling that gigs would just start lining up for us. We always had to hustle to find the next booking. If I'm being honest, between the two of us, I was probably more dedicated to seeing the act through. I always felt more optimistic about our chances for survival and, eventually, stardom.

However, I was beginning to fear that Tim had begun to express his frustrations to some close to him that he didn't feel we were getting anywhere and that he might have a better shot doing something else, on his own.

My fears were realized one cold winter day when I took an Illinois Central train from my neighborhood to downtown Chicago to meet with Alan Curtis, an agent who had booked several gigs for Tim and me. I was in Alan's office talking about scheduling new dates when he got a phone call from Tim, who didn't know I was there.

Tim had called from LA to ask Alan if he could start booking Tim as a solo act. When he hung up the phone, Alan looked me straight in the eye and told me that it was time I found a new partner.

I cannot begin to describe the bottomless pit I felt in my stomach. I was devastated, like being served divorce papers after an anniversary trip around the world where you felt more bonded to your partner than ever before.

The grand illusions of my mind painted a scene where we'd find success and follow in the steps of Dean Martin and Jerry Lewis. Sure, they had their differences along the way; all comedy acts do. But they stuck it out and then some, leaving behind a legacy of cultural impact, from movies to national tours in big arenas to a lasting career blueprint for those comedy acts that followed. Even in their own nasty breakup, they were still revered for what they had accomplished together.

Had we struck gold and found fame and fortune, I'm sure Tim and Tom would have run its course like anything else. At some point, like Martin and Lewis, we probably would have had creative differences leading to a bitter, public breakup. In my heart, I know it would have been worth it.

However, I'm not one to imagine what-ifs. My childhood conditioned me to find the lessons in everything that happens in life, good or bad, and to consider the alternatives. As I write this, I can pinpoint one life lesson I discovered almost immediately.

I was sitting in a Harvey tavern called the Sulky Inn around the time our comedy team was splitting up. I had played on the tavern's softball team and all my buddies hung out there, so I knew my way around the place. It turned out to be a fitting spot for a realization that was long in the making.

I had two fresh beers in front of me, along with two shot glasses turned upside down on the bar, meaning that a couple of friends had already bought my next drinks. In my fog of despair over Tim's decision to go his own way, my thoughts turned to the future: mine.

I loved show business so much and thought Tim Reid and I were going to become the greatest comedy team in America. That was my dream, but this was my reality. What were my alternatives? Simple: I could find another black comedian and do the same act, or I could get a job in a factory, like my wife wanted, and give up my dream once and for all. Or I could go it alone and fight to make it as a solo stand-up comedian. Those were my options, and I decided I could be a stand-up on my own.

Now I had a plan. With a strong beer buzz propelling me into the depths of my mind, I remembered something that Napoleon Hill and W. Clement Stone had written in their book *Success Through a Positive Mental Attitude*: "If you know what you want to do in life, and if it's a noble endeavor, then search your life and see if there's anything in your life that can deter you from that noble achievement."

Like a lightning bolt, I realized the only thing that could stop me from making it on my own was my drinking. This would be one of the toughest decisions and biggest commitments of my life, because I loved to drink. But I loved my dream far more.

I was wrestling this notion in my mind when my good buddy the bartender, Jimmy Lepore, came to my end of the bar and saw me pushing my two untouched beers back his way.

Jimmy said, "You done, Tommy?"

"No, I quit."

"Yeah, you done for tonight?"

"I quit."

"You said you quit drinking?"

"Yeah, I just quit drinking. Right now."

"Yeah, right. Get the fuck outta here. I'll see you tomorrow."

I may have chuckled to humor Jimmy, but my resolve kicked into gear. I didn't touch another drop of liquor for seven years, until I was finally making a name for myself in LA and went out one night with my wife. I thought I could handle a few beers just to unwind, but the moment the foam hit my lips, I realized that I had changed for good. The only thing that I tasted right then was my dream, and I knew it was close.

Meeting Tim Reid saved me in more ways than one. There is no telling how my life would have turned out had we not met at that Jaycees meeting in Harvey long ago. I'd like to think that I'd have become the CEO of Columbus Mutual, but more likely, I would have landed back in the bars of Harvey for years on end, dissatisfied with life and absent the knowledge that I had a chased down the end of the rainbow.

I always joked that Tim was an educated college graduate and that while I didn't have a degree from academia, I earned my doctorate from the streets. We were like two opposite characters in a buddy movie, enduring trials and tribulations together on the way to a happy ending. We found our individual callings in the experiences we shared together. The things that happened to Tim and Tom, the things we overcame, united us even more in our solo careers than they did when we were partners. It would have been different had we been two solo stand-up comedians who met and decided to team up. If the act didn't work out, I'd have gone back to my solo routine. However, I went onstage for the very first time in my life with Tim. Neither one of us had ever been onstage solo.

It wasn't until I started becoming good on my own that I understood I'd had it in me all along. And it was strangely liberating. I'm sure Tim felt the same way, because he made it too, going on to become a gifted actor and talented director.

With a few decades of perspective, Tim and I "reunited" in 2008 to collaborate with our friend Ron Rapoport on a book called *Tim and Tom: An American Comedy in Black and White*. It provided the chance to revisit the path we charted together. Looking back, I couldn't be any prouder of our shared history.

We remain dear friends to this day, brothers in every sense except by blood. His children, Tim Jr. and daughter Tori, call me "Uncle Tom," and I love them like they are my own. Tim's first wife,

Rita, and I have stayed in touch through the years, and we pray for one another whenever the need is there. Tim and I both agree that our relationship, that time we were show business pioneers, changed our lives for the better.

18

The earth of the entertainment world shook in 1972, when Johnny Carson moved *The Tonight Show* to the West Coast. Since the show first went on the air in 1954, it had been broadcast from NBC's Rockefeller Center studios in Midtown Manhattan. Johnny had determined that since most of the movie stars he wanted to book as the first guests of each show (the "A" guests) were based in Hollywood, it made sense to produce the show where those celebrities lived and worked. The show was also renowned as a breakthrough opportunity for standup comedians, who were normally booked in the "C" or "D" spots on many nights.

There was no better time to be a stand-up comedian. After a decade of music-driven culture in the 1960s, which began with the swinging heyday of the Rat Pack, gave way to the inspired groove of Motown magic, and ended with anti-war anthems warbled by Cat Stevens; Creedence Clearwater Revival; Pete Seger; Crosby, Stills and Nash; Bob Dylan; and others, it was now time for the joke makers to shine in the American pop spotlight. In many ways, comedy became the rock and roll of the 1970s.

No matter where you went in those days, if someone asked you what you did for a living and you said you were a stand-up comedian, the next question was always, "Oh, have you ever been on Johnny

Carson?" If the answer was no, well, the conversation about your career probably ended right there.

In the era of three TV network channels, long before the existence of 900 cable channels or YouTube, you weren't a professional comedian in the eyes of the American viewing public until you had walked through the multicolor curtain of Johnny's late-night show. Relocating *The Tonight Show* was a seismic event that forever changed the life decisions of stand-up comics across America, who ditched plans to move to a small apartment in New York and rerouted to find a small apartment in Los Angeles.

There were a few small clubs in LA at the time, where a new comedian might get up and try to develop an act. The Comedy Store was not a small club; in 1974, it was *the* club. Later, the Improvisation came along and, after that, the Laugh Factory. But none shone brighter than The Comedy Store, which was considered ground zero—the Atlantic Records of the hit-making comedy set.

All the talk and variety shows deployed their talent coordinators to these clubs to find new comedians, and all swarmed around The Comedy Store. Scouts from *American Bandstand, Soul Train, The Mike Douglas Show, The Merv Griffin Show, Dinah's Place, The Midnight Special,* they were all looking for hot new comedy talent. The constant buzz around The Comedy Store was indescribable, and once *The Tonight Show* set down roots in LA, that energy level shot into the stratosphere.

Tim Reid and I were still together when Johnny moved the show in 1972. We were doing pretty well, staying busy and always getting better onstage. We had dreams of doing *The Tonight Show* and catching the guaranteed rocket to national stardom.

As you now know, that never happened. When we parted ways in 1974, we still had one more gig booked, in Houston, Texas. Immediately afterward, I hopped a flight to Los Angeles. I told my wife I'd be home in a week. I thought that just by landing at LAX meant I was bound to "arrive" in LA, figuring that within one week, I'd get discovered and maybe become a star on my own. How fanciful and naïve I was. My wife was very happy, assuming I'd be home in seven days to trade in my stand-up routines for routines of a traditional life.

I arrived in LA and had no place to stay at first. There was a girl I knew who lived in Brentwood named Pat Hollis. She was originally from Texas, and we met in Chicago when we both performed at the Playboy Club. She was quirky but had great stage presence and could sing her ass off. I helped her get a job singing at Mr. Kelly's in Chicago, and she worked at good clubs around the country. She even appeared on *The Tonight Show* several times and should have been a major star. But that never happened.

She wasn't a girlfriend of mine. We never had an affair or anything. But I enjoyed being around her. Besides, she was going out with some guy named Gene, who, by her own admission, was a "nut case" and insanely jealous.

I got ahold of Pat and said I was looking for a place to stay. She told me that she was leaving town for a few weeks and asked if I wanted to house sit. I had never heard that term before; where I grew up, if someone was "sitting in a house," it meant they were about to steal some furniture.

I thanked her for her kindness and jumped at the opportunity. I ended up staying there for three weeks, making my way to The Comedy Store each night, hitchhiking down and back up Sunset Boulevard.

I had some glossy eight-by-ten pictures and bios made up, and during the day, I'd go around town looking for an agent to represent me, this surefire star about to explode. After the first week in LA, though, I realized that wasn't going to be so easy.

On top of it all, when Pat returned from travel, she was curt about my living situation. "Tom, you can't stay here anymore," she said. "My boyfriend will be coming around, and he won't understand this. I told you, he gets really jealous."

"I know, Pat, but I don't have any place to go," I said, begging her to let me stay. After some back-and-forth, she finally relented and said, "Look, I've got a room in the very back of the house, but you've got to use the back door. And if you see my boyfriend's car out in front, you have to wait until he's gone."

The room was clean and provided all I needed, with a mattress on the floor and an old lamp with no shade. I felt like I was back in a motel room on the road with Tim, waiting for a break. Still, I was glad to have a place to sleep, and it allowed me to continue my nightly trek to The Comedy Store.

The arrangement worked for about a week. Every night, I'd check to see if the boyfriend's car was out front, and if so, I'd walk around the block until he left. One night, I was coming back and saw that there was a party at a nearby house in the neighborhood, and the valet attendants had taken up all the parking spots on the street. I didn't see the boyfriend's car, but it turned out he was home. He must have heard me open the back door and thought I was an intruder. I heard him squeal as if terrified, followed by the sounds of his fat feet pounding on the wood-paneled floors as he lumbered to the back of the house to investigate.

Pat scampered after him and said, "He's just a friend of mine, Gene! I'm letting him stay here because he's a comedian trying to get discovered at The Comedy Store!"

I knew he was the jealous type, but by the way he responded, the thought crossed my mind that he must really hate aspiring comedians. He went absolutely berserk, just wacko. I tried to calm him down, "Look, look. She's just a friend trying to help me out. I got a wife and three kids in Chicago. I'm out here struggling…"

The wacko wasn't having any of this. He was convinced we were having an affair. In the middle of my fourth attempt to explain the truth, he said, "I ought to just kick your ass."

At that point, I lost it. All the pressure and emotion that had been ballooning inside of me for the last year was pierced by this prick, and my emotions detonated in his face, "I'm trying to tell you the truth!" He started saying something again, and I cut him off, "Shut the fuck up till I finish! This is a decent human being who's trying to help a friend, but you can't absorb that because it is too fucking deep.

You claim to love this woman? You couldn't possibly love her with that much hatred in your heart. You're calling me every name in the book, and now you want to fight? FINE! Let's go outside!"

I was basically taunting him at this point, because I was ready to continue my self-therapy by beating the ever-loving shit out of the guy. I stormed out the same back door that I had entered so quietly only five minutes earlier and stood in the alley. "I'm waiting, Tough Guy!" I shouted.

By this time, Pat was hysterical, standing in the doorway screaming, "Goddammit, Tommy! Just go back to Chicago, you crazy bastard!"

Her jab at my parents' supposed marital status at my birth was uncalled for; however, her diagnosis of my mental state was accurate. And true, I was also from Chicago. Pat slammed the door so violently that she broke one of its glass windowpanes. God only knows how her conversation with the wacko went from there. Moments later, she threw my few belongings out the back door, and I was officially homeless.

I spotted an old Nash Rambler up on cinderblocks in the alley where I used to dump her garbage. I climbed inside and fumbled with the lever on the front seat until it reclined almost horizontally, enough to serve as my makeshift bed. I put all my stuff in the backseat of the car, and that's where I slept for almost a month. My "master bath" was the restroom located behind a nearby gas station, where I would wash up in the morning before dropping in on agents and managers, hoping someone would sign me as a client. I was getting nowhere. I certainly didn't smell like the next big thing.

To make matters worse, just two days before the incident with the wacko, I had received a "Dear John" letter from Maryellen that said, "This is your dream, not mine. I wish you well, but I'm not moving to California. Good luck to you, but our relationship is over." If you've ever received one of those letters, you know how they sting—and that they rarely come when everything else is going right in your life. I'm not one to give in to bad times, but I felt like the world was coming down on me.

* * *

My saving grace was The Comedy Store, where magical things were happening every night.

I would stand in line and sign up and try to get on these Monday night auditions. While I hadn't yet made it onstage, I honed my craft by simply watching the parade of talented young comedians escort the audience into fits of hysterical laughter.

It took me about thirty days to get that coveted audition, when Mitzi Shore, the owner, finally gave me the chance to go on. Mitzi had cofounded the club in 1972 with her husband, Sammy. When they divorced a few years later, Mitzi got the club as part of the settlement, and she quickly settled into the role as "the grand dame who could grant fame."

I was at once ecstatic and terrified. I can't begin to describe the pressure of what it was like in those days to audition at The Comedy Store. If you did well, Mitzi might put you on the regular lineup. And if you got put on the regular lineup, you performed more nights, which meant that your chances increased of being seen by talent scouts from all the shows, as well as agents who might sign you on the spot.

That was the best-case scenario. However, if you didn't score in your audition, you were likely done on the Sunset Strip, returning to your personal boulevard of broken dreams in Chicago or Detroit or wherever you came from. The Improv and the Laugh Factory were not around yet, so it truly was The Comedy Store or bust.

Thankfully, I did well in my audition spot. I had the crowd right from the beginning and kept them there until my ten minutes was up. Mitzi was watching how the audience reacted to my set. She came up to me afterward and said, "Well, you seem like you've got some stage presence and that you've worked before. I think we can find some room for you." Thrilled but not taking anything for granted, I told her I could also serve as emcee some nights (I had actually started the first comedy room in Chicago inside a club called Le Pub, where I emceed every night), knowing that would provide additional stage time.

Mitzi said, "Yeah, maybe we'll try that. But first, I'm going to put you on the regular schedule," which meant that I'd get onstage at 1:30 or 2:00 in the morning, but it didn't matter. I was finally appearing at The Comedy Store.

Even though she had sent me a pretty declarative farewell note, I was still in touch with Maryellen and missed my kids. I managed to book a two-week gig back in Chicago, opening for Fats Domino at Mr. Kelly's, a famous nightclub that later became Gibsons Bar & Steakhouse. I returned home more confident about my career prospects than I had been in a long time, knowing that I was inching closer to a real breakthrough in LA. During my stint in Chicago, I somehow convinced my wife to return with me. I took the money I made at Mr. Kelly's and brought my family back to the West Coast.

Maryellen and I had ridden the roller coaster of marriage, and in my heart, I was unsure how long the ride would last. She made it clear that the dream I was chasing was mine, not hers. However, I was elated to be reunited with my children, who were living reminders for me that even in the darkest moments of my professional career, I could feel satisfied knowing that I had already won in life. The most important job a man can have is to be a father. To this day, my proudest achievement is the fact that Amy, Tommy, and Jennifer Dreesen are my children.

We searched all over and finally found an apartment on a tight budget. Now we had a place to live, I was working at The Comedy Store, and my family was reunited. Things were beginning to click. But my goal was to make the biggest leap of all and land a shot on *The Tonight Show.*

19

When I first became a regular at The Comedy Store, most comics were roughly on the same level. Jay Leno, however, was first among equals. Jay was flat-out funny. To this day, if you go see Jay perform, you're going to get two hours of solid stand-up.

A few comics from New York started hitting The Comedy Store scene. Jimmy Walker had been discovered in New York and found success on national television, playing "J. J." in the hit show *Good Times*. So when he showed up, he was already a name.

Freddie Prinze was the same way. Freddie got on *The Tonight Show* when he lived in New York, and within days, he had a TV series, *Chico and the Man*, and immediately moved to Los Angeles. I had known Freddie from way back, when he used to lie about his age so he could work in the New York Playboy Club. We became good friends and spent a lot of time together. He even came out to Chicago for Thanksgiving with me and my family. About six months later, when I saw Freddie in Los Angeles, he was the hottest thing in the country.

One night, I was out in front of The Comedy Store, still trying to get an audition with Mitzi, when Freddie pulls up in a new Corvette. All the young comics waiting in line were beside themselves, whispering, "Oh my God. It's Freddie Prinze!" I was quiet but beaming, because I knew that Freddie was going to see me and give me a big hug. And we'd pick up like old times.

Freddie got out of the car and started walking toward the entrance. "Hey, Freddie Prinze," I said, trying to kick-start the love-fest. He kept walking. "Hey, Freddie, how ya doing?" I said, a little sharper.

Freddie glanced my way for a split second and said, "Hey, man, how ya doing?" and kept moving. I was crestfallen.

I waited until he got offstage that night to approach him again. I was in the back of the club and got right in his face so he couldn't get by me this time and said, "Freddie, for the rest of your life, when you see me, walk the other fucking way. Don't ever say hello to me again."

He shot back, "Oh, hey man, what's up?"

I said, "What's up? I knew you when no one knew you. We hung out together. You came to my home, you met my family, you met my buddies in my neighborhood, and now you walk by me like I'm a piece of shit in front of these kids? Don't ever fucking talk to me again."

Feet firmly back on earth, Freddie said, "Now wait, Tommy, wait." I walked away, and he followed me and sat down. He said, "I'm sorry, man. I got my head in my ass," as he shook my hand and hugged me. "I'm sorry."

I forgave him, and we stayed friends after that night, and I always tried to look out for him.

Success happened very fast for Freddie. He was truly an over-night sensation. With that status came immediate access to all the drugs and other forbidden fruits you could imagine, and Freddie imagined with the best of them. Putting my Jaycees hat back on, I sat down with him one night at the Improv. He was doing Quaaludes and drinking a lot of Courvoisier in those days, and I was worried about him.

"Freddie, do you realize that you're putting one chemical in your body that's speeding up your heartbeat and another that's trying to slow your heartbeat down?" I told him. "That's very dangerous."

Freddie looked me in the eye and said, "You givin' me one of your classroom lectures?"

"Yeah, I am."

"Does that make me a student of yours?" he said, with his sly, boyish grin. We both started laughing.

"Freddie, I'm a student of *yours*, but I'm also a friend. And I know this is going to destroy you. I'm being serious. The most important thing a comedian has is that brain. And when you start filling it full of those chemicals, it's going to destroy your creativity."

Freddie grinned and laughed, and I thought he got the message. He'll be alright, I told myself. I was mistaken. Not long after that, he committed suicide. It was shocking news in the entertainment world, and it hit me hard, because Freddie was so talented and so damn young.

Johnny Carson once told me that for every one hundred people who can handle adversity, only one can handle success, because along with success comes a responsibility to remain successful. Freddie was a classic self-destructive comedian—all the talent in the world, but terrified that one day it would all be taken away from him. I said to him once when he was down on himself, "Freddie, look at you. You're nineteen years old and a huge star!" He said, "Yeah, but what if I have to make a comeback when I'm twenty-four?"

I'll never forget that. Make a comeback at twenty-four? Sadly, Freddie was one of those ninety-nine people who just couldn't deal with success or the thought of losing it all.

* * *

Another young comic I first met at The Comedy Store was David Letterman. I walked offstage one night and there he was, this tall kid with a red beard.

He said to me, "I really enjoyed your set, Mr. Dreesen," and then introduced himself.

"Dave, where you from?" I asked.

"Indianapolis."

"Oh, no kidding, I'm from Chicago. We're practically neighbors," I said. "What baseball team do you follow?" I thought he might say the Cubs, my favorite team, which would give us something in common.

Dave replied, "Uh, Cincinnati. It was closest." Well, at least we share the Midwest, I thought.

The next time I saw him, I watched his stand-up routine and gave him a compliment afterward. Dave hated compliments, and to this day, it's hard to compliment Dave. But I kept talking to him after sets and telling him he'd done a good job. After a while, I realized that Dave was a bit of a recluse, which, had I known earlier, I probably would've respected that more and not been so outgoing toward him.

Fortunately, by the time I realized this, we were already friends. Dave and I would play basketball and racquetball together at the Van Nuys YMCA. In fact, I taught him how to play racquetball, and he was a quick study. At first, I was beating him in games by the score of 21–2...then 21–5...21–8.... He was getting better. Before too long, it was Dreesen 21, Letterman 15.... And soon we were playing deuce games, 21–21. Then he started beating me.

For a socially shy guy, Dave was very aggressive on the racquetball court. If you're playing and standing in front of your opponent, there's always the chance you might get hit in the back by a ball off his racquet. If that happens enough, you learn not to stand right in front of your opponent on his serve. Now you're *supposed* to hit the ball off the gigantic wall in front that goes all the way to the ceiling, but Dave would sometimes hit that fucking ball as hard as he could straight into my ass. I'd turn around and flash an angry glare, to which Dave would simply shrug and say, "Oh gosh, Tom. Really, I didn't mean to."

To this day, I don't believe that. Dave was always competitive and wanted to win. He wasn't afraid to muscle around his opponent a little bit, which, deep down, I appreciated.

While most of The Comedy Store regulars were doing their best to keep getting onstage at the club, Dave was working hard to get off the stage. He didn't want to be a professional stand-up comic any more than I wanted to stand stationary in front of one of his faux-lousy shots on the racquetball court.

Dave knew himself and his skill set very well, and I think he ended up exactly where he belonged in his career—behind an inter-view desk with his own show, talking because he wanted to, not because he had to. Thankfully, he chose to talk to us for more than thirty years on one of the most successful television shows of all time. (Sorry, Dave, I know you still hate compliments.)

I don't believe it is a coincidence that some of our greatest TV talk-show hosts emerged out of the Midwest and found stardom as the last television voice Americans heard before going to sleep. Think about it: Jack Parr, Steve Allen, Dick Cavett, Mike Douglas, Johnny Carson, Phil Donahue—hell, even Oprah—and, of course, Dave. They all had Midwest personalities that exuded a certain warmth and authenticity that made it easier to connect with viewers. Across a career like Dave's, spanning more than three decades and thou-sands of nightly episodes, what could be more important than that?

Longevity in this business isn't an accident, especially on late-night television. You must be personable, appear to be honest, and the audience must believe that you mean what you say.

I live in California now, and if I'm out for a morning jog and someone says to me, "Good morning," I feel that if I stopped them and said, "You must be from the Midwest," they'd probably say, "Whoa, how did you know?"

Easy. If you're in Chicago and say to somebody, "Good morning. How are you?" what you really mean is, "Good morning. How are you?"

In LA, if you say, "Good morning. How are you?" you really mean, "I'm here for my therapist appointment."

And if you're in New York and say, "Good morning. How are you?" it means, "How long are you going to be away from your car?"

I think Dave's roots in the Midwest were an ingredient that made him one of the most relatable, easygoing, and successful personali-ties of our time.

* * *

Comedians protect their material like it is their lifeblood—which it is. Today's helicopter parents have nothing on comedians when it comes to lording over their fruits. As Rodney Dangerfield used to say, "If you steal one of our jokes, it's like eating one of our children." Back in my day, if somebody went on national television and did some of your material, those jokes were done, finished. From that point on, anytime you tried to do that material—*your own material*—people might say, "Hey, wait, that's so-and-so's line. I heard him do it on Carson. How dare you steal his jokes?"

We were all mindful of this, and we'd protect one another—the comedians' version of community policing. If I saw a comic doing something that even resembled another guy's material, I wouldn't be angry, but after the show I'd say, "We both know that bit you're doing belongs to so-and-so." And if the guy went on to be a repeat offender, word got out that he was a thief—the worst thing you could be labeled in the comedy community.

Most of the time when confronted, guys would say, "Gee, I really didn't know." Ollie Joe Prater was one of those comedians who lifted material all the time and didn't care. The classic line about him was that a comic confronted him and said, "Hey, you stole that piece from me." And Prater said, "You're a fucking liar. I stole it from Bob Shaw." Ollie didn't care. Stealing was what he did.

Sometimes it wasn't other comedians who lifted lines. There was a loose confederation of writers that worked for a group of comedians, some new and some well-established, whose side hustle was to write for morning-drive talk-radio hosts. They'd come to watch all the comics at The Comedy Store or the Improv and pull out tape recorders when the lights went down. They would record the acts and then sell the best jokes to other comedians or local disc jockeys around the country. I could do a joke at The Comedy Store at 10:30 p.m. on a Tuesday, and during rush hour on Wednesday morning, there would be some DJ in Lubbock, Texas, doing my bit.

There was really nothing you could do about it. You can't copy-right comedy material. I heard that W. C. Fields once paid fifty dollars to have a guy's legs broken for stealing a big chunk of his act. I'm not sure I blame him, because back then, if you had twenty minutes of good material, you could make a living off it for ten years. Jack Benny once told me, "Tommy, when I was doing vaudeville, I had a twenty-minute routine, and I took it around the country for years. Twenty minutes of your stuff right now, Tom, after three *Tonight Shows*, that material's gone."

Once you exposed your material to millions of people, it was a free-for-all. There were a lot of comedians working in the Catskills or on cruise ships who had good delivery and could deliver funny lines, but they weren't writers, so they just stole material. It's been happening since the age of court jesters. There's nothing you can do about it.

* * *

There was one legendary comedian who had a notorious reputation for lifting a joke here and there and making it his own.

When I was headlining at the Newport Beach Laff Stop, my opening acts were Roger & Roger (a comedy team), Willie Tyler and Lester (a black guy with a dummy, Lester), and a new kid named Robin Williams. When I first heard the name, I thought "he" was a "she." What a good lineup, I thought: two white guys, a black act with a dummy, Tom Dreesen, and Miss Robin Williams.

Robin burst out of the San Francisco comedy scene, and the first time I saw him perform, he blew me away. He had a brain that spun 360 degrees a second, all the time. Robin watched me every night and I watched him, and we became friends. He'd come up to me after my set and speak to me in a Russian accent, which always cracked me up. He soon landed the sitcom *Mork & Mindy*, where he played an extraterrestrial visiting Earth from the planet Ork trying to assimilate.

There was a recurring bit at the end of every show where Mork would talk to Orson, the leader of his planet. Robin usually improvised the monologue, and it always made for good watercooler banter in corporate America the following day. At the end of one episode, Robin as Mork did one of my jokes—some stupid line about marijuana or something—and immediately my phone lit up with friends calling to ask, "Did you see that Robin stole your joke?"

The problem with Robin lifting a line or two from you is that he took a piece of your material and made it far funnier than you could ever manage. He was brilliant at taking a little gem of yours and launching it into a different orbit, as only Robin could.

The next night at The Comedy Store, I walked backstage to find Robin and said, "Robin, the other night on *Mork and Mindy*, you did one of my routines."

"Oh, Tommy, oh, which one?" he said, in a serious, non-Russian accent. I told him the bit.

"Tommy, I'm sorry. Let me buy it. I'll pay you," he said.

"Don't worry about it. I just want you to know that I can no longer do that bit. You just did it in front of a big, national audience. If I do that joke in Vegas next month, people are going to think that I'm stealing from *you*."

"Aw man, I didn't mean to, really."

And I honestly believed him.

Robin Williams was the sweetest, kindest, nicest soul you'd ever want to meet in your life. He didn't have a mean streak in his body. When it came to pilfering jokes here and there, his problem was that he had a mind that was like a sponge and couldn't always differentiate between something he heard among friends and something he came up with on his own. I know other comics may take issue with me here regarding Robin, but I truly liked the guy and gave him the benefit of the doubt.

The greatest comedians who ever lived are those who are not afraid to take a risk. They'll go out with a fragment of material when they don't even have a punch line and make it work. Necessity is the mother of invention, and sometimes you roll the dice and a piece doesn't go anywhere, so you pull back or pivot to another bit. But some nights, you take a shot out of desperation and strike gold with something out of your creative mind.

Now, if a comedian does that once a month, that's pretty good. Robin did it every night, twenty or thirty times in one set. He wasn't afraid to fail. I forgave him for breaking the comedian's code because in the end, I didn't give a shit about a stupid little joke.

20

I had become a regular at The Comedy Store, working during prime time with some very talented and diverse acts. The lineup on any given night might include David Letterman, Jay Leno, Robin Williams, Elayne Boosler, Michael Keaton, and Gallagher, who, of course, became famous for his treatment of fruits and vegetables onstage.

I called *The Tonight Show* at least once a week. The talent coordinator was a guy named Craig Tennis, and I pestered him relentlessly, trying to get him to come to The Comedy Store to watch me. Finally, he agreed.

Something very interesting happened the night Tennis came to see me. It was a Tuesday, so I was expecting a small audience. I was hoping for a big crowd, because as every comedian knows, the bigger the crowd, the better chance to do well and feed off the energy. When I pulled in front of The Comedy Store, I was very excited and thought, "Oh my God, look at this crowd!" There had to be more than a hundred people waiting in line to enter.

As I walked by the crowd, I got very nervous, because I saw Norman Lear, then Carl Reiner, and all the major talent coordinators from all the variety shows, including Craig Tennis, who was scouting two other acts in addition to me that night. The first was a comedy team called Baum & Estin. Larry Estin later wrote for *Cheers*. And

Bruce Baum became "Babyman" Baum because always he walked out with a diaper on. They broke up not long after that night. The other young comic Tennis wanted to see was a kid named Billy Crystal. While the rest of us we were all being looked at that night for *The Tonight Show*, it seemed like Billy was being looked at by the entire industry.

The reason for the clamor out front was that Billy Crystal's management company, Rollins and Joffe, had arranged for all these people to see Billy. However, they wouldn't let anyone in until Billy went onstage—a very smart managerial move. They didn't line up all these people to launch the career of someone who wasn't signed to them. So, obviously, they wouldn't let them in during my show. I had to go onstage in front of about twenty people, although Craig Tennis came inside to see me, as he had promised. I did a good, strong twenty minutes, and after the show, Craig said, "I want you to come to my office next week."

I went to NBC the following Tuesday, and Craig told me I had *The Tonight Show*. Holy shit! Then he said, "Show me what you'd do." On the spot, I did five minutes of material. I'd been preparing for this moment for five years. When I finished, Tennis said, "Okay, take out this line.... Take out that line.... Replace this with something else.... Now do it again."

I did the routine again, and he said, "You're on. You'll be on the show a week from today." I was numb with excitement. I sent the word out all over the land. I told everybody I knew, and people I randomly met: "Yeah, I'm going to be on Carson...."

I got to *The Tonight Show* that next Tuesday, and I was ready. This was the moment I had been working and waiting for since Tim and I performed our first gig. I was in the dressing room when a producer gave me the news: I had been bumped. Another guest had run over the allotted time, and I was getting the squeeze. I was instructed to come the following Wednesday, which I did, and I got bumped again. And then I got bumped, again.

I was disheartened. During my fourth backstage appearance at *The Tonight Show*, the executive producer, Fred de Cordova, came in the makeup room and said, "Tommy, I got bad news for you."

"What?" I asked.

"You're going on tonight."

The nerves hit, and my world became a blur. I'm basically a calm performer. Throughout my life, I'd been in some high-pressure situations—hell, I was a crewmember on Navy planes that blasted off from and then landed safely back onto aircraft carriers in the middle of the ocean. I always put my faith in the pilot. This was different; now I was the pilot. Twenty-six *million* people were going to see me, including all the entertainment industry bigwigs and my buddies from The Comedy Store, who were huddled around a TV set in the kitchen of the club. Not only that, my mom had everybody in Harvey, Illinois, watching. If I bombed, I couldn't even go back home.

I had built my first *Tonight Show* routine based on something Jack Benny told me when I first met him. He said, "Don't go out there and talk about the government or the airlines. Talk about yourself. I want to hear six minutes of stand-up comedy about where you're from, your family, where you went to school, what sports you played. When you walk off that stage, you've had six minutes of good laughs, and we know something about you."

Oh, his name is Tom Dreesen. He had eight brothers and sisters. He went to Catholic school. He played basketball on an all-black team. He was in the Navy....

The other lesson I leaned on was to just have fun. After Tim and I broke up, my first solo stand-up gig was a return to Mr. Kelly's in Chicago. I was terrified that the press critics in attendance were going to write, "Tom without Tim is not an act...." Just before showtime, I was in the kitchen pacing around before my set when I ran into Cleveland, a black cook I had gotten to know over the years when Tim and I had appeared there. Cleveland would always joke with us before a show, trying to make us laugh. I saw Cleveland coming out of the restroom as the emcee was about to introduce me onstage, and I said, "Hey, Cleve..."

"What you want?"

"Please tell me you washed your hands."

"What for?" Cleve said.

I said, "Well, in my neighborhood, they teach you to wash your hands after you take a piss."

Cleve smiled and said, "White boy, in my neighborhood they teach you not to piss on your hands."

I started laughing right as my name was called, and when I hit the stage, I had this big grin on my face, laughing right from the start.

Ed McMahon, in his own way, shared the same truth in my dressing room before my first *Tonight Show*. He popped in and told me, "Tommy, good luck tonight. And remember this: no matter what's going on in your life—divorce, abscessed tooth, the flu—when you walk out there, have fun, and the audience will have fun too." This is a trick that I use to this day.

Ed's words were comforting, and I knew his advice was sound. The only problem was that I knew full well this was make-or-break time.

I was pacing around the green room when I realized that Bert Convey, the singer that night, had finished his song. Suddenly, I was next. Craig Tennis came to escort me to my spot behind the curtain, probably the longest walk of my life. We walked past the stagehands, and I remember hearing people whisper, "*It's his first time...*" before clearing out of the way and vanishing into the walls.

Doc Severinsen had the orchestra wailing, because the show was on a commercial break. Tennis looked at me and asked, "You okay?"

"Yeah, I'm great," I said as I began to feel drops of sweat running down my back.

"All right, have some fun out there," Tennis said and patted me on the back before vanishing himself. I was all alone now, save for the one guy who opened the curtain. I continued to pace and said an earnest prayer: "Oh God, you've got to get me through this. I know I can do this." As I was praying, I forgot my first line—what is my first line!? Oh yeah, that's right, that's right....

Then the music stopped. Perfectly timed, because my heart stopped too. The show was off commercial and back live, and I saw the big light coming through the curtain. Showtime.

Johnny said, "We're back now. And I'm glad you're in such a good mood tonight, because our next guest is making his first appearance on *The Tonight Show*. Will you welcome, please, Tom Dreesen."

"I'm glad you're in such a good mood tonight..." Johnny set the audience up for me, as if to say, "Give him a chance."

I felt something nudging my Adam's apple and realized it was my asshole trying to get out. The curtain opened, and I walked into the brightest lights I've ever seen. I felt like the lead surgeon walking into an operating room, but I couldn't see the patient. As a performer working clubs, I was used to walking onstage and seeing the people in the audience. On *The Tonight Show*, you could only see the bright, blinding lights. The audience was completely in the shadows. I saw the camera with the red light of reality on it, though, and I managed to hit my mark—a little green piece of tape on the floor in the shape of a "T," about three feet to the right of the blue-taped mark where Johnny did his monologue.

I waited for the audience applause to subside just a bit and then did my first joke, and it got a laugh. And then I did my second joke, and it got a laugh. And then I did my third joke, and I heard Johnny and Ed laughing behind me. I was on a roll.

The five-minute set was over in the blink of an eye, and I had scored. My last joke was: "You've been a wonderful audience. This is my first appearance on *The Tonight Show*. I'd like to ask you a favor. Show business is a tough life. It's not easy to make it. So if you liked what I did tonight and you're Protestant, do me a favor and say a prayer. If you're Catholic, light a candle. And if you're Jewish, somebody in your family owns a nightclub. Tell 'em about me, would you please?"

I got a big round of enthusiastic applause and went back through the curtain, where I was met by Tennis, who was running up to me and saying, "Tom, go back, go back!"

Excitedly, I said, "Where? Go sit by Johnny?"

"Jesus, no, don't sit by Johnny. Just go out there and take another bow. Get out there!" he said and shoved me back through the curtain. The audience was still applauding. I took another bow, and Johnny gave me that signature "OK" hand gesture that I had always dreamed would one day be directed at me. I left the stage for a second time and exhaled. Craig Tennis and all the stagehands reappeared, hugging me, patting me on the back, and telling me I'd done great.

I was euphoric. I scored on my first *Tonight Show.*

Johnny Carson didn't usually stick around after a show and mingle with the guests, but he came back as I was leaving the studio. "We'll have you back," he said, and my euphoria hit a higher level. I've never stopped working since that special night. Thank you, Johnny Carson.

Everything had paid off. The sleeping in cars, the hitchhiking up and down Sunset, the comedy team, the wife leaving me and then coming back. The bills I couldn't pay. And the birthdays for the kids when I had to scrounge up enough money for a card. It had all paid off.

Now my whole life had changed.

The next day, CBS signed me to a development deal. A CBS executive named Lee Curlin was watching and immediately called the William Morris talent agency, which immediately signed me to a deal. I got a check for $10,000 in addition to a guaranteed $1,850 a month for a year—a nice chunk of change. Our rent was $225 a month. Groceries were $75 a week. And now, I got a check for $10,000 and a guaranteed $1,850 a month?

There were so many things that zipped through my mind driving home that night, and I couldn't wait to hug my wife and kids. For all the dues I paid to earn this moment, they paid them right alongside me. I was now on the inside of this business I loved so much. It was no longer a hobby or fantasy. I basked in the glow of knowing that I could finally provide for my family and give them the things they deserved. But above all, I was excited—I needed—to see the pride on their faces when I returned home that night.

21

The floodgates opened after my first *Tonight Show*, and I became a sought-after guest for all the talk shows: *The Merv Griffin Show, The Dinah Shore Show, The Mike Douglas Show*, and even music and game shows *like American Bandstand, Hollywood Squares*, and *Soul Train*, to name a few.

The national exposure from these shows led to calls from different touring acts who wanted me to travel with them, including Vikki Carr, Natalie Cole, and Tony Orlando and Dawn. I also got a last-minute invite to appear on Sammy Davis Jr.'s variety show, *Sammy and Company*, which was taped live in Lake Tahoe. After the show, Sammy complimented my act and uttered four precious words: "You're coming with me." What? Sammy had a string of theater dates coming up on the East Coast, and on the spot, he asked me to join him on tour.

In the arc of my career, if Mitzi Shore gave me a big break in LA at The Comedy Store, and Johnny Carson gave me a huge break on *The Tonight Show*, then unquestionably, Sammy Davis Jr. provided a huge boost as a national touring act.

"Tommy, I'll bring you on tour in '77 and pay you seventy-five hundred dollars a week. We'll have a blast. And then I'm gonna let you go and find someone else, because I'm just a stepping-stone, baby. You gotta keep moving on till you become a star on your own."

Sounded like a plan to me! Sammy had just provided more of a career road map in one long breath than I had received in my entire life. Not to mention, I was making thirty-five hundred dollars a week at the time, and by more than doubling my salary, Sammy set a precedent and elevated my market value for what others would have to pay me in the future. Honestly, I would have taken a pay cut for the chance to work with Sammy.

I first saw Sammy perform live in 1971, and he instantly became one of my idols. Tim Reid and I were appearing at the Black Expo in Chicago, a weeklong celebration of African-American culture and art that culminated with a big show in a huge arena. On the bill that day were the major black acts of the time, including The Temptations, Smokey Robinson, and Gladys Knight & The Pips. Each came out and did three or four songs. Tim and I were in the wings, on standby as fillers to go out and do some comedy bits if the roadies needed extra time to strike the stage for the next singer.

Tim and I waited about six hours before we were called on to perform, but I didn't care because I had a prime spot to watch all these great acts do their thing. Then Sammy arrived backstage, and everyone started murmuring, "Holy shit, Sammy is here. He really showed up...."

I was confused by the reaction at first but then recalled that Sammy had been at the White House a few months prior to receive an award and was photographed giving President Richard Nixon a quick embrace—a very typical gesture because Sammy was a hugger. He hugged everybody, friend or stranger. He'd hug a stop sign on a busy corner to kill time. He was that kind of guy.

The problem was Nixon's policies were terribly unpopular in the black community, and that picture being splashed across newspapers and magazines created a sense of betrayal. Sammy became persona non grata in the black community.

The emcee welcomed the day's biggest star to the stage and fifteen thousand people began to jeer and boo, shouting horrible things like, "You Uncle Tom motherfucker, get off the stage! Get off the stage!"

Sammy didn't even get into the first song. George Rhodes, his conductor, had headphones on and couldn't hear the countdown to strike up the band, the jeering and booing was so loud.

There was a titter backstage; I had knots in my stomach seeing one of the greatest black entertainers of all time being rebuked by his own people. And what did Sammy do? He stood tall, absorbing each cursing taunt, every screaming catcall. He refused to leave the stage. The emcee scurried back out to calm the crowd and said, "Folks, what is our fight all about if it isn't about individual freedom? No matter Protestant or Jew, Democrat or Republican, tell me, isn't that what we're fighting for? This man flew all night from overseas to be here. Doesn't he at least deserve to be heard?"

The crowd began to quiet down, and sensing an opening, Sammy shouted out instructions to Rhodes and the orchestra, who flipped furiously through sheet music and suddenly broke into one of Sammy's signature songs, "I Gotta Be Me."

Halfway through the number, I could see that he was turning the hostile crowd around. At the end of the song, he received a standing ovation and earned back any lost respect.

I've been in this business for fifty years and seen it all, but I've never seen anybody take a hostile audience and, in one song, get a standing ovation. Only Sammy Davis Jr. could have done that. Frank Sinatra would've said, "Va fangool!" and walked off. Dean Martin would have shouted, "Up yours!" and turned up another drink. Sammy stood tall and effectively said, "Okay, you showed me what you've got. Now let me show you what I got!"

Sammy embraced the moment that night far more deeply than he embraced Nixon, and no one was going to take that stage from him. It was the most amazing performance I've ever seen.

* * *

More than an extraordinary talent and entertainer, Sammy was a gracious man. We were working the Mill Run Theatre in Chicago when Sammy came in my dressing room and said, "Hey, babe, have you ever worked Vegas?" I replied that I'd been trying for years to get there. Sammy smiled and said, "Well, you're opening for me there in January!"

I'll never forget that first time in Las Vegas, driving in Sammy's limo past the world-famous marquee at Caesars, where we were performing. Sammy saw they were updating the marquee, and his name was big and bold while mine was placed in small letters below, as was protocol for second billing. Sammy stopped the limo and shouted to the guys on the scaffolding, "Hey! No, no. I want Tom's name bigger up there so people can see it. This is my marquee. He's not my opening act; he's my co-star. Do it."

Once inside, we headed to rehearsal and were met by Nat Brandywynne, the entertainment director, who said, "Tommy, you'll come out and do twenty minutes, and Mr. Davis, you'll do an hour and ten." Back in those days, Caesars Palace was the absolute worst room to perform in for a comedian for one simple reason: the ceilings were too high. Comedians prefer to work low-ceilinged rooms since laughter is sound, and that energy needs to reverberate and come back at you. Later on, I came to love Vegas venues like the Desert Inn, the Sands, the Riviera, and the Golden Nugget. They're all great comedy rooms because they had low ceilings. Caesars, however, was a cavern. And like all Vegas dinner shows, they served food during your performance, which also was distracting.

Sammy knew this and said, "Hold on, Nat. This is Tommy's first time here. He's got to score big with all the critics in the audience who will be writing reviews. Here's what we're gonna do. I'll come out first and do a couple numbers while people are finishing dinner. Then I'll bring Tommy out before coming back and finishing my set. Tommy, trust me. This will be way better for you."

My mind flashed back to the Black Expo in Chicago and Sammy's resilient performance, where he refused to surrender the stage. Now here he was, volunteering to set the stage and open for me, no matter what the lettered marquee said. "And get this, baby," Sammy continued, "I pray you get a huge standing ovation, because that makes it easier on me."

I had known other artists who wanted their opening acts to do well but not "really well." Sammy wanted me to kill out there, because the better I did, the better the show was. He was determined to bring the house down every night, and he almost always did.

After rehearsal, I walked back out on that stage. There was no one there. I was just pacing around, getting a feel for the shape and parameters. Sammy saw me and, sensing the obvious, came out and said, "You nervous, babe?" I confirmed his observation. "Yeah, it's my first time in Vegas, and I'm performing with *you*."

Entertainers refer to the stage as "boards," the slabs of wood nestled together to create a platform for performances. Sammy said, "Tommy, you see these boards? You earned every single one of them. This is your stage. No one can take that from you, and don't you ever doubt that, because if they could do what you do, they'd be up here."

Sure enough, Sammy surprised everyone that night and opened the show. The opening act was the sacrificial lamb, always secondary to the entrees. This really confused the waitstaff, whose job it was to clear dinner plates before the headliner came on so that everyone paid attention. Those poor diners, who hadn't yet taken one bite, had their chicken parmigiana scooped up as the waitstaff hustled to clear tables. Sammy did three songs and then addressed the crowd: "Folks, you've been good to me. I think of my audience like family, because you've stayed with me through good years and bad, and I'm grateful. And it is special to have the chance to do something in return. So tonight, I've got a real present for you. Please welcome comedian Tom Dreesen...."

I breezed out there on the wings of a legend, confident and proud, and then I got down to business. "I always dreamed that one day I'd work Las Vegas at Caesars Palace," I said, pausing a beat for effect. "I never dreamed that the great Sammy Davis Jr. would be my opening act." The crowd exploded in laughter, but I only remember the sound of hearing Sammy laughing at that line from the wings.

As a rule, I would go out and do twenty-five minutes. But Sammy always told me to do as much time as I wanted, which was a perk that only a star like him could provide. The casinos were usually very strict and expected ninety-minute shows because they wanted those people to be gambling rather than sitting in a theater.

I remember a story about a comedian named Kip Addotta, opening for Andy Williams, who was supposed to do eighteen minutes and one night clocked in at twenty-four minutes. He was met offstage by two pit bosses, who informed him, "We make thirty thousand dollars for every minute a crowd this size is in the casino. You just cost us a hundred eighty thousand. Do you want that taken out of your check, or can you pay cash?" The next day, the joke was that Kip did eleven minutes to try and pay back the time.

Most artists, including Frank Sinatra, adhered to the time limit, believing ninety minutes was enough show for one night. But Sammy would sometimes do two hours or more. People would come to Vegas and say to a local, "Sammy Davis Jr. is in town. Did you see him?" And the local would say, "Oh, I saw him. He's terrific."

"You want to go see him again?"

"Nah, I saw him. He was great."

Conversely, the conversation might go, "Sinatra's still in town? I just saw him last week, but yeah, I'll go see him again." Sammy was a consummate entertainer, but he could also give you a little bit too much. I must admit, I never got tired of seeing Sammy work onstage, no matter how much money he cost the casinos in lost gambling time.

* * *

Sammy and Frank Sinatra had been incredibly close friends long before the summit of the legendary Rat Pack years. Sammy told me about the time Sinatra "discovered" him in the early 1950s at a club in Harlem, where he'd gone to check out the Will Mastin Trio he'd heard so much about. Frank went backstage after the show to pay his respects, and Sammy was beside himself that Frank Sinatra would come to see him. These were the years when Frank was down on his luck, and he invited Sammy to come see his show at the Paramount Theatre. Sammy promised to show up. Two weeks later, Frank returned to Harlem and said, "I'm disappointed in you. I've seen your show twice now, and you haven't come to see me once."

Sammy, head down, said, "Frank, I did come. They wouldn't let me in."

Sinatra understood. He went straight back to the theater, found the manager, ripped up his contract, and told the guy to stick the gig up his ass. He refused to perform in a venue that didn't admit blacks.

Whenever Sammy talked about Frank, he spoke with great reverence about Frank's loyalty and friendship over the years, that being just one of many examples.

When Sammy called me at home before our next stint at Caesars in Vegas, he was excited to inform me that we were following Sinatra. The two of them had not talked to each other for several years, mainly because Frank had learned that Sammy had developed an affinity for cocaine, and they had had a falling out over his drug problem. I knew that Sammy occasionally partied like that. One time at the Mill Run Theatre, Sammy came to my dressing room with a little vial of white powder and said, "Hey, buddy, you want some of this?" I declined, and Sammy didn't get upset, only saying, "Well, more for me."

Sammy told me that Barbara Sinatra and Altovise Davis, playing re-matchmakers, had arranged a dinner in Vegas for Sammy and Frank to make amends between Frank's two shows that night. "Hey, babe, I want you to come in early. We'll go see Frank's second show after my dinner with him," Sammy told me, excited like a little kid getting to invite a buddy to a ball game. "I want my peeps there," he said, which also included his conductor George Rhodes, Shirley Rhodes, Dino Meminger, and several others who worked for him.

We met up with Sammy at the Caesars showroom after his dinner with Frank, and he was giddy with excitement. Our table was right in front of the stage, and Sammy told me to stay tuned, because he and Frank had a surprise in store.

Frank came out delivered a command performance. Toward the end of the show, Frank segued into his rendition of "The Lady Is a Tramp," when, on cue, Sammy jumped up on top of the table, leapt onto the stage, grabbed the microphone, and joined in. When the audience saw this, just then realizing Sammy was in the audience, they went wild. Frank and Sammy, reunited again.

Sammy returned to our table as Frank, smiling, finished his set. Now Sammy was deep into his cups that night, and after the show, his bodyguard steered a wobbly Sammy and the rest of us through the kitchen area to avoid the mob of the crowd. We were walking through the kitchen when one of the waiters, a black guy, was yelling at another waiter for the steaks he needed for the next show. He didn't see Sammy behind him, and the waiter said, "Hey, Al, bring up the meat!"

Sammy stopped in his tracks. I remember nearly bumping into George Rhodes, who was in front of me, and we both watched Sammy confront the waiter, saying, "Who tha fuck you calling Buckwheat?"

The waiter turned around, and holy shit, there's Sammy Davis Jr. Now in his face, Sammy asked, "Who tha *fuck* you calling Buckwheat?"

"Sir, I didn't call you Buckwheat," the waiter said, shocked and embarrassed.

I was the only white guy there, and I said, "Sammy, he didn't say that."

Sammy gave me a mean look. "Say what?"

"Sammy, he didn't say that. I was standing right here," I said, repeating my stone-cold sober observation.

Time froze. The kitchen staff froze. The meat froze. Sammy looked at me sternly, then looked at the waiter. Then he walked away toward the elevator that took him to his suite. I went to my room, surprised at what I had witnessed.

A few moments later, the phone rang. It was Shirley Rhodes, Sammy's assistant. She said, "Sammy wants you to come up." I told her it wasn't the best idea, because I knew Sammy was still drinking. But I had also been around a lot of drinkers and knew I could handle it, so I went up to the suite.

I was sitting at the bar in the alcove of Sammy's luxurious suite talking to Murphy Bennett, Sammy's road manager, when Sammy appeared and took a seat next to me. Everyone scattered, leaving me alone with the shortest big man in the room.

Now whenever Sammy and I were alone, we'd speak to each other like a couple of street guys on the corner. "Let me see if I got this straight," Sammy slurred, "...and please s'plain this to me. I'm the nigga who pays you, but you stick up for the nigga in the kitchen who calls me Buckwheat?"

"Uh, Sammy the guy didn't call you—," and I couldn't say the word "Buckwheat." I just started laughing. Maybe it was nerves, or maybe it was the ridiculousness of it all. I was looking at Sammy Davis Jr. on a barstool asking me to "s'plain" this to him. Every time I'd try to s'plain, I burst into uncontrollable laughter.

"Sammy, please, the guy didn't call you—" I started laughing again. "Hold on.... Sammy, the guy didn't call you Buck—" And I lost it, laughing again.

Now Sammy ain't laughing. He was looking at me, stern again. Finally, I just got it out. "Sammy," I said, putting my head down, "the guy didn't call you that. He was telling someone to 'bring up the meat.'"

"Huh? That's your explaining?"

"That's it, Sammy, and that's the truth."

"Okay." And he ambled away.

The next day, Sammy came to my dressing room before our show. I had stayed away from him the entire day and wasn't sure what to expect.

"All right, babe, run it down for me again. What happened last night?"

I told him exactly what had happened. Sammy then asked, "Would you know this guy if we went in the kitchen?"

We went to the kitchen. I spotted the waiter from the night before and said, "Mr. Davis wants to talk to you."

The guy was distraught, cowering in front of his nemesis from the night before. Sammy said, "Tommy says that I owe you an apology."

Looking up, the waiter said, "Mr. Davis, you'll never know how much I looked forward to you coming here. My mother is your biggest fan, and she told me to make sure I got a chance to see you, because you're the greatest entertainer on the planet. And for you to think that I would call you or any brother 'Buckwheat'..." And he broke down.

Sammy said, "Well, son, I had too much to drink last night and I apologize." And then Sammy gave him a hug, and that was it.

The following day, Shirley Rhodes came into my dressing room and handed me a box with a ribbon on it and said, "Sammy wants you to take this to the kid." I found the guy, gave him the gift, and watched as he opened the box. It was a Rolex watch.

I immediately went to Sammy's dressing room, where I found him sitting in front of his vanity. I pulled up a chair and said, "I delivered the gift. Now please s'plain this to me. If I call you 'Buckwheat,' will I get one of them Rolex watches?"

Sammy smiled at me and said, "Yeah, because you're going to need to know what time the next bus leaves for Chicago, motherfucka." This time, Sammy joined me in laughing uncontrollably.

* * *

I worked consistently with Sammy from 1977 to 1980, and each night on tour was a party. What I remember most was the time he spent sharing his wisdom with me as veteran entertainer.

Sammy loved to tell stories about old show business and his days in the Will Mastin Trio, including one that I tell comedians to this day. Sammy only had one year of formal education, and he spent most of his time doing six shows a day on the Chitlin' Circuit as the youngest member of his Uncle Will's traveling act. In between shows, he'd go to the cinema and watch movies starring James Cagney, Jimmy Stewart, and other celebrities with unique, recognizable styles. Returning to his own stage, Sammy started doing impressions of them during shows to fill time in between songs. His Uncle Will would admonish him, saying, "You need to quit doing impressions of white people. You're going to get us in trouble."

Young Sammy kept doing the impressions, and the audiences kept warming up to the repertoire. One night, they were opening at Ciro's in Los Angeles for Janis Paige, one of the hottest live performers of the day. It was Oscars night, and Ciro's was filled with Hollywood stars intent on continuing the glamorous evening.

According to Sammy, the Will Mastin Trio came out and just knocked them dead, start to finish. For the encore, Sammy came back out and did impressions of many celebrities in the audience—except for Jerry Lewis, who was in the front row. Jerry stood up and yelled, "Hey, what about me?" Sammy then did a Jerry imitation that had the real Jerry doubled over in hysterics.

After the show, poor Janis Paige exclaimed, "I'll open for *you*. I can't follow that act." That night put the Mastin Trio on the map in new ways, and they were the talk of the town. Before long, they were opening for Jack Benny at Caesars, and once again, the Will Mastin Trio just destroyed the audience on opening night. They walked off with the room still buzzing. The lights dimmed, and Jack Benny slowly walked out to the center of the stage, which was a signature gag to get the audience giggling.

Into the microphone after this incredible standing ovation for the opening act, Benny starts and says, "A guy goes into a hardware store and says to the owner—"

Just then, Sammy walked back out and said, "Mr. Benny?"

Startled, Benny humored the intruder. "What is it, Sammy?"

"Mr. Benny, with all the excitement of opening night, we forgot to do our closing number."

Jack Benny, with his deadpan look said, "Your closing number?"

"Yes. Do you mind if we do it?"

"Well, no, Sammy. Of course not." Benny didn't leave the stage, though. He just moved upstage a little bit as Sammy swung into "Birth of the Blues" and, again, just fucking killed. Barely off the high from the first time Sammy left the stage, the audience again gave a loud standing ovation, and Sammy took a big, theatrical bow.

Meanwhile, Jack Benny had not moved from his spot upstage. He just stared at Sammy as he melted away into the wings. Then he slowly walked up to the microphone. "So, this guy says to the owner..." and the crowd burst into laughter. Benny just continued the joke. Do you know how fucking ballsy that is? That is one of the gutsiest things I've ever heard of—and another great lesson for comedians: don't be afraid to take a risk, no matter what.

Years later, I was working with Frank Sinatra at the Golden Nugget in Atlantic City when Sammy was appearing at Harrah's on the other side of town. After my set, I went Harrah's to catch Sammy's show and say hello. I was with a friend named Mike Goffredo, a PR guy from Philadelphia. We went backstage and saw all these stars who were assembled to greet Sammy after his closing number. When he took his final bow and came backstage, Sammy walked past all these stars and came right up to me. We embraced and talked for a few moments.

Afterward, Mike Goffredo said, "Did you see what Sammy did? He went through that whole crowd of stars, then came up and gave you a hug for the ages." I hadn't thought about it, but it hit me. "Oh yeah, wow."

Sammy and I were friends and had history together. I was touched by Sammy's gesture that night, and I was reminded how grateful I was for the experiences we shared and the lessons he taught me.

The eight Dreesen kids: Glenn, Darlene, Margie, Judi, me, Dennis, Alice, and Wally

Frank Polizzi as a young man

*Me at age sixteen,
in front of the shack
we called home*

*With Maryellen
on our wedding
night*

(Top) *With Maryellen and my
parents, Glenore and Walter
Dreesen*

(Left) *Navy Third-Class Petty
Officer Dreesen, taken aboard
the USS* Tarawa

(Right) *Home on leave after my first year in the Navy*

(Below) *Hanging out with Uncle Frank*

(Left) *Tim & Tom promotional photo*

(Below) *With my friend and fellow pioneer, Tim Reid. "Tim and Tom" was America's first— and last—black and white comedy team*

An early Tim and Tom promotional brochure

INTRODUCING

THE COMEDY TEAM OF: -TIM & TOM-

With Nancy Perry (L) and Kim Forbes (R). Three kids from Harvey working at the Chicago Playboy Club. I'm still dating Nancy...

*Early days at
The Comedy Store*

*My first appearance
on* The Tonight
Show *in December
1975*

Backstage with my Mom after a show at Field's Supper Club in Chicago

When Sammy Davis Jr. took me on the road, I found my big break as a touring comedian

(Top) *Fourteen years and a lifetime of memories with the "Chairman of the Board"*

(Right) *At former president Gerald Ford's house after a charity show, still in our tuxes*

Barbara Sinatra, my friend and part-time "lawyer"

I boldly asked Frank to take my photo with Frank Jr. before he began his first song on stage in Atlantic City. We laughed about it for years.

With Frank Sinatra and his road manager, my dear friend, Hank Cattaneo

Promo from my pilot TV show, "Dreesen Street"

My celebrity friends gathering around Darlene before we ran twenty-six miles

Appearing on The Tonight Show *when one of my dearest friends was the guest host*

Comedian Tom Dreesen

Ranked 3rd Best Celebrity Golfer
by Golf Digest Magazine

(Left) *My favorite pastime. In 2005,* Golf Digest *ranked me the 3rd best celebrity golfer.*

(Below) *An annual tradition of being picked up by the Bob Hope Classic Girls*

My good buddy, Clint Eastwood, showing me the way

If the Cubs had used this bat, they'd have won the World Series sooner

Goofing around with Cubs Hall of Famer Ryne Sandberg before a game at Dodger Stadium

Throwing out the ceremonial first pitch to Bob Dernier before a Cubs game

A silly joke became the "AHMO" battle cry for the Wylie Pirates (TX)

With Dr. Andrew Lowy. The ceiling lights make it seem we have halos. I don't deserve one, but he certainly does.

(Top) *My precious children: Amy, Tommy, and Jennifer*

(Left) *I received the Ellis Island Medal of Honor Award in 2005 and dedicated it to Frank Polizzi to fulfill my promise*

22

In March of 1979, I returned to LA during a break from appearing in Las Vegas with Sammy. As I normally did when I came off the road, I'd call The Comedy Store for time slots to get onstage and try out new stuff I'd written. I was regularly appearing on *The Tonight Show*, and every time they booked me, I'd have to come up with five minutes of fresh material, because Johnny Carson didn't want "Two guys go into a bar…" jokes. I'd go to The Comedy Store with my tape recorder and try out twenty minutes of material to see what worked. Then I'd go home and listen to the tape before going back to The Comedy Store to do it again. I'd repeat that process over and over until I had a tight five minutes for *The Tonight Show*.

Back then, there was only one room you worked at The Comedy Store, nicknamed "the Original Room," because that's where Mitzi's Comedy Store had started. There was an adjacent building owned by a guy named Art Lebeau, who had a fifties music kind of room and booked musical acts. Out of nowhere, he decided to open his own comedy club, and Mitzi put the word out to all of us that if we worked for the competition, she'd bar us from performing in her venue. Finally, she just bought out Lebeau, expanding her empire by creating what came to be known as "the Main Room," which had 400 seats.

The Main Room became the hosting ground for big name acts like Jackie Mason and Rodney Dangerfield. They'd take the door revenue, maybe thirty or forty dollars a head, while Mitzi took liquor sales. She made money, and the big acts made money.

The rest of us continued to work the Original Room, and we didn't get a dime. Mitzi's long-held theory was that The Comedy Store was a laboratory, a creative workshop for comedians to hone their acts, with the chance to be discovered by a talent scout for one of the national shows.

When I came off the road this time, I went to The Comedy Store and was informed I'd be playing the Main Room that night, along with Jay Leno, Robin Williams, David Letterman, and Elayne Boosler. When I did my new material, I felt like I was back in Las Vegas; there was a big crowd and great energy—just a top-class experience. After the show, we all went to Canter's, a restaurant on Fairfax Avenue and a regular post-show haunt.

I had been there for a bit when Jay Leno came in and declared in his signature high-pitched way, "Hey, guys, this is absolute bullshit. We go into the Main Room and work for free. The established comedians get the door, but we work for free?" Jay continued to rail, arguing that it may have taken five of us to fill it, but the room was packed, and Mitzi got the full pot while we got zip.

Some of the comics agreed with Jay and began to get agitated. I just listened. I was making a good living working in big venues around the country, and money had become a secondary concern for me. But I understood the imbalance Jay had identified. The group decided to have a meeting the following week and invited all the regular comics. I attended the meeting, along with about a hundred others, and it was utter chaos—disorganization that only a gang of comics could create. They were all talking at the same time, bickering about what should be done, cracking jokes, and getting nothing accomplished. The only thing they decided in the first meeting was that they should have a second meeting, which I also joined. Once again, they were all over the place. These were young, bright people coming out of college settings, as opposed to my generation, where many of us came from poor neighborhoods and straight off the streets. These kids needed to know how to operate, and I tried to bring a mix of that intellectual approach with some street smarts.

After listening to the unruly proceedings for a few minutes, I stood up and said, "Hold on. You're getting nowhere. Let me run the meeting, and we'll get organized." From my time in the Jaycees, I knew all about Robert's Rules of Order, which governed how a meeting was conducted, with action items, next steps, and deadlines. I played my card as the older "veteran" and took control of the meeting to create a structure and give folks a chance to speak, one at a time. The proceedings were...comical, but a bit more organized.

I'd say, "Wait, hold on, Jay, hold on, hold on. Gallagher's got the floor. Go ahead, Gallagher." And Gallagher would make some crazy point. Then Elayne Boosler would get up and have her moment. (Elayne is not only a wonderful comic talent, she's extremely smart, and I'm glad she was on our side because she contributed greatly to the cause).

Then I'd call for a motion and ask someone to second that motion. We set up committees and subcommittees to discuss and debate clear objectives. Finally, we were getting organized about what the comics really wanted, which forced everyone to talk about the issues that mattered most.

The group decided that I should be the one to approach Mitzi on behalf of everyone else, so I went to talk to her about the comedians getting paid.

Mitzi was insulted. She said there was no way she was paying the comics, and to my chagrin, I couldn't make any headway with her. I had charmed my way into the hearts of many smart and tough women in my day as an insurance salesman, but Mitzi was undeterred. I continued to try, and we agreed to meet again. The next time, Paul Mooney, Tim Thomerson, and George Miller came along. We went to Mitzi's home at ten o'clock one night and shared our proposal to get paid. By two o'clock in the morning, she still would not budge. Paul Mooney was sitting in a chair half asleep. Miller was lying on a couch out cold. Thomerson was in a chair snoring. And I was still trying to reason with Mitzi. She would not blink.

The comedians kept meeting to discuss what we should do. This was becoming an all-consuming endeavor. One night after a meeting, I was tossing and turning in bed, trying to come up with a solution. I fell asleep—and then woke up with an idea, a silver bullet that worked for all. I jumped up out of bed, in the process scaring the hell out of my wife, who, in a ruined slumber, said, "What's wrong with you?"

"I got it!" I told her. "I've got the solution!"

The next morning, I went straight to Mitzi's office and told her, "Look, you're charging four-fifty at the door. Why don't you charge five-fifty and let the comedians have that extra dollar?"

The math made sense to me. If a hundred people came to the club one night, the comedians would split a hundred bucks. If two hundred people showed, they'd share two hundred bucks. "Mitzi, this is the solution, and it doesn't cost you a dime," I said. "Just add another dollar onto the door for a cover charge. There's no cost at all to The Store."

Mitzi dismissed me faster than a beleaguered teacher sick of a rowdy class on the last day of school. And then, tellingly, she said these cutting words: "They don't *deserve* to be paid." I was stunned. I always thought the issue for Mitzi was about money, and if so, then we could solve this problem. But it wasn't about money at all. It was about pride and control. Power.

Her motives were now clear, and even though it made no sense to me to quibble over one hundred cents per customer, she rejected the idea. I took her response back to the comedians, whose resolve continued to harden. Rather swiftly, they voted to go on strike. I called Mitzi from a phone in the room and said, "Mitzi, the comedians are planning to go on strike. Would you please consider paying the comedians?

Her answer? "Not one red fucking cent." I asked her to repeat what she said as the comedians gathered around me, leaning in to hear Mitzi say even more sternly, "Not. One. Red. Fucking. Cent." Well.

And then, like a crowd of jazzed-up union members pissed off at working conditions on the dock, they all began to yell in unison, "Strike! Strike! Strike!" Plans for picketing The Comedy Store began in earnest.

Several weeks before the strike, Mitzi held a meeting inside The Comedy Store, where one of her loyalists, a rough-around-the-edges comedian named Biff Maynard, observed that we wouldn't go on strike because we needed some place to work.

The fact of the matter was, there was another comedy club in LA on Melrose Avenue that was becoming popular, the Improvisation, which was owned by a guy named Budd Friedman. We hadn't discussed the reason for our strike yet with Budd, because The Comedy Store was still the mother ship—the Yankee Stadium of the comedy circuit.

Mitzi said to Maynard, "Well, if they want to work, they can go to the Improvisation." Another Mitzi loyalist, Ollie Joe Prater, allegedly then said, "What if there was no Improv?" Two days later, somebody threw a Molotov cocktail on the roof of the Improv and burned down half of the building.

23

Steve Bluestein was the head of our publicity committee. Once the decision was made to strike, he immediately began reaching out to media outlets like *Variety*, the *Hollywood Reporter*, ABC, NBC, CBS, and others to invite them to The Comedy Store to witness the first night of picketing comedians on strike.

With all the media planning to descend upon The Comedy Store, I was once again nominated to be the spokesman to ensure we had one voice speaking on behalf of the entire effort. I didn't want to be involved to this degree, but I also wanted to see my friends prevail in what I believed was a noble and just fight.

That first night, more than a hundred comedians marched out front. But nineteen crossed the picket line—the biggest name being Garry Shandling, who wasn't well known back then and was just trying to get onstage at The Comedy Store. Had they not crossed that picket line I don't believe the strike would have lasted more than twenty-four hours. But because they did, it gave Mitzi a small but vocal contingent of her own, and the strike lasted nearly eight weeks.

We walked the picket line night after night. All sorts of things happened in that parking lot, including comics getting into arguments and fights with fellow funny people. It was all so insane, and it became clear that nobody was giving in.

Around that time, Budd Friedman, the owner of the charred club, the Improv, came to me and said, "Tom, I can still have a comedy stage in the front of my building while I'm trying to rebuild. If you guys strike, I'm out of business. Please don't strike me now."

I told him we didn't want to strike anybody. The comics just wanted to be paid. I asked Budd if he would sign a memo agreeing that, once he rebuilt, if we worked at the Improv he would sit down and negotiate fairly with us. "Absolutely," Budd said and signed the document.

Walking the picket line, we would approach patrons arriving at The Comedy Store and ask them not to cross our picket line, but instead go to the Improv, where we were all doing a show later that night. Once we arrived at the Improv to do our renegade show, you could smell the burnt wood from the fire, a pungent reminder of the seriousness of our situation—not to mention the collateral damage that had come to a rather innocent bystander in Budd.

Meanwhile, the strike kept going night after night, and we were getting more and more attention. Johnny Carson talked about it during his monologues and had guests on the show who debated both sides, including Buddy Hackett, who said he thought the comics were wrong. We had supporters of our own, like Bob Hope and Richard Pryor, who applauded our fight for fairness and equal treatment.

The momentum and energy of the striking comedians began to slip after about two weeks walking the picket line. People began to worry that they would never have a steady place to work because of their affiliation with the cause. Panic started to set in, and it became harder to keep the kids in line. I was a little bit senior to them. I'd also been in the military and had experienced some hard times, so I kept trying to hold them together. I'm not one to look for a fight, but when I do, I sure don't want to lose. A guy I grew up with in Harvey used to say, "I don't want to fight Dreesen. I could whip his ass, but I know he's going to come back tomorrow, and I'll have to whip his ass again. And then, he's going to come back the next day, and I'll have to whip his ass again. He won't quit." I always loved that observation about my commitment to never giving up, because sooner or later, I'm going to find a way to prevail.

I may have been "winning" in that the strikers were holding together at my direction, but I was beginning to lose income myself. I turned down gigs on the road with Sammy Davis Jr. to the tune of nearly fifty thousand dollars, but Sammy got word to me that he was proud of what we were doing. I kept telling everyone to stay the course, and Sammy was telling me the same thing, even as I began to wonder about my own future.

Things seemed to be at an impasse. Finally, Mitzi came to us with a counteroffer: She would not pay in the Original Room or the Belly Room, another stage inside the club, on weekdays. But on weekends, she would pay in the Original Room. She pledged to give comedians twenty-five dollars a set. I brought the offer, which I would have settled for, back to the comedians, knowing that we'd get something and could claim victory. But the majority of comedians said no, arguing that she charged a cover in the other two rooms, so why shouldn't we get paid whenever she charges a cover?

I went back to Mitzi to report that her offer wasn't good enough; the comedians wanted to be paid anytime they appeared on any of her stages that charged a cover. Furious, Mitzi decided to start paying any comedian who crossed the picket line twenty-five dollars a set on weekends.

There were two key moments during the strike that, looking back, turned out to be pivotal in our favor.

David Letterman was understood by all to be one of Mitzi's favorite comics. She felt she had nurtured and readied Dave's career for prime time, culminating in several appearances on *The Tonight Show*. As a result of his command performances on hallowed grounds, it was hardly a secret around town that Johnny Carson had also taken a real liking to Dave. This was punctuated by the fact that Carson had asked Dave to guest host *The Tonight Show* the night that Carson served as emcee for the Academy Awards that year. This was the biggest night of Dave's young career, and I accompanied my buddy to the show that afternoon.

Dave claimed he was petrified—just scared to death of the task to carry the show of his television idol. No matter what I said or did to try and calm his nerves, all Dave could say was that this was certainly the end, a direct bus ticket back to Indianapolis. I think he was joking, and of course Dave went out and did what he's always done best. He had the crowd on a tight string, delivering an impressive and well-received turn as host that night. And he provided a perfect landing spot for TV viewers across the country after Johnny bid goodnight to the assembled crowd of Oscar-goers a few channels away.

After Dave's triumphant showing, we got into his car and drove back to The Comedy Store, where he walked the picket line for the first time. As Dave received thumps of praise and high-fives from his fellow comics after the performance of a lifetime, Mitzi watched the scene unfold from a window inside her cavernous club, heartbroken at how her Chosen Ones had chosen each other over her.

Around that time, the Screen Actors Guild held a big event for their members and had invited representatives from both sides of the strike to attend and speak. I was accompanied by Mark Lonow and his wife, JoAnne Astrow, who were very involved in our efforts. Biff Maynard represented Mitzi's team, and during his remarks, he made a stupid comment.

To a room full of unionized artists and actors he said, "Comedians are artists, and artists need not be paid." There was a groan of incredulousness across the room, and I seized on the remark when I got up on behalf of the strikers. "We've been walking the picket line for almost eight weeks. Halfway through, Mitzi decided she would give those who worked the club twenty-five dollars a set on weekends only." Directing my ire at Biff as an example, I said, "Do you know what this man did last weekend? He worked The Comedy Store on Friday and Saturday night, and because of our efforts he got twenty-five dollars each night. Do you know what he did with that money? He put gas in his car, had a nice dinner, and then drove here to tell you not to pay us."

The crowd began to murmur in agreement. In closing, I said, "If you don't support us, I don't know how much longer we can last." The murmur from the crowd swelled into a big ovation of applause, and I walked offstage.

Afterward, one of the Screen Actors Guild's leaders informed me that, while their bylaws prohibited them from publicly supporting non-members, they planned to take out full-page ads in *Variety* and the *Hollywood Reporter* to encourage those in the creative industry not to attend or appear onstage at The Comedy Store while we were striking, which was a really big boost to us.

I was excited to drive back to The Comedy Store with Mark and JoAnne to share this news with our front-line marchers that night. I didn't realize I was about to witness the second turning point in our campaign.

When I arrived, I began to tell the clamoring crowd what happened at the SAG meeting. I was facing east and noticed a few comedians in the nearby driveway that led to the parking lot. Looking over, I saw Biff Maynard in his car on Sunset Boulevard facing east, waiting for the westbound traffic to pass so he could pull in that driveway. He was gunning his engine as if on the starting line of a drag race. The comedians milling about in the driveways were clearly in danger, and I shouted at them to get out of the way.

Just then, I heard his tires screech, and he came flying in there, followed by a loud thud of human flesh hitting the pavement. People shrieked as the rest of us hurried over, where we found Jay Leno laid flat on the ground, motionless.

"Oh shit!" I yelled as Maynard pulled his car way in the back corner of the parking lot and slammed on the brakes. People started yelling, "He ran over Jay!"

At that moment, I found my breaking point. I could not take any more of this bullshit over a few dollars. I was done with all of it and decided my next act would be to break the sturdy jaw of Biff Maynard. I wanted to annihilate the guy.

But first, Jay. I ran over to kneel next to him and yelled for someone to call an ambulance. I put my hand on Jay's head and asked him to respond to me, at which point, he looked up and gave an unmistakable wink before closing his eyes again.

Shocked and impressed, I whispered down to him, "You sly son of a bitch...." Jay had thrown his hand and smacked the side of Biff's fender hard before falling to the ground, as if he had been hit.

Biff came running up, and joining the act, I screamed, "What the fuck is wrong with you? You hit Jay!" Biff stammered and began to argue that he didn't mean to mow Jay down, which led to a loud if contrived argument on my part. Sensing the opportunity, I decided not to deck Biff, which was probably smart since I knew Biff could hold his own.

An ambulance arrived to take Jay to the hospital, which he protested at first, because he wasn't actually hurt, but the EMS workers had protocol to follow. Plus, it made for a continued theatrical statement. Meanwhile, Biff had run inside The Comedy Store and informed Mitzi about all the commotion outside. About twenty minutes later, one of Mitzi's staff came out and said she wanted to speak with me.

I walked inside and saw that Mitzi was rightfully shaken. She looked me in the eye and simply said, "Enough. Let's settle this tonight." I told her that it was time and the right thing to do. I left the brief meeting and called our lawyer, Ken Browning, who used to work with Henry Bushkin, Johnny Carson's longtime personal attorney. Browning arrived half an hour later, and we sat with Mitzi until 4:30 that morning, when she finally agreed to negotiate a settlement contract.

The strike was over. The fallout from the strike and the personal toll rendered on the family of comedians who called The Comedy Store "home," however, was not.

* * *

Three weeks after the strike ended, thanks in part to the manu-factured drama of Jay Leno's pratfall onto the dark asphalt of The Comedy Store parking lot, I was ready to resume my actual job and rejoin Sammy Davis Jr. on the road as he headed to Lake Tahoe for a two-week engagement. But first, the comedians gathered one last time to commemorate the victory we had achieved in our fight for fair pay. Our motto of "No Money, No Funny" had won out, and the comedians were slowly beginning to find their way back onto the nightly bills at The Store.

I took the opportunity to deliver a farewell speech, acknowledg-ing what we had accomplished by sticking together and standing up (pun intended) for what was right—not just for us but for any kid who wanted to be compensated for performing at one of the hun-dreds of comedy clubs that had sprung up around the country in recent years. From then on, kids would perform stand-up, and they would get paid.

To this day, comedians will approach me—young kids in their twenties and thirties whose parents hadn't even met when the strike took place—and say, "I know what you did for me. Thank you." And I always give the credit to the comedians who walked the picket line, because by that point, my career was established, and they had more to lose than I did.

I heard about a comedian who got an offer to travel to Denver for a couple of hundred dollars for five days. The kid said, "Gee, Denver for just a couple of hundred dollars?" and the club owner said, "Well, you work at The Comedy Store for free. At least we'll pay you to come here and try out new material." There was a certain logic to that argument. Then, once The Comedy Store began to pay enough so that young talent could make enough for food and gas, while being able to plant a flag in Hollywood to audition for TV shows or commercials, it was a new day. Those clubs outside of LA really fell in line, having to pay a little bit more money to attract performers.

The New York comedy clubs started paying too. Silver Friedman, Budd's wife, had won the Improv in New York during their divorce. She told me once that she pulled up in a cab in front of the Improv one night when her club manager, Chris Albrecht, came running out. (Albrecht later became the head of HBO and Starz.)

Albrecht met her at the curb in a panicked state and said, "Silver, our comics want to get paid because the comics in LA won the strike." Silver calmly asked how much they were demanding. Albrecht told her they wanted thirty-five dollars a set. "What are we offering?" she asked. "Fifteen dollars a set." Silver thought about it for a moment and said, "We're not that far apart. We'll give them twenty dollars a set." And it was settled.

Our win reverberated internationally as well, and I remember getting letters from comedians in London reporting that the comedy clubs there, upon hearing about the comedians' victory in LA, started paying their regular acts.

We had achieved something monumental for comedians around the world, and that remains one of my proudest career memories.

After my remarks, before I left, many of the comedians gathered around to say goodbye. I felt like a presidential candidate leaving a fundraiser, surrounded by supporters and well-wishers, off to the next city and the next event. I was humbled and grateful for their kind words about my small role as the de facto head of our movement.

I was speaking with my friend George Miller when Steve Lubetkin approached, a funny man who had worked for years to establish himself as a regular comic in our orbit, and who had struggled with the disappointment of having not yet made it big.

"Tommy, please don't leave the group. She's going to retaliate against us," Lubetkin said, speaking of Mitzi. "I've called in three weeks in a row for times to appear, and I haven't gotten any slots. And it's happening to others too," he said, speaking of several whom Mitzi had seemingly singled out for punishment, given their involvement with the strike.

"No, Steve it's in our contract," I said. "She can't retaliate because we walked the picket line. You have nothing to worry about."

"Tommy, I called three times already, and nothing!" he said, sounding familiarly despondent. He looked so forlorn and desperate that I turned around and said, "Steve, I give you my word. I won't go back onstage there until you go back. You got it?"

Joining the moment, comforted perhaps by hearing someone in his corner, he said, "Okay then. Okay." I gave Steve a hug and said goodbye, shook a few more hands and shared a few more celebratory hugs with folks, and then I headed to the airport for the short flight to Lake Tahoe.

One week later, around midnight before my second show opening for Sammy Davis, I was sitting in my dressing room at Harrah's in Lake Tahoe when Jay Leno called. He thought he was reaching me just after my show, but I still had one more show to go and was about to go on.

"Well, this is really hard," Jay began, the emotion punctuating his words. "I need to let you know that Steve Lubetkin just committed suicide. He jumped off the top of the Continental Hyatt House."

I was stricken, unable to form proper words as Jay continued to share the morbid details, saving the saddest bit for last: Steve had left a suicide note, which said, "My name is Steve Lubetkin. I used to work at The Comedy Store...." Those were the last words of a man who had the same hopes and dreams as all new comedians but had been rejected for a fourth time from performing at The Comedy Store. That was his suicide note. For all the good the strike seemingly brought to the lives and careers of young comedians, the collateral damage was the career, and ultimately the life, of one of our own.

In the professional language of stand-up comedians, if you bombed onstage, you'd say, "I died up there. How'd you do last night?" "I died like a dog." That was the sad double entendre conveyed in the title of Bill Knoedelseder's excellent book *I'm Dying Up Here*, about the full history of the strike.

Many of the senior comics still do not talk to those who crossed the picket line. There is still animosity. Personally, if anyone comes up to me from that era, I'll talk to them, no matter on which side of the line they stood.

Biff Maynard and I ran into each other once at a party at Richard Belzer's house, and Biff said that he was wrong and felt terrible about his decision to cross. Mike Binder was another one of the comics who crossed the picket line, yet we were always friendly. He told me the same thing when we ran into each other one night outside the Improv.

Binder had gone on to become a successful director, and he called me one day to ask that I appear in a documentary about The Comedy Store he was doing. As part of my appearance, he wanted to film me going back to perform at The Comedy Store for the first time.

Mitzi's son, Peter Shore, also called, asking me to return. Peter had taken over The Store and said that it would be as a favor to his mom, who had recently passed away.

For more than forty years, I kept my promise to Steve Lubetkin to not appear onstage at The Comedy Store. I wrestled with the choice for several days, and then finally agreed.

It was eerie to return after so many years away, but it was time to close that chapter and begin a new one. I went into the Main Room and did a set, filmed for the documentary.

The truth is, I always liked Mitzi. Before the strike, Mitzi and I did a couple of radio shows together and had a lot of fun. She was very shy about doing interviews on the air at that time, but we always had fun together. After the strike, Argus Hamilton got us on the phone together. We talked just like old times and began to heal our relationship.

I never wanted to be enemies. I just thought that it was reasonable that Mitzi should pay the comedians who gave light to her star power. Still, through it all and to this day, I owe Mitzi a debt of gratitude and have never forgotten the outsized influence she had on my own career.

Had Mitzi not taken me under her wing and given me a shot to score on her stage, I never would have made it on *The Tonight Show*. And had I not made it on *The Tonight Show*, which opened the floodgates of my career, I never would have found myself touring the country as the opening act for so many great artists, which put me on a path to the greatest adventure of all.

24

The author Christopher Morley once said, "Success is living the life you want." Being the opening act for Sammy Davis Jr. further established me as a national act, and I began to gain notice from other performers who wanted me to open for them around the country. I was as happy with my career as I had ever been and couldn't imagine things getting better.

I was touring around the country with Smokey Robinson, the legendary torch-holder of Motown, and we were appearing at Caesars Palace in Lake Tahoe. Frank Sinatra was appearing next door at Harrah's Hotel with his daughter Nancy, a major talent in her own right. I always loved to see Frank perform anytime I could. Frank Sinatra created more excitement walking to the microphone than most entertainers create during their entire act.

After my show one night at Caesars, I ran next door to Harrah's and into the showroom to catch Frank's set. I didn't even change out of my stage clothes. As I walked through the gaming area of the casino and toward the door of the showroom, I saw Holmes Hendrickson, who was the vice president of Harrah's and a very powerful man. He was standing with a rather heavyset gentleman chomping on a cigar. I had worked Harrah's many times with Sammy, so I was familiar with Mr. Hendrickson, but I didn't know the guy with him.

Holmes said, "Tommy, come here." I walked over, and he introduced me to his friend, Mickey Rudin, who happened to be Frank Sinatra's manager. Holmes said, "Mickey, this is Tom Dreesen. I think Tom would make a great opening act for Frank."

Rudin furrowed his brow and rolled his eyes, reluctant to be put on the spot, and then he winked at Holmes. I caught the wink. Rudin turned to me and said, "Hey, kid. If I gave you a week with Frank Sinatra, would you want more than fifty thousand?" I reflexively said, "Mr. Rudin, put it this way: If you gave me a week with Frank Sinatra, would *you* want more than fifty thousand?" He started laughing, looked back at Hendrickson, and said, "I like this kid."

A few days later, my manager got a call that Sinatra's people wanted me to open for him at the Golden Nugget in Atlantic City. I thought, "Wow, this is great. I'll work with him for a week, and I'll get a picture taken with him, which I can hang inside every tavern in Harvey, and that'll be that."

After the second show, Frank and his wife, Barbara, invited me out to dinner. In the middle of the meal, Frank set his knife and fork down and said to me, "I like your style, Tommy, and I like your material. I want you to do a few other dates with me, if you're interested." Unlike in my response to Mickey Rudin, I resisted the urge to be glib and say something like, "Well, lemme check my calendar." Instead, I simply said, "Yeah, that would be great."

As excited as I was to be touring with Frank, my manager and agents advised me not to stay with him too long. They thought I should do six months and then leave, telling me, "You'll never become a star in your own right in the shadow of such a great star." From a business standpoint, they were right. Sammy Davis Jr. had advised the same, but I didn't care.

The dream of a lifetime had come true for this skinny, raggedy kid from Harvey. It was a long way from those tavern floors, shining shoes on my knees while hearing Sinatra's songs on the jukeboxes. Now, I was standing tall, watching him perform live from only thirty feet away as he sang those same songs to thousands of fans. This was truly the life I wanted. From my vantage point every night, there was no TV series, no radio show, no movie deal that compared to what I was experiencing. I thanked my manger and agents for their input and said, "I'm staying with Sinatra as long as he'll have me."

* * *

For years, people have asked the question: "What was it like to open for Frank Sinatra?" I always give the same answer.

"Let me tell you what it's like. Imagine there's an arena packed with twenty thousand people. You're standing in the wings five minutes before you go on. Someone says, 'Okay, I want you to go out to the center of that stage. And for the next thirty minutes, your job is to hold the attention of that crowd. I want you to make them laugh for thirty minutes. I want you to pull the strings on their every emotion, with no props, no tricks, no special lighting, no special arrangements, no orchestra, nothing. Just you and twenty thousand people. And one more thing: Remember, not one of them came to see you.'"

That's what I had to do every night for the biggest headliner in show business—and it never got old. I was as excited on the last night as I was the very first.

There were many nights when I was onstage opening for Sinatra and everything was working. The material, my timing, and the audience were all clicking in perfect rhythm, that beautiful "give and take" that stand-up comedians live for. When I reached the last line of my final joke and the audience roared their approval, I was flying higher than the eagles. And then the nights got even better.

Every night, as I was heading for the wings after taking a bow, Frank Sinatra was coming toward me on his way to the microphone. And every night, the first words he spoke were in my praise. "Tommy Dreesen, ladies and gentlemen, Tommy Dreesen. Come out and take another bow, Tommy. Funny man. He's marvelous, isn't he?"

On the road, I quickly picked up on the fact that Sinatra didn't trust a lot of people. And as monumental as it was in my life to be around him, I understood that Frank didn't need another fan, so I kept my distance between shows. I was always polite and respectful. If he invited me to dinner, I'd accept, but I didn't dominate the conversation and honestly tried to just absorb what was happening around me, thrilled to be in the same room. If someone turned to me and asked me to weigh in, I'd add my two cents, but that was it.

It took a while for me to get more comfortable around him, because Frank had the same people around him all the time, tending to his every need. Hank Cattaneo was Frank's road manager for all of my years with him, a great guy who had perhaps the hardest job in the world: managing an international star who was very precise and particular about the way each evening must go with stage setup, sound, and band rehearsal, while balancing his responsibilities to make sure the show went exactly as Frank Sinatra planned it.

His secretary, Dorothy Uhlemann; his house manager, Elvina "Vine" Joubert; and his publicist, Susan Reynolds, would often travel with us, and they all had specific duties to make sure Frank had what he needed to step out every night and give the audience all he had. In my opinion, they were all great ladies who were very proficient in their responsibilities.

And, of course, there was Jilly Rizzo. Anyone who knows anything about Frank Sinatra knows how important Jilly was for many years as Frank's protector—his bodyguard and best friend. Like me, Jilly was educated on the streets, and for that reason more than any other, we got along and learned how to coexist in the small bubble of those who orbited the world of Frank Sinatra. Jilly was a tough customer, and he worked hard to keep his reputation as a fierce guardian of "the Boss," as we called him.

Jilly held a special place in the entourage because he was a personality in his own right, inside of our circle and far beyond. For years, he owned a saloon on the west side of Midtown Manhattan—called Jilly's—that was to the jet set of the '60s and '70s what the Stork Club and Toots Shor's were to earlier decades of New York saloon-goers. For a glorious spell, Jilly's was an almost singular place to be and to be seen. Many famous celebrities and entertainers logged time in Jilly's as patrons of the arts—the arts of drinking, carousing, and hanging out—but none more so than Frank himself. Jilly was never happier than when playing host to the biggest names of the day in his saloon.

When I first joined Frank, I was simply a fly on the wall. A very happy, well-fed fly. Over time, I began to find my niche in his circle when Frank got to know me and my style and began asking me to serve as the emcee at charity events where he had agreed to appear. I always made myself available. I later found out that Frank wanted me to emcee because I knew how to keep the program moving and on schedule, which got him out of the events on time and back home where he wanted to be. He was the most impatient man I've ever known, and he hated when an evening's program dragged on for no reason. A good emcee knows how to streamline a program and keep it flowing. I earned my keep in this regard.

The other valuable skill of mine was one I had developed when I was much younger. Long before I got into show business, I worked as a private detective for my cousin Don Polizzi. He was a bail bondsman and had his own private detective agency. My many adventures trailing cheating spouses, sitting in a car for hours on stakeouts, and providing security for people concerned about being confronted (for good or bad) taught me how to inconspicuously position myself in a crowded setting to help protect Frank from a mob of people. While doing so, I never wanted to insult them by seeming to keep Frank isolated from his admirers. If we were walking out of a bar or a building past a throng of fans, I knew how to be the "lead blocker" and stay close enough to Sinatra to ensure an unscathed exit into a waiting limo. There were many times when just the two of us were out together, without his official security detail, and he noticed my efforts and appreciated the quasi-security I provided.

My mom came to a show when I performed with Frank in Chicago for the first time, and I took her backstage afterward to meet him. She knew how special this was and understandably felt very nervous, but she finally mustered enough courage to say, "Thank you for taking care of my son." With typical Sinatra charm, wooing the former bobby-soxer standing in front of him, he said, "Your son takes care of *me*," which was a classy if embellished thing to say. But, wow, did it make her feel proud.

Frank also entrusted me to hold my own around his celebrity friends, many of whom often came to see Frank perform before going to dinner or spending the rest of the evening with him. By then, I understood the contours of my job. I remembered when Sammy Davis Jr. sketched my role as his opening act: "Get that audience up, get them in a good mood, and get them ready so that I can just skate out on top of your performance."

Frank had hired me to do the same and to keep coming up with new material, because we often performed in the same city each year for fans who were repeat customers and enjoyed a comedian who could freshen up the act. Many nights, the biggest names in show business would be in attendance to see Sinatra once again, including the likes of Gregory Peck, Kirk Douglas, Robert Wagner, Jill St. John, Jack Lemmon, and Angie Dickenson, to name a few, as well as governors, senators, and even US presidents.

After the show, either backstage or at Frank's house, they all welcomed me and made me a part of their conversations, treating me as if I were a peer, even though I certainly was not. I always felt like I was breathing rarified air in these moments, but I never let them know. I never gushed or fawned over them. Instead, I'd go back to my bungalow and then marvel, "How 'bout that? You just visited with Gregory Peck for forty minutes about baseball, movies, and Broadway," and I would literally pinch myself.

Still, nothing was more fulfilling to me than turning in a good show for Frank every night. I was especially proud when *Variety*, the Bible of the entertainment world, reviewed our show one night and said:

> "...Dreesen has that show of elegance, also sported by Sinatra, which
> is why the two are fine partners on nitery and arena ventures.

Dreesen's ability to fit his observations into streams of conscious laugh-getting is the mark of a thorough pro.... Dreesen doesn't let a moment of his half-hour sag."

I knew this was a special opportunity, and I never took it for granted. I was constantly aware and amazed by the fact that it wasn't long ago that I was just another kid on the streets of Harvey, Illinois, scrapping for jobs to feed myself and my family. Now, traveling in the most distinguished of circles, I was careful not to violate the trust that had landed me in the room in the first place.

I always joked with my Catholic friends that opening for Frank was like a former altar boy serving Mass with the Pope. Whenever I'd go back to my old neighborhood, before I started with Frank, folks would ask in passing, "What's Johnny Carson like?" or, "Sammy Davis Jr., is he a good guy?" Once I joined Frank, people would corner me, asking question after question about Frank. "Did you ever see a bunch of mob guys around him?" "Does he really drink?" "Did you ever talk about *From Here to Eternity*?" Does he ever talk about Ava Gardner?"

I would answer them as honestly as possible, but I was also very careful. There were some things I didn't talk about or confirm, because I knew an amazing truth about show business: If you tell a saxophone player in Kansas City that you think the drummer for a band playing in Reno is lousy, somehow, the drummer will hear about your jab two days later. Words travel quickly in show business circles, and by the fourth time your story is retold, it's incredibly exaggerated.

I was always cautious not to say anything too personal about Frank or reveal too much of my privileged view of him as a man offstage. Oftentimes, I would meet people who claimed they knew Frank personally and later find out they did not. More than once I heard a story that began with, "Let me tell you about the time that Frank..." and then say things that I knew to be untrue. I always avoided discussions or arguments with people like that, even though there were times I really wanted to set things straight.

Later, Frank described it to me best. We were flying to New York in his private jet, high above Ohio, when I joked and said, "If we landed right now in Akron and drove to the nearest Italian bakery, I bet there'd be a picture of you on the wall and an owner who swears that you don't go onstage in Akron unless you've had one of his cannolis." Frank laughed and said, "Tommy, the guy who owns the bakery is probably married with kids. If that story helps him sell a few more cannolis to provide for his family, then God bless him. Let him have that story."

Frank continued, "Now when somebody says I hit someone over the head with a pool cue or something that isn't true, I don't like that. But a story that's harmless? Let them have it." I never forgot that. From that point on, when people approached me and started telling me fanciful, exaggerated stories about Frank that I knew to be untrue, but innocent, I'd let them have their story.

Fandom is an interesting thing. I've always been curious to know how people become fans of an entertainer, and what I learned in my time with Frank is that Sinatra fans were a different breed, created out of circumstances that few other celebrities could claim.

Frank's following was incredible, and by the time I joined up with him, the fan base spanned generations. I remember one evening when Frank and I were appearing at the Centrum in Worcester, Massachusetts. After the show, I went across the street to a restaurant with the guys in the band. Frank's guitar player, Ron Anthony, said, "Tommy, see those two young girls over there across the room? They came up to the front of the stage tonight and laid flowers at Mr. S's feet. Then they went back to their seats and wept all though the performance." I thought that was kind of odd. I was also surprised they were Sinatra fans because they looked so young, probably no more than twenty years old.

As I was leaving, I went to the coat check. By coincidence, the two young girls came up to get their coats at the same time. One of the girls commented to me that they thought my act was funny and enjoyed the show.

I said, "Can I ask you a question?" She said yes, and I continued, "The guitar player noticed that the two of you placed flowers at Frank's feet and wept during the show. You both seem very young to be Frank Sinatra fans."

The older girl said, "Our parents loved Frank Sinatra and had all of his albums. They even put a big picture of Frank over our fireplace mantle. Our dad died last year, and our mother died four months later."

She continued, "Before my mother died, she, my sister, and I were having 'girl talk' one evening, and she told us that she and my father used to make love to Frank Sinatra's music and that both of us were conceived to Frank's music. So tonight, while watching him sing, we felt our parents' presence. That's why we wept."

Several weeks later, I was having dinner at Frank's house, and he made a comment to Barbara that a lot of young people seemed to be coming to his performances lately. Frank was about seventy-five at the time. He asked me if I had noticed that trend, so I told him the story of the two sisters in Worchester.

Frank was very moved by the story and asked if I had gotten their names. I admitted that I had not—which was a big mistake, because I know Frank would have sent them something special to honor their parents.

That was a memorable example, to be sure, but there had to be hundreds of thousands of other couples across the country who achieved the same special bond because of Frank's musical poetry.

I had worked hard for years to earn my stripes as a performer, and from my time with Tim to The Comedy Store to appearing on *The Tonight Show*, I had really honed my craft. As a comedian, you must consistently be nimble and alert, always listening to the internal clock that helps pace your set, being mindful of the acts that follow. That training helped me many times when opening for Frank, who was often moody on the road and would tailor his performance to how he was feeling on any given night. As a rule, he liked to do a ninety-minute show. On other nights, he'd say to me right before a show, "Tommy, do twenty-five minutes tonight. I'm going to do an hour and five."

As an established comedian with a bunch of set routines in my arsenal, I could unload and do two hours straight if I had to. The trick as an opening act is condensing your best material to fill a much shorter set. Do twenty-five? Okay. Well, I'll start with this bit, then do this, and then pivot to that, and then close on this. With Frank, that mental planning sometimes went out the window. After readying myself for what I planned to do in my twenty-five minutes, Frank would come back and say, "You know what, Tommy, my reed's a little sore," talking about his throat. "Do thirty tonight. I'll do an hour. Got it?"

No problem. I'd adjust and add a couple more jokes that layered into what I already planned for my twenty-five-minute set. Then I'd be walking up to the wings, getting ready to go on, and the road manager would suddenly come running up to say "Never mind! Frank decided he wants to add another song, so just do twenty."

Can you imagine what this does to a comedian's brain? You plan and do twenty-five minutes of solid stand-up, then thirty, and then down to twenty. It zaps you of a lot of that mental energy you're counting on to carry you through. You've got to recalibrate and keep adapting your material. Fortunately, I could always do that; it never rattled me. And that's one thing I believe Frank liked about me. Whatever he asked me to do out there, I could adjust seamlessly.

Despite calling the occasional audible just before a show, Frank was a man of habit and routine on the road; he liked familiarity. During the swirl of life on the road, he found comfort in the things that stayed the same, beginning with where we stayed. For the most part, he only stayed in three places while on tour—that's three places in the nation to cover more than fifty dates a year. Here's how it worked. If we were doing western states (Colorado, New Mexico, or Arizona—and even Oregon or Washington), Frank would stay at his home in Rancho Mirage, California, and we'd take the private jet to Denver, Albuquerque, Phoenix, Portland, or Seattle. Then we'd fly right back after the show. The exceptions were Las Vegas and Lake Tahoe, where we normally did a full week or two in residence in those locations and just stayed at one of the casinos.

When we went to New York City, we would only stay at the Waldorf Astoria, and we would satellite out of there every night to Hartford, Philadelphia, Atlantic City, Washington, or Boston—all the eastern cities.

For all the midwestern markets, we'd stay at the Ambassador East in Chicago and launch out of there to do St. Louis, Detroit, Omaha, and Lincoln, Nebraska. I'd always stay at the Ambassador with him, but I'd make it a point to go to the South Side some days to see family and friends before returning for the show and to hang with Frank in downtown Chicago. We'd go to Gibsons Steakhouse on Rush Street. Then we'd visit a nearby bar or come back to the Ambassador to hang out in his suite or at the famous Pump Room just off the hotel's main lobby, where we'd stay parked in a private booth for hours. They still have a picture of Frank hanging over that booth, his home away from home.

When my mom was a bartender in Harvey, she would come home in the early dawn hours sometimes and sit at the kitchen table. I had an early paper route and would bring home the *Chicago Sun-Times* every morning, which had a bold-faced-name column that would tell you which celebrity was spotted where. Mom would have coffee and a cigarette, and she'd read the column and say, "Oh Tommy, you won't believe who was eating dinner in the Number One Booth at the Pump Room last night...."

Celebrities like Humphrey Bogart, Betty Grable, Ava Gardner, and Marilyn Monroe—any stars who found themselves in Chicago found their way to the Ambassador East. I joked to my mom that she should try to get a job tending bar at the Pump Room so she could see all the celebrities. Mom said, "Oh, honey, they don't hire the likes of us, you know that."

I reminded my mom of this story as I escorted her for the first time into the Pump Room years later. We walked into the room and the maître d' came up and inquired, "Number One Booth, Mr. Dreesen?" The next day, that bold-faced-name column read, "SPOT-TED in the Number One booth at the Ambassador's Pump Room was Glenore Dreesen and her son, Tom...." She cut out that column and kept it on her dresser for the rest of her life.

25

I had been touring with Frank for about two months when he first invited me to his home in Palm Springs. It was the summer of 1983. I was honored by the gesture and thought, "Wow! Frank Sinatra's house. This is gonna be an exciting weekend!"

I made the two-and-a-half-hour drive to Palm Springs from my home in Sherman Oaks, listening to a cassette of Sinatra's music the entire trip. I arrived in the late afternoon, pulling up to this huge compound on Frank Sinatra Drive in Rancho Mirage, California. This became a ritual for the next decade, and I never once tired of or took it for granted. Entering through a big iron gate that swung open, the security guards directed you further into the large and fascinating property, a playground for your eyes. Sinatra's beautiful home was situated in the center, surrounded by an outer perimeter of bungalow guesthouses that were named after Frank's popular songs, "Strangers in the Night," "My Way," and "New York, New York." I usually stayed in the one called, "The Tender Trap."

On my first trip, Alan Shepard stayed in the bungalow next to mine. He was the first American to venture into space and later landed on the moon during NASA's fifth lunar mission. We developed a great friendship, in part because I had been in the Navy as an enlisted man and he was an admiral. In the evenings, after dinner with Frank at the main house, as we headed back to our bunga-lows, Shepard would say, "Petty Officer Dreesen, prepare to 'pipe me aboard!'" a Navy term for the whistle you hear on ships when the skipper comes aboard. I'd always stop and salute and do my best tin-piping sound, which resulted in both of us laughing hysterically.

We often played golf together at the Tamarisk Golf Course, which was just outside the compound. Later, we played in several tournaments together, and I would often do some stand-up to close the proceedings.

I used to tell audiences what it was like to be a former enlisted man, the very bottom of the naval pecking order, playing golf with an admiral. "The only experience I had with brass was when I would shine it," I'd say, "and now, after a bad shot, I could say to him, 'Shit shot there, Al.'" He always got a big kick out of that line, and so did the audience.

In the other bungalows that first time, were Gregory Peck, Robert Wagner, Kirk Douglas, Jack Lemmon, Clint Eastwood, and the Ital-ian ambassador to the United States. The next morning at breakfast, in front of everybody, Frank said, "I'm going to drive the ambassador and his wife to the airport. Who'd like to go along with me?"

I wanted to volunteer on the spot but didn't want to act too eager, because these were all his old friends, and I was sure someone with more tenure would enjoy the private time with Frank. However, no one took him up on it, and the room seemed to empty out almost immediately. Suddenly, I was the only one standing there with Frank and the ambassador.

I said, "I'll ride with you, Frank."

"Okay, let's go." We went outside and there was a line of cars he owned to choose for the short trip, including a Rolls-Royce, a Mer-cedes-Benz, a Jaguar, and a Chrysler station wagon that Lee Iacocca had given him. Frank said, "We'll take the station wagon."

This was something: Frank Sinatra driving a station wagon! He instructed me to jump in the back seat with the ambassador's wife, a nice Italian woman who spoke only broken English.

The security guard opened the gate, walked onto Frank Sinatra Drive, and waved us out when traffic had cleared. As soon as the gate slid back far enough for Frank to squeeze the station wagon out, he hit the gas, and we hurtled straight into traffic. Cars screeched to a stop on both sides, and the ambassador's wife looked at me, concerned, wondering who this madman was driving her to the airport. I looked at her with eyes that said, "This is my first trip too."

At every stop light, Frank rolled through the crosswalk, almost into the middle of the intersection. By the third stop light, I was a little anxious. By the fourth light, the ambassador's wife had her rosary beads out and was praying to high heaven. She looked nervously at me, and I just shrugged my shoulders and turned my palms skyward as if to say, "Whattaya gonna do?"

For someone who drove cultural norms for so many years, Frank was a terrible driver of automobiles. When he wanted to change lanes, he'd dart either left or right to suit his desire—no checking the rearview mirrors, no signal, nothing. He just moved over. We arrived at the airport, and the ambassador's wife got out, clearly shaken. As Frank was saying goodbye to the ambassador, she looked at me and asked, "Do you hafta rida back wida him?" I nodded yes. And then she extended her finger and made the sign of the cross on my forehead.

I jumped into the front seat for the drive home, and sure enough, Frank drove the same reckless way he had on the way there. For the entire ride back, he kept talking, telling me these interesting stories about when he toured with Count Basie and the kind of music they played in those days—all the while shifting lanes without realizing there were cars with sensible drivers next to and behind him. At one point, he veered from the right lane into the left lane, not seeing another station wagon in his path. This caused the other car to swerve and run up the embankment of the center divider. "Holy shit! He just cut that guy off," I thought.

I looked back and the guy was now chasing us. Frank kept talking, unaware. Finally, the enraged driver pulled alongside on the passenger side, next to me, cursing. I could read his lips, and he was saying, "You son of a bitch, you cut me off!" I shrugged my shoulders, as if to say, "Hey, I'm not the one driving."

Then he looked past me and saw that it was Frank driving, who was still talking while I played charades. The realization changed the guy's complexion, and he moved his lips to ask, "Is that Frank Sinatra?" I nodded in the affirmative. He smiled wide and made a signal gesture like he was Johnny Carson as if to say, "Ah, if it's Sinatra, it's okay." I imagine he went home and said to his wife, "Honey, you'll never guess who cut me off and nearly killed me today...."

Mercifully, we returned to the compound unharmed. Frank wandered back to his room as if nothing had happened, and I beelined to the pool where the guests were lounging to share my near-death experience. Robert Wagner looked up with a slight grin on his tanned face. "Hey, Tommy, you enjoy the drive to the airport?"

"Guys, you're not going to believe this..." I said, and started to recount the adventure. Wagner was the first to start laughing, "Hell, we all know, Tommy. Why do you think that room emptied so quickly when he asked for volunteers?"

There were other surprises in store for me during weekends at Frank's place. One Sunday, Frank invited some of the guests to join him for Mass at his church, Saint Francis of Assisi. Roger Moore, Gregory Peck, and I were the Catholics staying there for the weekend. On the way to church, Frank said that we were each going to read from the Gospel in front of the congregation and that he had already worked things out with the clergy.

When the service started, the priest made the announcement: "Reading from the Gospel this morning will be Mr. Frank Sinatra, Mr. Roger Moore, Mr. Gregory Peck, and Mr. Tom Dreesen." The whole church began to buzz, and I'm sure they collectively wondered, "Who's Tom Dreesen?"

To make matters worse, I had to follow Gregory Peck. Now when Gregory Peck reads the Gospel, people in the church lean over to each other and say, "Didn't he write this?"

I followed Peck's masterful interpretation and got up to read my assigned verses, finally relaxing when I sat back down next to Frank in the pews. As most Catholics know, at the end of the Mass, the priest always says, "Go, the Mass has ended," and no one leaves the church until the priest departs. This morning, however, after concluding Mass, the priest said, "Perhaps some of you have seen Tom Dreesen on television telling jokes about his Catholic upbringing. And perhaps he would honor us today with a joke before we go."

My heart sank. Frank hit me with his elbow and said, "Get up. Tell 'em a joke, Tommy." I walked toward the lectern, but my mind had gone blank. I couldn't think of a single joke—at least one that I could tell in church. I'm normally pretty good on my feet, but I began to panic as my mind raced in circles, hoping to run into a joke that would be appropriate for this congregation.

At that moment, steps away from the lectern, I remembered something that Morey Amsterdam taught me many years ago. He said, "If you ever forget your lines, and you can't remember what to do, just start talking and your brain will catch up."

I started babbling, "Gosh, it's great to be in this beautiful church. I remember as an altar boy, serving Mass..." And I kept going. Suddenly, like precious manna from the skies, I remembered a joke that I could tell in church. "Many years ago, in the middle of Mass, a priest turned around and faced the congregation and began to chant, 'I'm the priest in this parish, and I make two hundred dollars a week, and that's...not enough.' Moments later, the bishop came out of the sacristy, walked to the middle of the altar, and began to chant, 'I'm the bishop in this diocese, and I make four hundred dollars a week, and that's...not enough.' Then, way up in the choir, the organist began playing very loudly and sang, 'I'm the organist in this parish, and I make two thousand dollars a week, and...there's *no* business like *show* business!'"

The church erupted in laughter and applauded. I went back to my seat next to Frank, who looked at me and winked and said, "Atta boy. Good joke. Now let's get the hell outta here."

I always enjoyed staying at the Sinatra compound. It was a special place to just get away from it all. Frank and Barbara were the greatest hosts I have ever known, supported by an outstanding staff, and guests wanted for nothing.

Breakfast was provided to your bungalow, lunch was served around the tennis court, dinner took place in the main house—or we went out to a local restaurant, like Dominick's or Lord Fletcher's, before enjoying post-dinner drinks and wonderful conversation until the wee hours of the morning. When you awoke, you could swim, play tennis or golf, lounge by the pool, or just relax; there was always a massage therapist on call. If you chose to play golf, your clubs would be on a cart in front of your bungalow, and the side gate would be open so you could drive right over to the first tee. For me, it was paradise, the most peaceful place I'd ever been.

In February of 1984, Frank asked me to do a charity show with him for the Eisenhower Medical Center and then invited me to spend a week at the compound. One night, we started talking and talking, and by the time we retired, I only got about three hours of sleep—and I had to get up early to play golf with Johnny Bench, the Hall of Fame baseball player who had secured a 7:45 a.m. tee time at PGA West. I stumbled from my bungalow into the main house to get some orange juice and toast and immediately encountered Frank in his bathrobe (and with no toupee, which he rarely wore in private); he had obviously stayed up all night. He asked my plans, and I told him I was playing golf with Bench. "Make sure you give Johnny my best, please." I promised I would, and as I looked out the window, I noticed there was snow on the mountains. I remarked how unusual it was for a guy from Chicago to look out and see snow while knowing I would soon be out playing golf.

Frank took the opportunity to point at a particular mountain and said, "My children call that Grandma's Mountain. My mother was killed when the airplane she was on flew into that mountain."

Frank was performing in Las Vegas and had arranged a private jet for his mother to come see his show. As he was preparing to do his second show that night, he was told her plane was missing. When Frank finished the second show, he flew back to Palm Springs, fearing the worst. The next day, the plane was still missing. Helicopters searched the area but couldn't find anything.

As he was telling me about the search, he got tears in his eyes. I remember this moment well, because it was the first time he opened up to me on a personal level.

Frank said he even went up in one of the helicopters with the searchers. Eventually, they found several trees that had been sheared off and determined that the plane had gone somewhere under the snow. They soon found the wreckage. (A sad irony is that several years later, Dean Martin's son Dino was also killed when his plane flew into the opposite side of the same mountain. Frank remarked at the time, "Someone should just tear down that goddamn mountain once and for all.")

Frank buried his mother at Desert Memorial Park in Cathedral City, California, next to his dad, who had passed several years earlier. Then Frank told me an interesting story about the memorial service. Pat Henry, a comedian who had been an opening act before I came along, was one of the pallbearers that day, along with other Sinatra family friends. A writer from a desert newspaper made a rude comment about how the pallbearers looked like a contingency of the Mafia, an unsavory remark that really angered Frank.

Frank had Jilly Rizzo find out who the writer was and where he lived, and then they paid him a visit on a Sunday where he was hosting a barbecue for guests in the backyard. Jilly rang the doorbell, and the guy came to the door by himself. Jilly asked his name and then said, "I want you to meet somebody."

The writer stepped out onto the porch and said, "Wow, Frank Sinatra! I ca—" Frank decked him cold, knocking him into the bushes next to the stoop. At that moment, some of the guests came around the house and saw the guy in the bushes. They asked what had happened, to which Jilly responded, "I dunno. We came to ask for directions, and your friend fell over. I guess he fainted when he saw Frank."

There was an element of dark humor in that story, but as Frank was sharing all this, I realized how much he needed to just talk about it at that moment. To be honest, I was also thinking about Johnny Bench pacing and cussing me at the first tee for being late. But I wasn't about to tell Frank, "Boss, I'd love to hear this story, but I'm late for golf."

* * *

One night around two o'clock in the morning, there was a knock at my bungalow door. "I couldn't sleep," Frank said. "Let's take a ride."

I pulled on my pants, and we got into one of Frank's cars. And I drove us all around the desert. It was a very hot night, and we had the windows open. We talked about many different things. He began opening up about things in his childhood before getting very personal and sharing a story I promised to never repeat.

When he finished, he said, "I shouldn't have told you that story. It was too personal, although I feel much better getting it off my chest." I looked him in the eye and said, "Well, it won't go any further than this car. I give you my word."

"Thank you, Tommy."

"Of course. Men need someone outside of family to confide in, knowing it won't go any further. I call that person a 'go-to guy.' But it should be a friend, and I consider you a friend."

Frank retorted, "Or maybe it should be a stranger, someone you'll never see again."

"Yeah, maybe you're right."

We were both quiet for a moment when a ridiculous urge overtook me. I began to softly sing, *"Strangers in the night...exchanging glances."* Frank looked at me quizzically and groaned, "My God. If you're going to sing the song, could you try doing it in the right key?"

Then he began singing the song back to me, in perfect voice, *"Wonderin' in the night..."* And we started trading lines back and forth, laughing almost uncontrollably.

When we returned to the compound, I parked the car and started toward my bungalow. "Good night, Tommy," Frank said, giving me the traditional Italian embrace and kiss on the cheek. "Good night, Frank," I replied, still absorbing the arc of our desert conversation from the serious to sublime. I couldn't help but imagine what my buddies back home would say if I told them I was riding around the desert with Frank Sinatra, singing a duet of "Strangers in the Night."

* * *

Luckily, Frank kept me around for doing material that got audiences in a good mood before his shows, because my singing abilities are limited. When it came to true professional singers, Frank was often complimentary, but there were only a few for whom he had a deep and abiding respect.

I once asked what performer gave the greatest concert he ever saw. Without hesitating, he said, "Judy Garland." I was surprised, but Frank began to describe how meek and vulnerable she seemed at first onstage. "Judy would walk out toward the microphone, and you'd think she wasn't going to make it there," he said. "And when she reached the microphone and started singing, you didn't think she'd make it through the first song. But she would get stronger and stronger, and before long, she had you captivated."

"When she sang," he explained, "you could feel it in your chest. She literally penetrated your whole being, because she sang from her guts. She wasn't afraid to bare her soul." Most people didn't realize how vulnerable Frank Sinatra made himself in the comfort of performing a song. Perhaps he identified with Judy Garland for the same reasons.

Frank also had a strong artistic appreciation for Billie Holiday. His admiration was so well known, in fact, that Barbara Sinatra always suspected that Frank and Billie may have had an affair when he was younger.

He told me once about the time he walked out of a hotel in New York on a rainy, gray day and saw Billie Holiday on the street. He said to her, "Can I give you a ride somewhere, Lady?" (People who knew her well called her Lady Day.) She said, "No, I need to be alone today, Frank." And he said, "I understand."

Billie started to get into a cab but paused and said, "You're doing well, aren't you, Frank?" And he said, "Yeah. Things are going well. I'm just lucky, I guess." And she turned around and sharply said, "Oh, Francis, you know why you're doing well.... It's because when you sing, you need somebody." She turned, climbed in the cab, and drove away.

Frank said he never forgot that. Only another singer like him who sang from the soul could recognize that characteristic in his own performances. He needed somebody.

Imagine an addict in rehab who stands up in front of his peers to share his life story but refuses to go deep and reveal his true pain. The group leader would probably tell the addict, "You're denying us the truth. You're scared to go there. We need you to take us there, so we understand." The addict would probably get defensive and try to veer away from his pain, but the group would steer him back until he finally admits the source of his life's pain, finally sobbing out the truth as the group comforts him by saying, "It's okay to go there. You have to go there."

If a singer doesn't "go there" with authenticity and introspection, they cheat the audience. Billie Holiday, Judy Garland, and Frank Sinatra never cheated an audience. They always bared their souls in their songs and onstage.

Another singer Frank respected, as much for his natural gifts as his interpretation of song, was Luciano Pavarotti. They were both appearing at a charity event, and Frank was talking to Pavarotti, just two Italians swapping stories from their respective corners of the entertainment world. Frank said, "Luciano, during the aria on that one song, there's a moment when you take a breath and...." Then he asked Pavarotti a very technical question.

Frank asked, "How do you do that?" Pavarotti paused, thinking, and everyone in the room got quiet, anxious to hear the profound response. Pavarotti looked at Frank and said, "I don'ta know. I justa open my mouth and ita comes out...."

Frank totally cracked up, and for the rest of his life, he retold that story with glee about his fellow professional singer.

26

Frank Sinatra loved women. That is a well-documented, indisputable fact.

Barbara Sinatra used to tell a funny story about when she was with a group of friends at her tennis club in Palm Springs. She was having lunch with ten of her girlfriends at a big table, when a woman walked by and stopped to talk to Barbara for a moment. When the woman walked away, one of Barbara's friends said, "Barb, how can you talk to her? Don't you know she used to fuck Frank?" Barbara said, "If I quit talking to every woman who used to fuck Frank, I wouldn't have anyone to talk to—including half of you sitting at this table."

What perhaps is misunderstood is that Frank respected women beyond measure, and he took every opportunity to demonstrate that when in their company. While I can't speak to anything that happened before my time with him, I only saw Frank act as a perfect gentleman. If we were at a dinner and there were ten or twelve people at the table and a woman got up to go to the ladies' room, he'd catch her from out of the corner of his eye and gallantly rise from his seat in a courteous gesture before sitting back down to continue with a story or conversation. When the woman returned, even if he was in the middle of another story, he would stop and rise again until she sat down. He believed in that old-school kind of chivalry.

Despite his reputation as a man of many conquests, in all the years that I spent with Frank Sinatra, he never talked about his lovers. Unlike most men in the competitive boys' club of one-upmanship, he would never say anything intimate about any previous relationship. Even one-on-one, on a golf course, in a bar at 4:00 a.m., or driving through the desert, Frank never talked like that. If asked about someone he was rumored to have dated, he'd dismiss you by saying, "That's none of your business," and that was that. A lot of other people spoke of Frank's alleged adventures, but you had to always accept it with a shade of understanding that it might be embellished for the story's sake, since it never came directly from Frank himself.

That being said, one of my favorite Frank stories was told to me by Jim Mahoney, who was Frank's publicist long before I went on tour with him. He told of the time years ago when Frank was recording in New York and they would go to Patsy's Italian Restaurant on West 56th Street for dinner after finishing the evening's recording session. Patsy's has been owned and operated for generations by the Scognamillo family, and long was Frank's favorite restaurant in the city. According to Mahoney, one night they had technical problems and the studio session was canceled, so they went early to Patsy's. Frank immediately went over to the phone near the front desk and called a girl. "You can't? Really? What time you gotta get up? Oh, all right," he said, and hung up. Then he dialed the phone again and called a second girl. "You can't? Why not? All right," he said, and hung up again. Frank called a third girl and said, "Oh yeah? Good. Patsy's. Get here as fast as you can." Fifteen minutes later, Marilyn Monroe walked into the restaurant. Mahoney turned to Frank and said, "I want to know who those first two girls were."

27

Frank Sinatra once gave me a compliment I'll never forget. We were sitting around at Rocky Lee's in New York City one night after a show when a reporter from the *New York Times* came up to the table and asked Frank why, of all the performers in the country, he had kept me as his opening act for so many years. "You mean besides the fact that he's funny?" Frank retorted. The reporter chuckled as Frank continued. "If I'm a saloon singer, then Tommy is a saloon comedian. By that I mean we're just a couple of neighborhood guys."

There were many similarities in our upbringings, which we talked about often in reflective moments after a show or in the limousine or driving to nowhere in the desert in the early morning hours. I grew up on the streets of Harvey, Illinois, shining shoes and chasing dreams in the taverns of the neighborhood. Frank grew up in Hoboken, New Jersey, sometimes as a little boy singing for patrons in the saloon that his father owned. Over the years, I'd come to understand this was the foundation for the natural bond and affinity we had for each other. From Frank's perspective, I knew my way around a tavern environment, and he appreciated those qualities in me. Although I never heard him use the word "tavern." He always called them "saloons." Hell, I remember one night when he referred to Caesars Palace as a saloon.

Frank would often ask about my childhood. I'd share stories about growing up poor and how I'd work the streets to help make ends meet for the family. Invariably, I'd end up talking about my Uncle Frank and the impact he had on me, which Sinatra enjoyed hearing about. One night, after a charity show in Palm Desert, we returned to his compound, where I was staying. Everyone had gone to bed except for Frank and me, and he asked about the origin of my name, Dreesen, since I was Italian. "Did you change your name for show business?" he asked. "No, Dreesen is my real name," I said and then proceeded to share with him the story that I had kept bottled up inside me for years.

* * *

Growing up in Harvey, I would go places and people would see me from across the street and say, "Hey, Polizzi!" I'd say, "My name isn't Polizzi. It's Dreesen. Oh yeah, but he's my uncle. You're confusing me with Frank's kids." I certainly had a cousin's resemblance to Frank's sons, Don and Buzz.

Around the age of thirteen, I started to learn about where babies came from, talking to friends in hushed, scandalous side conversations. As an altar boy in Catholic school going to confession every Friday, these were impure thoughts as far as I was concerned, and I tried my best to redirect my mind from them.

The tale of the birds and bees coincided with an unshakable realization that persisted in my mind: I looked so much like my cousins, and I didn't understand why. I didn't want to think my mom and dad ever did *that*, let alone my mom and my uncle, her brother-in-law.

I carried this around in me for a couple more years, and it became too much for me to handle on my own. I finally turned to the one man I knew would shoot me straight.

I went to Uncle Frank's home and found him cleaning his garage out back. "I need to talk to you," I said firmly. He looked up slowly, as if he knew what was coming. We took a walk, and he finally broke the thick, awkward silence between us.

"What is it, Tommy?" Uncle Frank asked.

I stammered for a bit before finally uttering the words that had been written on my heart for longer than I had known: "I think you're my father."

"What on Earth makes you think that?" he said, with a slight edge in his voice.

At that moment, I got a little nervous, because as much as I loved this guy, I knew his temper could flare at any moment, though I'd never borne the brunt of it before. As a kid, I'd watched him throw steelworkers out of the bar two at a time if they got out of line. If you started a fight or caused problems, Frank Polizzi was going to come around the bar, and may God help you then. He wasn't a big guy, but he was a tough son of a bitch.

Dad used to tell the story of Uncle Frank singing onstage with his band one night. Some guy in the audience started messing with Uncle Frank's sister, who was in attendance. In the middle of the song, Uncle Frank walked off the stage and knocked the guy out with one punch before going back up onstage and finishing the number. The band didn't miss a beat, Uncle Frank didn't miss a lyric, and in between verses, a loudmouth got whacked in the kisser, laid out on a cold, musty club floor for all to see. A lesson.

In a lower tone, I continued, "I don't look like my brothers and sisters. I look like Buzz and Don. And everybody calls me 'Polizzi.'

"I just want to know."

We walked a bit further, as I desperately waited for him to say it was untrue, that I was crazy. Suddenly, he stopped cold and looked me in the eye.

"Yes, it's true. Tommy. You can go tell the world if you want. But you'd ruin your mom and dad's marriage. And you'd ruin mine. Your Aunt Marge would be devastated. But yes, it's the truth, and you should probably know."

My heart fluttered, and my mind raced with the revelation. Uncle Frank asked if I had discussed this with my mom. I told him no. "I don't want to ruin anybody's marriage," I said. "I just needed to know. I promise that I won't tell anybody."

"Well, it's your choice," Uncle Frank said.

"It's just between us, you and me," I promised.

My heart was still beating fast, my emotions swirling. The agony of being the result of a betrayed promise between my mom and dad impacted me deeply, yet I also felt a suspended vindication from finally knowing the truth of my own existence. I was grateful my uncle had shared the truth, painful as it was.

I thought back to my childhood and how Uncle Frank had conducted himself around me. The gifts. The money he slipped me. The preference he showed for me even at large family gatherings, surrounded by my siblings—his other nephews and nieces. It all made sense now.

Uncle Frank was a proud Sicilian and occasionally would tell me an Italian word and say, "Tom, you know what that means?" I figured he was just pointing out the correct dialect he used, sharing more about his own heritage. In retrospect, I realized he was teaching me something because he felt that I should know.

I had my truth now, and I felt very uncomfortable around Uncle Frank for a long time. We didn't make eye contact when we saw each other on the streets, or when I was setting pins at the Bowl Center, where his tavern fielded a bowling team every year. He'd see me and nonchalantly say, "Hey there, Tommy," and I'd nod and say hello and then find somewhere else to be.

It was not until I joined the Navy, where my life experiences blossomed, that I began to accept my reality. I remember coming home on leave and realizing that I had come to terms with things. Who cares? It didn't matter anymore. I started being friendlier to him, but I still mostly kept my distance.

When I returned home after my Navy discharge, I began to reestablish a solid relationship with him. If I saw him on the street, I'd be the one to call out and say, "Hey there, Unc," and we'd hug and visit.

There were still awkward moments.

One night, I walked into a neighborhood bar called Phil's Polka Club, where Uncle Frank and Aunt Margie were drinking at the bar. I joined them for a few beers. At some point, they got into a minor argument over something silly. I weighed in on the matter and took Uncle Frank's side. She smiled and said, "You know what I don't understand? All your life you've stuck up for him. But I'm your blood. He's not."

A thunderbolt sliced through my body, and I felt a rush of blood that made me sway a little. My reaction was to chuckle; she got off her stool to give me a hug, at which point I locked eyes with Uncle Frank over the bend of her shoulder. He looked at once anxious and sad, and I tried to communicate with my eyes that he had nothing to fear in the moment. The secret remained ours.

Another time, my cousin Buzz had a party at his house. Buzz had an undiagnosed bipolar disorder and was going through one of his erratic veers between high and low. He was running around the house, tending to guests one moment before descending over the edge of mental canyons the next.

I was standing against a wall, talking to my mom and Uncle Frank. Buzz was zooming around the room erratically. He stopped at our group and blurted, "You know what I think?" He pointed at my mom. "I think that one day you..." He moved his extended right index finger in the direction of his dad. "...and you, got together, and that's where he came from." Buzz pointed at me and kind of jabbed his finger and then walked away. We were collectively astonished.

Uncle Frank looked at my mom and said, "Tommy knows, Glenore." My mom turned as pale as the wall I was standing against. Shocked, she stammered, "Well, you boys can think whatever you want. But please, I—I don't want any part of this," and then walked away, leaving me and Uncle Frank alone. The circle had widened, but the secret remained ours.

I was determined to keep it that way. If my mom knew that I was truly wise, it would bother her deeply. If she thought her sister knew, it would have destroyed her. And despite Walter Dreesen's alcoholism, which exacerbated his shortcomings as a father, I still considered him my dad. I loved him as much as I could; therefore, I honored him by keeping my mouth shut. I'm not sure it mattered.

Walter Dreesen was a very intelligent man who had been around the block of life. The realization that he must have known was one of the greatest heartaches I experienced, and it brought me to tears. He couldn't possibly look at me and think I resembled any of my siblings. My older brother, Glenn, had blonde hair; my sister Darlene had blue eyes. The younger kids looked like Dreesens too. But I had coal-black hair, brown eyes, and a nose of a certain Italian distinction. Every time I walked into a room, it must have hurt my dad. I shudder at the thought of how it must have felt for him to look at me and internalize the pain while remaining silent.

I felt bad for my dad, but now I had a contrast in my mind of what a relationship between father and son could be. Walter Dreesen never put his arm around me, never said he loved me, none of that. On the other hand, even as a tough guy, Frank Polizzi always showed me great warmth and was a world-class hugger. He'd hug his friends every time he saw them, and he'd pull me into his arms when I saw him, gregariously saying, "Hey, how you doin', Tommy?" Perhaps this was inherently passed on to me, because I've always been an outgoing and affectionate guy myself, which I could now trace back to something. I guess the nature of my DNA was stronger than the nurture I received at home.

Although my dad exhibited very little love toward me, I gained a kind of respect for him knowing that, in the dozens of arguments he had with my mom over the years, I never once heard him throw this grenade in her face. He was either man enough to look past it and shut up when tempted, or perhaps he was fooling around himself for so long that he felt guilty for his own behavior. He also may have been afraid of what Frank Polizzi would have done if he attacked my mom in such a way.

Uncle Frank's documented hair-trigger, volcanic eruptions may also have kept Dad's frequent physical outbursts directed solely toward Glenn, because Dad never laid a hand on me. Now, I began to wonder if the reason was because Dad figured if he did anything to me and Uncle Frank heard about it, he might end up laid out on the floor like that loudmouth in the club.

After Walter Dreesen died in 1973, I finally confronted my mom. She denied it at first, still ashamed and holding tight to the façade she'd maintained for more than twenty years. I tried to assuage her sense of guilt.

"Mom, I know it's true, and I want you to know that I don't care. I'm here and I'm yours. And it just doesn't matter, because you always hugged and kissed me and, on many occasions, told me you loved me. You wrote to me so often when I was in the service and genuinely cared about me. Dad never did any of those things, so it doesn't matter to me who planted the seed."

I got up and hugged and kissed her and said, "I'm sure you went to confession years ago and made your peace with the Lord. I spent a lot of time talking to the Lord as a young guy, and I too have found peace." She said, "When we're young, we sometimes do things that seem right at the time but, when you look back, shouldn't have happened." I said, "Well if it didn't happen, I wouldn't be standing here telling you I love you." I turned to leave, and she said, "Thank you, Tommy." We never talked about it again.

For years, I was asked to appear at all kinds of Italian charity events, which I loved doing. Now, I was free to embrace my identity in a way that endeared me to so many fellow entertainers of Italian descent. I could share memories (or make gentle fun) of my true backstory. I didn't mind telling my friends out there that I was Italian, or anyone else for that matter.

Except for my older brother, Glenn. I knew we had to talk, and he did too. I called him on the phone and told him. Given his tortured history with Walter Dreesen, Glenn didn't share the same regret I had. But he shared concern for me. Glenn was always a surrogate father to me, and to this day, his support means everything.

I also confided in my older sister, Darlene. I was not as up-front with my younger siblings for a simple reason: I knew it would hurt them badly. Years later, I gave an interview to Rick Kogan of the *Chicago Tribune*, and in the moment, I decided to come clean. I don't know why I did it, because when the article came out, it really hurt my sister Margie, and it took a long time for her to get over it, which bothered me deeply. I'm not sure she's completely over it now, but we communicate almost daily and always express our love for one another.

People might wonder why I just didn't keep it a secret. One reason is that many times during TV shows or interviews, I'd be asked, "How are you Italian?"—much like Frank Sinatra asked me the night I shared my secret with him—and I'd have to meander to deliver a logical answer. Finally, I came out with it in that *Tribune* article and put it all out in the open.

All of my siblings bear the scars of neglect from our childhood, and each has had to deal with it in their own way. I'm proud to say they've all carved a niche for themselves in life, and save for our sweet Darlene, who passed away far too soon, all my brothers and sisters are doing well.

I never wanted to hurt anybody in my family over this, but it was the truth. I remain very close to my siblings. Still, we never discussed it much after that.

* * *

In 1980, Uncle Frank's health began to really deteriorate. After years of gently guiding patrons out of his tavern at 2:00 a.m., he was sternly admitted into the hospital for what would be his last call. By that time, I was in show business, doing TV shows and finally finding my way. I went to the hospital to see him, and people were coming in and out of his room; it was clear to me that the end was near.

Soon after I arrived, the room cleared of nurses and doctors, and I found myself alone with him. He called me over to his bedside and said, "Tommy, I don't have long to live, and I need to know something. Do you have any bad feelings, anything that you want to talk to me about? Is there anything you want to get off your chest?" I said no.

"Hey. Don't feel sorry for me because I'm laying here weak and frail. Get it off your chest."

"No, I have nothing."

"You don't have any animosity?"

"None," I said. "In fact, everything I have, everything I am is probably because of you, because I came from your genes, and I emulated you as a comedian and a performer. I'm forever grateful to you."

And then I asked him, "Do you have any regrets?"

It was quiet for a moment. He finally looked up from his bed and looked me straight in the eyes and said, "Tommy, the only thing I regret is that every time I saw you on TV, in a bar or somewhere, I couldn't tell those people, 'Hey, that's my kid up there.'"

I was so moved by his words, by his acceptance of me. Now, with tears in my eyes, I made a promise, "One day, I'll receive an award in show business, and I'll accept it in your name."

He turned his head away, and I could see that he had tears in his eyes. It was the only time I ever saw him cry.

* * *

I ended this long, personal tale by telling Frank Sinatra that Uncle Frank used to razz me about not drinking once I got sober. He'd say, "I don't trust a man who doesn't drink."

Sinatra said, "Your father was right. I don't trust a man who doesn't drink either." Then he looked up from his Jack Daniel's, smiled, and said, "Tommy, that kind of thing happens in more families than you can imagine. The only difference is you learned the truth."

The two Franks in my life had a lot in common. They were about the same size and build, both were unmistakably tough, and both had incredible presence that would change the psychology of any room they entered. And there was no greater delight than spending time with a group of guys they enjoyed being around.

Polizzi's Tavern was my training ground for how to relate to people of all stripes, how to perform and get along with strangers, and how not to take shit from anyone. Watching him night after night for more than a decade, I never met anyone who embodied those same characteristics more than Frank Sinatra.

Uncle Frank passed away on November 11, 1980, a few years before I began touring with Frank Sinatra. I never had the chance to introduce the two men who had a major influence on my life. I did, however, keep my last promise to Uncle Frank. In May of 2005, I went to Ellis Island, where he had arrived in 1913 as a six-year-old off the SS *Italia*, and where I was honored to receive the prestigious Ellis Island Medal of Honor Award for Humanitarian Service to my country. I dedicated it to Frank Polizzi, my father.

28

Looking back on my childhood, I finally saw clearly that Italian heritage was more inherent to my sense of self than I ever realized.

When I was a little boy, I always remember the natural affinity and appreciation I had for Italian culture. Simple things, like going to Blue Island, the town next to us, where the Catholic Church had an Italian parish called St. Donatus that put on a grand carnival every year. I remember the smells of the food wafting through the cool September air, the sounds of Italian dialects being spoken all around me, and, of course, the music coming out of the speakers set up around all the booths. There was something about that carnival that made me feel so comfortable in that environment. It sounds silly, but I felt Italian before I even knew I was one. I felt at home.

In Los Angeles, some of my closest friends in show business were Italian: Dennis Farina, Frankie Avalon, James Darren, Johnny Dark, John Romeo, Frankie Valli, Joe Pesci, Joe Mantegna, Ed Marinaro, and others. We used to jokingly have a thing called the IMO, "Italian Men Only." Once a month, we'd go to a neighborhood Italian restaurant and get a big table in the back. The guys would bring their wives or girlfriends, and we'd have a good meal, sharing laughs and stories from our respective old days. We were all just a bunch of neighborhood guys from Philadelphia, New York, New Jersey, Chicago, and Harvey.

And now, I was hanging out with the greatest Italian icon of them all, an affiliation that served me well in more ways than one.

Frank and I were appearing at the Golden Nugget in Atlantic City one night. I was onstage opening, about halfway through my set, when I heard some guy holler out of nowhere, "*Hey, Dreesen. You ever have your nose broke?*"

Wait…. What did he say?

Now I'd handled plenty of hecklers in my day, but this line landed strangely with me and sure didn't sound like a regular jeer. There was a certain personality behind the line, an underlying menace in the tone that stopped me cold for a second.

Fishing a bit in my response, I said, "I'm sorry. I didn't hear what you said. Did you ask if I've ever had my nose broken?"

I couldn't see much of the audience because of the lights. But I found a strategic moment to coyly dip my head under them long enough to see long rows of tables where people were seated near the front of the stage and where I think I spotted the clown talking to me. He had moved his chair away from the table and was kind of arrogantly leaning back in the seat, but I couldn't make him out beyond blurry features.

I started doing jokes about how big my nose was because of my Italian heritage and the fact that I had had my nose fixed because of a deviated septum, and so on. But this heckler wouldn't shut up. He threw other taunting barbs my way, each of which I responded to, making the audience chuckle and side with me during the verbal joust. We went back and forth a couple of times before I finally pivoted away from the guy and continued my act.

As I finished and exited the stage a few minutes later, I kept thinking, "Who the fuck would say something like that?" I was a bit shaken but took comfort in knowing I had plenty of backup that night.

My half-brother, Don Polizzi, was in town and hanging out backstage that night. After the show, I said, "Don, do me a favor. Go down to the maître d' and ask him if there's a guy named Denardo on the guest list." My mind had gone to that chickenshit who ambushed me outside the Blue Goose bus years earlier in my Navy days. I wondered if he had serendipitously found his way into the crowd of high society that night in Atlantic City and was looking to get even after I had repaid him with a beatdown in Brooklyn.

Don came to my dressing room and reported that there was no "Denardo" on the guest list. But there were several large groups with a lot of Italian names in attendance. Who knew if he was guest at one of those tables?

I never saw my verbal assailant, just as I didn't see Denardo when he first ambushed me. To this day, I believe that he was in the audience in Atlantic City, probably with a crew of wiseguys that he had linked up with after being dishonorably discharged from the service.

The thought occurred to me that the only reason he didn't track me down after the show to try and finish the conversation was because I had a reputable crew of my own—headed by the one and only Frank Sinatra—whom he perhaps admired enough to just let things be between the two of us.

29

The first year I was touring with Frank, we performed at the Waldorf Astoria in New York for an event honoring Barbara Sinatra. At the cocktail party, I was standing off to the side next to Frank when Henry Kissinger, the former secretary of state, walked up to Frank and said, "Francis, how are you?" Frank said, "Dr. Kissinger, it's good to see you again. This is Tom Dreesen, a comedian who's been touring with me." Kissinger took his fist and kind of punched my arm and said, "I've seen you on *The Tonight Show*. You're a funny lad." "Holy cow," I thought, "Henry Kissinger watches Johnny Carson, just like everyone else."

Frank smiled and turned around to speak with Donald Trump, who was just a young real estate executive at the time, leaving me alone with Kissinger. I wanted him to know I was worldly and more than a funny lad, so I said, "Dr. Kissinger, I was watching *Nightline* the other night, and they were talking about the West Bank and…" I started to ask him a serious question when Lee Castle, the Italian bandleader, brushed by Kissinger and said, "Excuse me," and then approaching me said, "Tommy, did you hear about Tony M. from Milwaukee? The fucking feds busted him. He got two years."

I was mortified. I didn't know who he was talking about. Castle walked away, and Kissinger was now looking at me like I was Al

Capone. I mustered the only appropriate response to Kissinger I could muster, "Well, you know how them fucking feds are," and then we awkwardly continued our conversation.

Afterward, I found Castle and said, "Lee, who the hell were you talking about?" He said, "Tony Machi, from Milwaukee. He bribed a judge, and they gave him some time in jail. Can you believe that shit?"

"Jeez. I met the guy once at the Italian Fest in Milwaukee. I walked offstage, he handed me a check, and I left. That's the only thing I know about him."

Castle said, "I thought you'd want to know." I said, "It's no fucking wonder why everyone thinks all Italians are in the mob when you interrupt a conversation and share a story like that."

Later, Frank and I were sitting at Rocky Lee's restaurant with some other friends when he said to me, "What were you and Kissinger talking about for so long?" I told Frank he wouldn't believe what Lee Castle had said in front of Kissinger. Frank shook his head and said, "Tommy, guys like that just don't think," and proceeded to tell me a story of his own from years earlier.

Frank was at a big political fundraising dinner with a lot of construction company executives in the audience. He was sitting on the dais next to the governor of New York. During the salad course, one of the wiseguys got up from a table, walked up to the dais, and knelt between Sinatra and the governor. The guy said, "Frank, I don't know if you heard about Paulie, but he died last night—in the electric chair." The guy jabbed a finger at the governor and said loudly, "...'Cause this *fuck* right here wouldn't pardon him." Frank told me he fell off the chair laughing, shocked the guy called out the governor like that.

I often speak to groups—particularly young comedians—about my experiences in show business, and anytime I open the floor to questions from the audience, there is one query I have come to expect: "Was Frank in the Mafia?"

Let's put this question in context. Frank Sinatra went into the recording studio 1,431 times in his career. He recorded more than

200 albums and debuted over 1,200 songs. That's unheard of. He's the only male artist ever to record in seven decades, from the 1930s through the 1990s. He's probably on every jukebox and every streaming playlist in the world. He appeared in more than sixty movies and won two Academy Awards. He is the most complete global entertainer in history, and the one question I always get is if Frank was mobbed up.

The truth is so simple it's complicated. Back when Frank was starting out and for many years after, the Mafia had an outsized presence in the casinos of all the great gambling cities, like Las Vegas, Lake Tahoe, Reno, and even Havana, Cuba, along with hundreds of popular night clubs across America. Sure, he *knew* those guys; everybody in our business did. They owned the venues and booked the acts to bring in big crowds every night—and what they did with their cut of the proceeds was none of our business. Normally after a show, the club owners wanted to take pictures with their headliner, and speaking for myself, what was the harm? I was always happy to comply, and so was Frank, but that didn't mean we were secret members of the mob.

Still, I'll never forget the advice I got once from Dean Martin, who was no stranger to this conundrum. Dean was really a tough guy. As a kid in Steubenville, Ohio, he boxed professionally under the name "Kid Crochet," as Crocetti was his actual surname. You couldn't tell it from his stage persona, but Dean was not a guy to mess with.

Speaking of wiseguys he'd encountered over the years, Dean offered me some advice: "Tommy, keep them at arm's length. Show respect, be polite, but find your distance." Dean was known not to take shit from anyone, including the biggest mob boss. There's the old story of how Johnny Roselli, the don of Miami, contemplated putting a contract on Dean's life over a jumbo shrimp. The story goes that Roselli and Dean were at some banquet dinner, and Dean was sitting at the table eating his appetizer when Roselli reached over Dean's shoulder to take a shrimp off his plate. Indignant, Dean slapped his hand hard and said, "I don't like people messing with my food when I'm eating."

Roselli was embarrassed—and fucking livid. Later, it was revealed on an FBI wiretap that Roselli told Sam Giancana, another notorious mafioso, that he wanted to kill Dean Martin because of the slight. Mind you, this was over a shrimp cocktail. Dean didn't give a shit.

Frank himself shared privately with me the burden he carried of being considered guilty by association with that crowd. He once told me how he regretted that his early career had been dominated by the necessary affiliation with club owners with Mafia ties. "I rue the day I ever made friends with some of those guys. They won't get out of your life, Tommy." He explained, "If you're young and trying to make it in show business and somebody does you a favor, that person expects a payback someday. Years go by, and that guy's son will come backstage and say, 'You know, my father did you a favor once,' and then ask for something in return himself. Years after that, you might meet the grandson of the guy, who says, 'I heard my grandfather did you a favor once.' They won't get out of your life."

Still, when you're the biggest Italian star on the planet and a hero of the toughest of tough guys, there are going to be times on the road when some of those people gain access to be around you—and no one understood the effect he had on others more than Frank himself.

Sinatra once said during an interview early in his career, "In order to become a major star as a boy singer performing with a big band, you had to have four qualities. Number one, young women want to make love to you. Number two, older women want to mother you. Number three, little children wish you were their dad. Number four, the guys want to hang out with you.

Most singers I know had the first three of those qualities, but not the fourth. Sinatra had all four. All the guys wanted to be around him and be like him. I've never seen another performer that possessed the sheer magnetism of Frank Sinatra.

That's one reason all the top casinos in Vegas, many operated by the mob in those days, always wanted him to perform in their hotels.

He had an incredible ability to draw in crowds of long-drinking, free-spending high rollers. In casino parlance, the "drop in the pit" is an expression for how much money is brought in from gambling on a given night. When Frank was performing in a casino, the drop in the pit was often double, if not triple, what it would be for other entertainers. Guys just wanted to occupy the same space as Sinatra.

Jeanne Martin, Dean's wife, once said something about her husband that exemplified Sinatra and a lot of other guys, including me. She said, "Dean would come home, we'd have a cocktail or two and then dinner, and we'd spend a nice evening together. But I knew that given the choice, he'd rather be in the back of a restaurant hanging out with the guys."

Next to playing golf, "hanging out" is my favorite pastime. Sitting around with a group of friends and telling stories about recent events and those long forgotten is my happy place. Not everyone is a "hangout" person, but no one loved to sit around with friends over drinks and reminisce more than Frank, and he could do it every night.

Jilly Rizzo was one of Frank's original hang-out guys, and he could hang out better than most. Jilly and Frank spoke the same dialect when it came to humor, finding comedy in the everyday things in life that plague us all. He was quick with jokes and one-liners—and he also enjoyed being the subject of them now and again. Years later, Jilly was the guest of honor at a Friars Club Roast in New York City, and I was on the dais as one of those chosen to roast him. When I got up to speak, I told the following story:

"Before Jilly met Frank, he worked construction in New York. One time on the job, a guy named Eddie Johnson was killed in a tragic accident when a concrete truck rolled over him. Somebody had to go tell his wife that her husband was killed. The foreman said, 'I gotta get somebody who has tact,' so he called Jilly into his office. 'Jilly, you've got to go tell Mrs. Johnson that her husband was killed, and please, use a little tact when you break the news.' Jilly went to the Johnson house and knocked on the front door. When a woman answered, Jilly said, 'Are you the Widow Johnson?' The woman said, 'I'm Mrs. Johnson but I'm not a widow.' And Jilly said, *'The fuck you ain't.'*"

The joke was a huge score, and for years after that, when we were out to dinner with a bunch of guys who hadn't heard it, Jilly would say, "Hey, Tommy, tell that story about me working construction." It remains one of my favorite hang-out jokes.

30

'll never forget a story that Jilly and Frank told me on separate occasions, about the time Johnny Carson got completely sideways with the infamous mobster Joey Gallo.

We were on Frank's jet heading to a gig. I had done *The Tonight Show* a few days earlier, and Johnny's name came up in conversation. Jilly had told me a story a week earlier that I found hard to believe, but then Frank validated the same story verbatim.

Johnny used to be a frequent patron of Jilly's bar in New York back when *The Tonight Show* was still broadcast from Manhattan. Every night, Jilly's brought together big-name celebrities, police captains, FBI guys, and the gangsters they chased—one big melting pot of interesting clientele.

Johnny Carson had a reputation as a calm, cool, mild-mannered guy—a former naval officer who also seemed to be a gentleman. However, what the studio audience never saw was Johnny after a couple of drinks, when he could become a paradox of his image and act more juvenile than an eighth-grader crashing the senior prom. Johnny was a young star and still relatively new as host of the show. After tapings, he and his sidekick, Ed McMahon, would often hop over to Jilly's for a few pops.

On this particular night, Joe Gallo strolled into Jilly's, accompanied by two guys and two girls dressed for the evening. At the time, Gallo was one of the most notorious mobsters in America. Anyone who knew Gallo knew he had a hot temper and a fast trigger finger. His well-earned nickname was "Crazy Joey," because as much as he was feared by others, Gallo feared nothing and no one.

As they entered, Joey dispatched the girls to the wood-paneled bar near the front. He approached Jilly, who was tending bar, and asked for a private space for a discussion with his two "associates." Jilly obliged and directed them to a back room. Shortly after, Carson and McMahon strolled in, and it was apparent that they'd already had a few drinks. Johnny scanned the terrain and spotted the two girls standing alone at the bar nursing their drinks. Johnny tiptoed up behind them and shoved his hand up the miniskirt of one of Joe's gals. Big mistake.

The girl started screaming at the top of her lungs, and the whole place came to a screeching halt. Sensing how bad things were about to get, Jilly turned around, jumped over the bar, and grabbed Ed by the collar, "GET HIM THE FUCK OUT OF HERE! NOW!"

Ed took his orders without argument and sternly escorted Johnny by the elbow out of the bar, marking the quickest exit Carson ever made. Meanwhile, the violated girl continued wailing to the point she began hyperventilating when Gallo returned from the back room and said, "What the fuck is going on?"

Through sobs, the girl explained what happened and that Johnny Carson was the perpetrator. Gallo immediately turned to his two associates and barked, "Find him! Beat his fucking brains out. Then cut his cock off and stick it in his mouth! Stick it in his fucking mouth!"

As the two capos scurried out into the night in search of Carson, Crazy Joe turned his angry attention to Jilly and shouted, "You fucking prick! You let this go down?!"

"I was doing stuff behind the bar!" Jilly exclaimed, "I didn't even notice anything till I heard her scream!"

Five minutes later, the two guys came back, covered in sweat, reporting they couldn't find Carson. Now Gallo was really pissed, and word quickly spread that he was going to whack the up-and-coming king of late-night television.

Carson knew he had fucked up big time and that Crazy Joey Gallo wasn't one to bluff. The next day, Dave Tebet, an NBC executive and acquaintance of Johnny's, walked into the bar and asked Jilly to talk to Gallo and smooth over the situation.

"You want me to talk to Gallo?" Jilly asked, finding himself in the middle for the second time in as many days. "The Five Families can't even talk to Gallo!"

The guy then asked Jilly, "Well, can Frank talk to him?"

"Are you fucking crazy? You want me to ask Sinatra to intervene?"

"Jilly, please, this guy's life is on the line. Frank knows John. You gotta do something here." Reluctantly, Jilly agreed and shared the situation with Frank, who happened to be performing in New York that week. Frank agreed to do what he could, and he started by inviting Gallo to his show. Gallo was apparently honored that Frank would show him that respect, arranging for two tables near the stage: one for Joey and his mother, and the other for guys in his crew.

After the show, Gallo and his mother were invited backstage, and Frank continued the charm offensive, signing autographs, taking pictures, and doting on Joe's mom. Eventually, most of the room cleared out except for Jilly, Joe, and Frank.

Gallo said to Frank, "I'll never forget what you did for me, what you did for my mom. You made her life tonight. If you ever need anything, Frank, anything at all, just ask."

Frank quickly responded, "There is something, Joe."

Joey was standing in front of Frank and extended his arms out wide, in the shape of an inverted "V," palms ups, as if to say, "name it."

"Johnny Carson—" No sooner had Frank clipped the final consonant in Carson's name, when Gallo's open right hand lasered up and landed squarely on Frank's mouth, squeezing his cheeks inward.

"You're sticking up for that fucking piece of shit? A man of your caliber? This punk thinks he can get away with shit like that because he's got a TV show? He's a fucking dead man!" Joe violently released Frank, allowing him to catch his breath and speak.

"Joey, please, he didn't know that broad was with you. He knows he made a terrible mistake, and he's very sorry. He knows you're a man of respect. He's scared shitless. If he were here right now, he'd be on his hands and knees, begging for forgiveness."

Joey started pacing around Frank's dressing room, breathing heavy and mumbling to himself. Sensing his contemplation, Frank continued, "Joey, you just said to me, 'If there's anything that I ever need,' and I'm asking you to forgive this kid."

Joe looked at Frank with his crazy, wild eyes and started walking again in circles. This request was really testing his patience. Finally, Gallo marched to the dressing room door, turned around, and loudly said, "You tell Johnny Carson that the ONLY reason he breathes is because he knows Frank Sinatra."

Gallo swiped his arms horizontally clean in the air, like a Vegas blackjack dealer does when exiting a table, and then wiped his hands as if to signal to Frank, "This is finished." The matter was concluded. Crazy Joe walked out of the door, and that was that.

Frank Sinatra saved Johnny Carson's life that night. I don't doubt that for one moment. I've heard several versions of this story over the years, with similar outcomes but different heroes, and I'm here to tell you, I believe Jilly and I certainly believe Frank. If there was ever a man who had absolutely zero need to embellish or pretend to be a hero, it was Frank Sinatra.

And while it is the most extreme of examples, this was a classic gesture of loyalty by Frank Sinatra, who was always willing to stand up for his friends—in this case, both Jilly and Carson.

31

For many years, the arc of Frank Sinatra's career rose and dipped from hot to cold to hot again. Frank once told me that when he was hot, he could call the White House and ask to speak to the president of the United States, and the president would immediately take his call. The same went for any record executive or movie producer in the land. But when his career hit a snag and he got cold, he couldn't get anybody's attention. Frank reminisced how he'd go to parties or social events after he got hot again and see a powerful guy across the room, and that person would put his head down, unable to look him in the eye knowing that he had ignored Frank during a cold spell. "I wasn't bitter," Frank told me. "I couldn't do business for him anymore. That's why he didn't take my call. My fault was, I thought we were friends. But, Tommy, don't ever forget, show business is two words: 'show' and 'business.'"

Throughout the career ups and downs, the one constant that defined Sinatra's life was his generosity—to friends and strangers alike.

Frank Sinatra was the most generous man I've ever known. I'm a man of faith, and I know Frank was too. He understood that he had been blessed with a talent beyond measure, and that along with fame and fortune came a responsibility to care for others. The

Gallo-Carson incident aside, Sinatra's many other, less dramatic acts of generosity were well known and spanned his entire life.

Everybody knew Frank Sinatra was a big tipper, and the one hundred-dollar bill was his favorite denomination to dole out. If some kid working in a club ran out to fetch him a pack of cigarettes, Frank would pull out a roll of bills and hand him a hundred dollars. If a waiter brought him another Jack Daniels, he got a hundred dollars. Frank didn't show off with it, though. He'd slip the bills to you quietly. There's the legendary story about Frank coming out of a restaurant and when the valet pulled up his car, Frank asked, "What's the biggest tip you ever got?" The valet said, "One hundred dollars, sir." Frank gave him two hundred bucks and said, "Here you go. By the way, who tipped you the hundred dollars?" The valet said, "You did, Mr. Sinatra, last Friday."

Frank also helped people without them ever knowing. Frank read the newspapers most every day, and if he saw a story about a child who had a brain tumor and lived in a boxcar with her mom and six siblings, the next day, somebody would deliver an anonymous check to that mother. This exhibition of grace and goodness happened many times. That's the way Frank Sinatra lived.

To his friends, Frank's big-heartedness was so abundant that you had to be very careful not to say that you wanted or needed something, because he would always fill the order. If you said in an offhanded way, "I like your watch," Frank would take it off and place it on your wrist, and if you tried to refuse or give it back, you'd end up insulting him. If you admired a painting in his house, he'd take it off the wall and give it to you. You couldn't say you liked his jacket, or it was yours.

One night in New York, we were leaving the back exit of the Waldorf Astoria to get into the limousine to go do a show. A woman who had been hiding in a doorway ran up, shouting, "Mr. Sinatra, please!" The security guys stopped her, but she kept calling for him. Frank was almost in the limo when he turned around and asked, "What is it?" She explained, "My husband adores you. He is home very ill. If I could get your autograph, it would mean the world to him. Could you make it out to him?" Frank agreed, and while he was signing her piece of paper, making nervous small talk she said, "Those are beautiful cuff links." After breaking the stroke of his pen, Frank took off his expensive cuff links and handed them to her. "Give them to your husband." The woman was flabbergasted, unable to form a response as Frank said goodbye and we sped away.

During the limo ride, I asked him why he'd done that. Frank said, "Tommy, if you possess something that you can't give away, you don't possess it; it possesses you. If someone says, 'That's a beautiful pair of cuff links,' and you don't give them to that person on the spot, you're forced to admit that the cuff links own you." He continued, "Think of Aristotle Onassis. He had billions of dollars and all the toys you could imagine. The second he died, everything he owned—the yachts, the mansions, the jewelry—it all belonged to someone else. Nothing we have is ours, we're just using it."

That observation had a profound impact on me. Possessions in life are fleeting, and I often hear Frank's voice in my head, advising me not to let anything own me, lest they be false idols.

Some may define power and influence as reaching the status of not having to care anymore, because you have enough wealth or power to overcome just about any adversity. In my view, Frank had achieved that stature, but he always remained a gentle and benevolent steward of his power, one who always cared, and someone who always shared the generosity of the light that surrounded him.

We were at a restaurant in Chicago once called Doro's with a table full of people, including Barbara, Jilly, and some others. Frank and I were talking about some moment in my career where I felt I didn't have any leverage over a situation, and Frank started giving me advice on what he would have done in that same situation. I chuckled and said, "Well, I couldn't have done that."

"Why not?" he asked

"Frank, I'm not a star."

"Well, you're a star in my eyes," Frank said, sweetly and earnestly.

I laughed again and said, "That's nice. Thank you. But I don't have power like that; I'm not a superstar."

Frank said, "Tommy, you have power. Because you have *my* power." The others around the table began to key into our conversation, and everyone got quiet. Frank continued, "Any power I have, you have. And if you ever need anything, you call me." Then he looked over at Barbara and said, "If Tommy ever calls, I want to know."

I cut the mood and said, "Frank, if Barbara ever tells you I'm on the phone, sit down, because I ain't gonna be asking for two tickets to the Engelbert Humperdinck show."

Frank doubled over in laughter because he knew it was true. If a man of power ever says to you, "If you need anything, call me," you sure don't waste that offer on something trivial.

In 1986, I was approached by Multimedia Entertainment about filming a television pilot where I would basically host a talk show in my own bar. The concept was that celebrities and athletes and other famous people would walk into my bar, and I would proceed to interview them. Knowing that the pilot had to include the most impressive guests I could book, I turned to my friends. There was no one more notable in sports at the time than Johnny Bench, the Hall of Fame catcher and spirited spark plug of the Cincinnati Reds baseball team during their historic "Big Red Machine" years. Johnny checked his calendar and said, "I'm in."

Of course, there was no one in the entire world more famous than the guy I was touring with, and I decided to spend some personal capital and ask Frank if he'd do me the favor of appearing on my show. We were performing at the Golden Nugget in Las Vegas, and I went to his dressing room before the show to float the idea. Frank willingly agreed. I was over the moon and began to endlessly thank him. Finally, he said, "Tommy, stop it, please." And I said, "I know how busy you are, so this means a lot to me." Frank said, "Tommy, we do these shows for strangers all the time. Why wouldn't we do them for friends?" I said, "Well, I didn't want to impose on you." He grabbed my shoulder and looked me square in the eyes and said, "Tommy, please. Friends are never an imposition."

In my own small way, it was important for me to occasionally reciprocate the generosity Frank always showed me. While on tour, once a week, I insisted on taking Frank out to dinner, and I'd arrange ahead of time to pay the bill, no questions asked. Frank certainly didn't need my charity, but I know he always appreciated that I made the gesture. To arrange the schedule and location for our weekly "Dinner on Dreesen," I'd call his assistant Dorothy Uhlemann and tell her the restaurant I had selected, and she would run the place by Frank, who always gave his approval. Frank could bring anybody he wanted. Normally it was Barbara and perhaps a few other friends they had previously planned to have dinner with that night.

To round out the table, I'd also invite people I thought would be interesting dinner companions. Once, we were in Chicago, and I called Dorothy and said, "Okay, this week I'd like to take the Boss to Kelly Mondelli's on Clark Street. And oh, I've invited Irv and Essie Kupcinet to join." Irv Kupcinet was a well-known and influential columnist in Chicago. Kup had such a powerful pen that if your name was mentioned in one of his columns, well, then you were a somebody. He was to Chicago what Liz Smith or Page Six became to New York City. Everybody read Kup's column, every day. He was one of those old-time reporters who always checked the story out. He would never run with something until he called the sources and verified what he planned to report. He was a true journalist.

My phone rang about an hour before dinner, and Dorothy said, "Tom, he's not happy with Irv Kup." "Why?" I asked? "Apparently, Kup wrote something about him that made Frank upset."

"Oh my God, I've already invited them, what should I do?" I said. Dorothy said, "Look, he'll come there, but he might get mad and let Kup have it. You never know. Just be ready."

As it turned out, we got there and Frank sees Kup, and they immediately embrace. "Kup! It's great to see you, you look good!"

Frank bleated in praise. Kup reciprocated, and nothing happened beyond having a wonderful evening together.

* * *

Frank had a classic love/hate relationship with the media: they loved to write about him, and he hated it when they did. Frank was always very cautious of the media, which came after decades of experience being in the public eye. He had had more than a few heated and well-documented run-ins with critics and gossip columnists over the years, like when he slugged Lee Mortimer not long after Mortimer had written another unflattering item about him.

That wary approach to media extended to me. "They're not your friends, Tommy," Frank would say, and I regularly declined interview requests to talk about Frank, except for one notable exception. There was a local pub in the San Fernando Valley that I used to frequent when at home, just to see some guys and hang out. Another regular in there was a reporter, a good guy and someone I got to know and like, but he was always asking about Frank. One day, for some reason, I relented. I gave him a great interview, sharing all the wonderful things I knew to be true about Frank as a person and as a friend. At one point, trying to make this clear, I mentioned in an aside, "Now don't get me wrong, Frank Sinatra is no saint, but he does saintly things." And wouldn't you know it? When the story appeared in the paper a few days later, the headline was "Frank Sinatra Is No Saint." I was mortified. I knew Frank read the papers and would see that headline soon enough. I also knew that I had no choice but to come clean with Frank and let him know what had happened, from my perspective. "Better that he heard this directly from me," I thought, so I made my way to his place in Palm Springs and I brought a copy of the article with me.

I showed the paper to him and began to explain how this was a total puff-piece profile and that I had been so complimentary the entire time, save for that one out-of-context comment that became the unfortunate headline. Frank looked at me and smiled, sort of. "Tommy, what did I tell you? You can't trust them." And then he let it go. In an instant, all was forgiven, and we never spoke of that article again.

Frank Sinatra was no saint, but he did saintly things. I can say that now in perfect context, and I will never compromise my belief of that statement, because there were so many times I witnessed or was the beneficiary of Frank's graciousness and generosity.

32

When you are in the regular presence of a celebrity the magnitude of Frank Sinatra, there are naturally going to be some interpersonal dynamics to navigate among his regular aides. As the "sun in our solar system," Frank relied primarily on a few trusted individuals to mind his interests. First and foremost, Barbara Sinatra was without peer—she was truly the first lady of our entourage, and what Barbara said became doctrine—because whether people accepted it or not, she was speaking for Frank. In my experience, there was never anything Barbara said as a directive that was not blessed by Frank himself.

Now this was good for me. Barbara and I got along very well, and she wanted me around Frank all the time, because she knew that I looked after him when she wasn't there, especially out in public. When I was a bartender in Harvey, I learned that alcohol affects everybody differently, and after a couple of belts, the most loyal drinkers could be categorized by one of "the Three Rs." They either became Rocky Marciano and wanted to fight everybody in the place; they became Rudolph Valentino and wanted to fuck everybody in the place; or they became Rip Van Winkle and went to sleep. Frank Sinatra was an "R" of the Rocky Marciano variety. After a couple of drinks, he tended to get aggressive.

My experience as a bartender gave me vision to look around the corner when Frank might get pugilistic, and I'd spring into action. I'd say, "Hey, Frank, remember that night you told me about the time when you and Dean..."

And Frank would say, "Oh yeah, yeah, yeah." And I'd get him laughing. I could always redirect him in these moments when he drank like that, and we averted some problems over the years as a result. I did my best to look out for her guy over the years, and so Barbara looked out for me.

Before I arrived on the scene, Jilly had worked a deal so that he got paid a commission by whatever comedian was opening for Frank. I'm not sure who agreed to this, but I was brought on tour by Frank's lawyer and manager, Mickey Rudin, so I never knew about any previous arrangement.

Early in my tenure, Jilly came up to me and bluntly told me that he wanted 10 percent of whatever Frank paid me. Somewhat taken aback, I looked at him and asked why. He said, "Because that's my deal. I get the comic." And I said, "Well, I'm sorry, Jilly, but Mickey's the guy who hired me," and I walked away. I didn't say anything more, but it struck me as odd. At the same time, Frank was always checking to make sure I was happy with things and often said to me, "Tommy, is everything working out for you? Don't bullshit me. I want to make sure you're getting what you need." I would always say, "First of all, Mr. S., you are beyond good to me, flying in your private jet, taking care of me on the road, inviting me to your home several times a year, and yes, the money is good." "Okay," Frank would say. "You let me know."

Mickey Rudin, too, was always inquiring about my happiness and offered to boost my salary on several occasions. He'd say, "If you're not satisfied, let me know and we'll work something out."

After Jilly approached me, I told my manager, Dan Wiley, who was also perplexed by the demand. I decided to let it go even though it bothered me. Not long after, I was having dinner with Frank and Barbara, and once again, Frank asked if I was happy with our arrangement. I assured him I was, and in a passing reference, I joked, "I even have money left over after I pay my manager, Dan, and my new agent, Jilly...."

Barbara said, "What do you mean 'your agent Jilly?'" And I said, "Well, I'm told he gets the commission for comedians."

Barbara said, "No, he doesn't." Frank chimed in and said, "Like hell he does." The saga of who my new agent was ended right there.

I was with Frank for a total of fourteen years. For the first six or seven years, Mickey Rudin was out on tour with us almost all the time. When Mickey left, a guy named Eliot Weisman took on the role of managing Frank's bookings and traveled on the tours. Eliot was an interesting character of some renown; for one, he was involved in the infamous Westchester Theatre scandal and did some prison time as a result.

In addition to Sinatra, Eliot managed a couple of comedians, and he was always trying to get them booked on the tour in my place. (Eliot later managed Don Rickles, a partnership that lasted only a short while.) When I wasn't booked to tour with Frank, my manager would keep my schedule full by booking corporate gigs, either as a stand-up act or by serving as an emcee at business conferences and awards dinners. But I remained close personally to Frank and Barbara, who often invited me to spend time with them.

One time I was at their house for a party, and Frank said, "Tommy, I hear you've not been available to open for me lately because you're doing a lot of corporate dates. I thought you were happy with things between us?"

I said, "Frank, I'm always available for you—you're my number-one priority—but your guys don't let me know about dates until about a week beforehand, and sometimes I've already been booked for other gigs." When Rudin was there, the Sinatra office would send me Frank's updated tour schedule every six months. In that moment, I realized they weren't doing that any longer because Eliot got a commission from booking his other comics. I was getting shut out. When Frank heard that he said, "Barbara, get Eliot on the phone. Tell him that Tom gets first crack at every one of our gigs. Every single one. And if Tommy can't do 'em, that's okay, but he gets first shot."

Soon thereafter, Eliot and Jilly started referring to Barbara as my lawyer. I'd see Eliot in passing, and he'd say, "Yeah, your lawyer and I were talking the other day and..."

"Yeah, she's pretty good, isn't she?" I'd shoot back, because I didn't take any shit from either of them—especially Eliot, who sure as fuck didn't control me, and I made sure he knew it.

Jilly was a good person, and I truly liked him; we had a lot of good times and many laughs together over the years. At his core, Jilly was a fun-loving guy who loved Frank Sinatra and, like all of us, simply wanted to be around him. Still, even though Jilly was a tough guy who had Frank's ear most of the time, he never tried to pull rank on me after that first encounter, because by then, I had established a strong relationship of my own with Frank.

I had my ups and downs with Eliot over the years, and things finally came to a boil when we had a run-in one night at the Civic Opera House in Chicago, my hometown. Frank and I were getting ready to do the show, and I was in the dressing room, with about five minutes to go before showtime. The production manager knocked on my door to escort me to the stage, and in the hallway stood a security guard, who said, "Mr. Dreesen, Jack McHugh and his wife Brenda are out there looking for their seats. They don't know where to go." Jack and Brenda McHugh were longtime friends of mine—and of Frank's. They were supposed to be sitting with Barbara that night.

The show was about to start. I should have been behind the curtain ready to kick things off. Instead, I went to find Eliot, who was supposed to handle things like this. I tracked him down in a tiny office near the stage, sitting with his feet up on a small desk, talking to two "wannabe wiseguys" from Chicago he was clearly trying to impress. Calmly but urgently, I said, "Excuse me, Eliot, I'm about to go on, but Jack McHugh and Brenda are wandering around. They don't know where to go. They're sitting with Barbara and—"

He cut me off and sarcastically said, "Forget about it, will ya? Forget about it."

I went berserk. "Who the fuck do you think you're talking to? You trying to impress these fucking guys, big shot? Kiss my fucking ass. I'm going onstage now, but I'll see you when I walk off. You want to go in the fucking alley? We'll go into the alley and see how tough you really are."

I stormed out of there, and the last thing I remember is seeing Eliot with his mouth open in shock and his two companions just sitting there. When I went onstage, my heart was pounding so loud that I thought the audience might hear the cardiac rhythms in my microphone when I sailed into my first joke. I felt like I was in a combat zone; however, the added adrenalin to my material set the pace, and I killed onstage that night.

After my set, I was in the dressing room getting out of my tux when Eliot knocked on my door. He said, "What was that all about?" Hot again, I said, "Look, Mr. Tough Guy. There's an alley right outside of here. Do you wanna show me how tough you really are?"

"Tommy, what are you talking ab—"

I cut him off this time and said, "Ever since you came on this tour, you've given me a fucking bad time. I'm sick and tired of it. When Frank doesn't want me around anymore, he'll make that decision, not you." Eliot walked out, and we stayed away from each other for a while. He knew I was pissed at him. I knew that he would continue to try and sabotage me every chance he got. And we both knew was that as long as Frank wanted me around, I was going to be around.

Many people in Frank's midst got jealous of any relationship that might threaten their own standing with the king. There was a jealousy with a few there that Frank and I were so close. I think Eliot fell into that category.

However, as confident as I was in my personal relationship with Frank—and in my ability to perform the job he hired me to do—I never took it for granted. I always considered this opportunity a temporary gift, because as much as I absolutely loved the job, I didn't need it. I knew that if or when my career chapter with Frank ended, I was going to continue to work. My life didn't depend on him, unlike many of the others. And I think Frank knew that about me. We had established our street-guy credentials and bonded early and easily because of our shared upbringings on the streets of hard-knocks, blue-collar America.

Frank was known to have mood swings, and I had witnessed his volatile temper when he sometimes went off on people. I had seen him do that to other comedians. When Pat Henry opened for him, he would yell at Pat sometimes. Years before I went on tour with him, I went to see Frank perform in Las Vegas. Jackie Gayle was opening for him, and Frank hollered from the wings, not joking, "Get off the stage already!" He never did that to me. Never.

When I first started touring with Frank, I made up my mind that if the day ever came when he shouted at me from the wings, or said something rude to me in public, I was going to grab his hand, shake it, and say, "Frank, it's been the thrill of a lifetime. Thank you for everything." And then I was going to walk out the door.

I'm grateful that day never came. But I was prepared if it did. I honestly loved him and thought the world of him, but I knew he was volatile. I also knew that life had taught me not to be a whipping boy for anyone—not even Frank Sinatra.

* * *

In politics and corporate America, there is a thing called "walk-in privileges," where someone who works for a principal—or a star, in my case—is allowed entry to the private sanctum at any time. I had that privilege on the road with Sinatra.

Susan Reynolds handled Frank's publicity for many years and was often on the road with us. Susan was very good about reading Frank's moods, which was a helpful skill to me and others around him before and after shows. Sometimes I'd be walking toward Frank's dressing room and Susan would intercept me and say, "Don't go in there.

He's in a bad mood today," which I appreciated, understanding the weather report. But most times, I would enter the sanctum anyway and take my chances. I'd go in there and pretend I didn't know he was in a bad mood. I'd say something about baseball like, "Hey, Boss, did you see what happened today with the Dodgers?" I'd work to change his mood, and over the years I had a pretty good record of success. Frank also liked to watch the game show *Jeopardy!*, which is funny if you think about it. I'd sit and watch the show with him sometimes, and we'd try to outduel each other on who could provide questions to the answers given.

One time, however, I saw Frank sink back into a funk and throw a fit after my show when there were twenty thousand people in the audience waiting for him to take the stage, when he had a bug in his ass and didn't want to go on for some reason.

Hank Cattaneo was Frank's road manager for all my time on tour with him. Frank thought the world of Hank, who was truly the Boss Whisperer. He was the only person I ever saw, other than Barbara and me, who could get Frank out of a momentary funk. In one of his pre-show moods, Frank, in his dressing room, would say to no one in particular, "Get the fucking jet ready. I'm not doing this shit."

Hank would come to the dressing room and calm him down and say, "Mr. S., what do want to do here?"

"I'm not doing the fucking show. Get the jet ready."

And Hank would say, "You got it. Tommy, what I want you to do is go back out there and tell the sold-out crowd tonight that—"

Frank stopped him and asked, "Who said it's sold out?"

And Hank said, "Boss, it's completely sold out. So, Tommy, you go out there and tell them that Mr. S. has fallen ill and that you're sorry, but people will get their tickets refunded and—"

Frank would say, "Wait a minute, wait a minute." And before you know it, Hank would gently coax him into doing the show.

Hank not only whispered in Frank's ear but also spoke to his stomach. Hank cooked sometimes for us on the road and always knew the precise preferences of the Boss. In fact, there was a special note card that Hank carried around to remind him of Frank's meal requirements:

$400 Bottle of Petrus. Cold. Put on Ice.

Before dinner drink: dry martini.

Italian cold cuts, sliced thin.

Antipasto sliced salami, thin.

French fries, real small and thin.

One clove of garlic. Never let it stay in the oil too long. Just long enough to give flavor to the oil.

Piece of filet. 6 oz. Medium.

Veal Cutlet Milanese, breaded thin, lightly floured. Dip quickly in egg batter, then into breadcrumbs, then into a frying pan with oil and butter. Fry very quickly at high temperature and serve immediately. (He wants to hear the crunch when he cuts it. He also enjoys pasta fagioli.)

We had many terrific meals on the road prepared by Hank over the years, and they rarely wavered from this script.

* * *

Eliot Weisman's attempts to sideline me aside, there was one time when a scheduling conflict led to the only instance in my fourteen years with him that Frank Sinatra got mad at me.

In between my time on the road with Sinatra, I'd often book a couple of solo dates here and there. To stay in sync, I would always call Frank's office to get the list of upcoming gigs so that I could plan around them. One time in late summer, Dorothy Uhlemann called me to say that Frank had just been booked at the MGM Grand in Vegas for a week, the day after Christmas through New Year's Day, and asked if

I was available. I told Dorothy to count me in—except I had already committed to one gig during that week to open for Glen Campbell, who was performing in Lake Tahoe on New Year's Eve. Dorothy said it was no problem, they'd just hire a substitute for that one night.

They went out and hired another comedian to fill in for me and open for Frank that night, and all seemed well. Except no one told Frank. Before he went on for his set, Frank would pace behind the curtain in the wings. He liked to listen to my material and hear the reaction of the crowd; it helped him size up the room and the night in front of him.

On New Year's Eve, Frank was backstage with Jilly and Eliot, and they both knew that Frank had no idea I was working in Tahoe the same night. As Frank was pacing behind the curtain, he heard another voice telling strange jokes out on the stage. Frank turned to Jilly and said, "Wait, who's that?"

"Uh, that's Brad Garrett." Jilly replied.

"Where's Tommy?" Frank inquired, thinking I may have gotten sick or something.

"Uh, he had a gig. In Tahoe," Jilly said.

"This ain't a fucking gig?" Frank said, sternly.

The next day, I flew in from Tahoe, and the first person I saw when I got to the hotel in Vegas on New Year's Day was Hank Cattaneo.

"Hey, Tommy, just so you know, the old man is pissed that you weren't here last night."

I just assumed Frank knew. I said to Hank, "Jesus. Everybody knew. I told the office..."

"Yeah. He's still pissed." Hank said.

I went up to his suite and said, "Frank, I'm so sorry. I told the office I could work every day this tour except for one night."

Frank said, "Oh, Tommy, don't worry about it."

I said, "I feel bad that you weren't informed."

"Ah, don't worry. It's over," Frank said.

That's the only time in all the years I was with him that he ever was mad at me, and it was only temporary. I'll take it.

33

One of the things I enjoyed most was making Frank laugh. Anytime I scored with a story or wisecrack that made him smile, I felt like a kid swinging the mallet at a carnival game who rang the bell and won a prize. Honestly, Frank was an easy audience; he loved to laugh. One time, we were in Las Vegas after a show and it was around 4:30 a.m. I was beyond ready for bed, but I could tell Frank was just getting started. I saw that twinkle in his blue eyes and thought to myself, "Oh my God, we're gonna be up again all night long."

There were maybe five people at the table, and finally I just stood up. Frank said to me in a gruff voice, "Where you going?"

"I'm going to bed."

"What for?"

"I gotta get up early in the morning and go to the cemetery to visit those guys."

"What guys?"

"All those guys who died trying to stay up with you every night."

Frank and everyone else at the table boomed with laughter.

Another time I cracked him up with a joke about a guy who died and went to heaven. As Saint Peter met him at the pearly gates, the guy heard an incredible orchestra playing "Come Fly with Me," "Summer Wind," and other songs made famous by Frank. The guy asked Saint

Peter, "Can I go there?" Saint Peter said yes. The guy approached the orchestra, which was playing in the most magnificent bandshell. Suddenly, a man appeared stage left and began walking to the microphone. "Who's that?" the guy asked Saint Peter, who replied, "That's God...he thinks he's Sinatra."

Frank let out a belly laugh, and I smiled, again taking pleasure in making my friend laugh like a schoolboy. Frank looked out the window, then looked at me again with those clear blue eyes and said, "That's the worst joke I've ever heard!"

There were also times during a show when I found his funny bone. We were at the Fox Theatre in Atlanta, Georgia, and I walked out and started my show. I was several jokes in when some guy just screamed out as loud as he could, "Where's Frank Sinatra?" Knowing Frank was in the wings listening to my set, I shot back, "He's outside, looking for your manners." The audience roared and clapped, and Frank told me after the show, "I loved the way you handled that."

Frank had a legendary wit of his own, and we connected well because we found humor in many of the same mundane things in life. Frank, on occasion, was also good at poking fun at himself, which to me is a sign of someone who has complete self-confidence. We were flying back after a gig to Palm Springs one Thursday evening, and he asked if I was staying the weekend. I told him no, I had to go to Los Angeles to do *The Tonight Show*.

Normally, the plane would drop Frank off in Palm Springs and then continue to Van Nuys Airport, where it was hangered. I lived in Sherman Oaks, so I would often stay on the plane and go into Van Nuys, which was fifteen minutes to my home.

Frank said, "Why don't you come back after the show and stay the weekend?" So I said, "I think I will." Then Frank said, "You've done a lot of *Tonight Shows*, haven't you?"

I said, "Yeah, this is like my fiftieth appearance."

"Is that a record?"

"No, there are a lot of other comedians who have done more than me." And I named a few, like Rodney Dangerfield, David Brenner, and Joan Rivers. "But you know what, Mr. S? I could do ten thousand *Tonight Shows*, or I could find the cure for cancer. But when I die, my obituary is going to say, 'The comedian who toured with Frank Sinatra.' And I'm happy with that."

"Well," he said, "maybe my obituary will say, 'The singer who toured with Tom Dreesen.'"

He looked at me with a smirk, and we both started laughing uncontrollably. It was one of those silly moments. Maybe it was because we had been on the road for a long time and we were punchy, but we just couldn't stop laughing. Tears were running down both of our faces. It was such a ridiculous thing for him to say.

Another time, we went to a bar down the street from his place in Palm Springs called Chaplin's Bar, which was owned by Sydney Chaplin, Charlie Chaplin's son. Sidney had been on Broadway as a star of the smash hit *Bye Bye Birdie*, and with the money he had saved, he bought this bar. Around two in the morning, we were the only ones in there. They were closing, but the manager left the front door unlocked so the rest of the staff could leave. As I was standing there with Frank, I saw a car pull up in front with two ladies inside. The woman on the passenger side got out of the car and came into the bar as the driver stayed in the car. Frank had his back to her, and I watched her as she walked up to him. She said, "Excuse me, do they have a jukebox in here?"

And Frank turned around and looked at her and said, "I'm sorry, what did you say?"

"Do they have a jukebox in here?" Frank looked around the bar and said, "Uh, I don't think so." Then, as an afterthought, he said, "I'll sing for you."

"No thanks," And she turned around and walked out.

He watched her like a little boy who had been turned down for a dance at a junior prom, just staring at her in disbelief. I said, "She obviously didn't recognize you." And Frank said, "Maybe she did...."

I wanted to go after her and tell her she had just turned down a guy who's on every jukebox in the world. However, then I'm sure we never would have gotten rid of her.

34

It's hard to describe what it was like for a kid from Harvey, Illinois, to see my name just below Frank Sinatra's on the marquees of the Golden Nugget, MGM Grand, Desert Inn, Sands, Riviera, and Bally's in Las Vegas—not to mention all the great casinos in Lake Tahoe, Reno, and Atlantic City. We also performed in the biggest arenas in Boston, New York, Pittsburgh, Chicago, St. Louis, Detroit, Cincinnati, Omaha, Denver, Los Angeles, Toronto, and a night I'll never forget in front of forty thousand people in Hawaii.

We returned to many of those cities every year, and the years on tour with Frank began to fly by. Traveling with Frank for so long, watching him do his show every night, there came a point when I could tell that he was beginning to struggle to remember the lyrics of the standards he had sung thousands of times. This was a subtle observation and probably something the audience didn't notice.

Sammy Davis Jr. sometimes used a teleprompter whenever he was singing new material—maybe a cover of a song by another artist or an obscure Broadway show tune. As someone who had seen Frank at the top of his game for so long, it occurred to me that maybe Frank should employ a teleprompter like his buddy Sammy, just in case. I didn't want to be the one to suggest this, so I gently floated the idea with Hank Cattaneo, who agreed and finally persuaded Frank to give it a try.

Teleprompters, when positioned strategically on the stage, look like feedback monitors to the audience. Frank could glance down casually at a teleprompter and see the next lyric, and it would seem like he was just looking at the audience. He was very good at the technique, and there were times when he didn't even look at the teleprompters, but they served a purpose as a security blanket. He was more comfortable knowing the words were there. He was like a new man onstage and more confident—to the point that he brought back songs to his live shows that he hadn't done in years.

Encouraged by what the teleprompters had done for his shows, Frank started encouraging other showbiz pals to try them out, beginning with Dean Martin, who was reportedly having trouble himself in Las Vegas, forgetting lyrics and quitting halfway through some songs.

Frank said, "Look, you know we're getting older, and you should use those teleprompters." But Dean just dismissed him. Dean was a tough sell, and he humorously feigned indignation that Frank had even suggested that he needed assistance onstage, but Frank persisted.

One day, we were appearing at the Fox Theatre in Detroit. We had done a matinee, and we had an evening show to do. We were sitting around Frank's suite watching football when Frank got a call from Mort Viner, Dean's manager, who said that Dean had used a teleprompter the night before in Las Vegas and loved it. According to Viner, as Dean came offstage that night, he said, "Book me on a world tour!" Frank smiled and said, "Damn it, he's finally listening to me! Get Dean on the phone."

Viner got Dean on the phone, and Frank started chewing him out. He said, "Goddammit, Dag..." (He always called Dean "Dag," an affectionate term among the two of them.) "I've been telling you for years, we're not getting any younger. So, what if you've gotta use those teleprompters? For Chrissake, we're not kids anymore...."

Dean wasn't about to admit that Frank was right. He didn't want to hear the gloating. Dean said, "Yeah, yeah, yeah.... Hey, where are you guys tonight?" And Frank said, "Hold on one second. Hey, Tommy, where're we at?" I reminded him we were in Detroit. Frank said, "Detroit." And Dean said, "Well, did you have to look in the fucking teleprompter to see what city you're in?"

Frank dropped the phone and with a huge laugh he roared, "Dean did it again! The bastard got me again!"

* * *

Age eventually did catch up to the otherwise timeless entertainer, and he was aware of this fact. We were performing in Salt Lake City when Frank was seventy-eight years old. He was in rare form, and the audience responded so well, loving every moment. Many people brought flowers up during a song and laid them at his feet, until a pile of floral arrangements cluttered the front of the stage. He received ovation after ovation, and as we were leaving the arena, people continued to cheer, and the crowd in the balcony began dropping flower petals from above so that they rained down softly and landed on his tuxedo. The guy was surrounded by flowers from head to toe, and the crowd noise was deafening.

Seconds later, we were in the limousine, surrounded only by an eerie silence as we sped to the airport. Frank had a solemn look on his face and was staring out the window. Feeling the mood, I broke the silence and said, "Great audience tonight, huh, Boss?"

"Yeah..." he said, pausing. "Y'know, I think they feel they're seeing me for the last time."

He had read the audience correctly. From my perspective, that had been happening everywhere we went. People were coming out to see him, afraid he wouldn't be coming their way again. I said, "Well, you know, we haven't been in Utah in a long time." And Frank said, "I know." He looked out the window again and was quiet for a while. After a couple of minutes, he said, "They came to say goodbye to me, Tommy."

He knew. Those last days on tour, people were coming to say goodbye and thank you to Frank Sinatra. It was most apparent to me when he would go into his signature rendition of "My Way," which had been written specifically for Frank by the brilliant Paul Anka.

Over the years, the audience always seemed to sigh, somewhat sadly, when he started that song, because it signaled that the show—the shared experience in the presence of a legend—was drawing to a close. "*And now the end is near, and so I face that final curtain...*" By the middle of the song, the melancholy gave way to joy, because the moment was ripe to be enjoyed. "*Through it all, when there was doubt, I ate it up and spit it out...*"

By the end of the song, the audience was on their feet, cheering as he rounded the turn and entered the homestretch, a thoroughbred galloping to the wire. "*The record shows I took the blows...and did it my way....*"

In the later years, that emotional crescendo of each show became more poignant. This was a moment to be savored, something you could boastfully tell your coworkers about the next day, and a treasured memory to be shared with your kids and grandkids for years to come. "*Did I ever tell you that I saw Frank perform for the last time in Salt Lake?*"

There was something about Frank's singing, the impact he had in our lives. We fell in love to his music. We got engaged and married to his music. We got divorced and maybe married again, encouraged by his sentiment, as Frank once sang, "that's life." Most of all, we took chances to his music. We maybe got knocked down as a result, but we always got back up. Our way.

People were coming to say goodbye, all right, but not just to Frank and not just in praise of the mark he'd burned on our hearts. They were coming to bid farewell to the moments of innocence and experience that he chronicled for us in songs that so perfectly mirrored our daily lives. As long as Frank was singing somewhere, we were still young. The thought of him not performing anymore meant that our time was running low as well. Those fans knew that the next morning when they awoke, the sun would still shine. But if you loved Frank Sinatra, the days weren't going to be as warm as they used to be.

35

About seven years into my time as Sinatra's opening act, Frank's only son, Frank Jr., joined us on the road as the conductor for his dad's world-class orchestra. "J. R.," as we called him, had, like his sister Nancy, embraced the gift of his DNA and was an accomplished musician and singer who had worked hard to make his own name for himself. Of course, when you bear the exact name of a legend, that road can be a challenging one.

Perhaps as a result, Frank and Frank Jr. didn't have the kind of father-son relationship you might expect. J. R. loved his dad so much and respected his talent greatly. I know Frank was quietly proud of J. R. and fully aware of the predicament his shadow created for his name-sake. Still, in public, they didn't seem like they had a warm, embracing relationship. J. R. acted tough sometimes, but in my opinion, he was not. There was something distant about him, a certain loneliness.

It was a strange relationship, and I always kind of felt bad for the kid, who happened to be brilliant in many ways, about many things. If you asked J. R. what time it was, he'd tell you how the watch was built. One time, we were on the plane for an overnight flight, and I said, "These seats are really comfortable..." Before I knew it, we were talking about how the bolts were beveled on the wings. He was just a brilliant guy and, therefore, a very competent choice as the leader of the musicians who played for his father on the nightly musical journey. He took a great deal of pride in selecting the show songs to present to his dad before each performance.

I really liked J. R., and we established a good relationship of our own, built on many memorable moments. Perhaps the funniest was a night onstage at the Sands Hotel in Atlantic City, when I was overcome with an urge to have a little fun with Frank as he took the stage.

I was about to walk out onstage when a stagehand said, "Mr. Dreesen, could I have a picture with you before you go out?" I agreed, and we took the picture. Then I asked him mischievously, "Hey, can I borrow your camera?" He handed it over, and I took it out onstage with me, keeping it in my jacket pocket. I did my set, and as I was closing, I was just goofing with the audience and said, "You're such a great audience. I don't want to sound patronizing, but you're probably the best audience I've ever had in my whole career. I've never seen an audience this wonderful! I don't want to forget this.... Do you mind if I get a picture of you?"

The audience began applauding, and I took the little tiny camera out of my pocket and snapped a picture of the huge crowd. Looking through the lens, I joked, "Wait. Can you get in a little bit closer?"

I snapped another picture, did my closing joke, and then started to walk off. Per our nightly routine, Frank crisscrossed me as he took the stage to begin his show. Instead of continuing past him and walking offstage, I pranced straight up to him while J. R. had the orchestra vamping, waiting for Frank to sail into his opening number. Frank's eyes got as big as a couple of Frisbees. He looked at me and said, "What are you doing?" He was surprised, because usually I'd take a quick bow and be gone.

I said, "Can I ask you a favor?"

"You want a favor? Right now?"

"Yeah, can I get a picture?"

I had the camera in my hand, and Frank, turning to acknowledge the audience, said, "Look at this guy. I'm trying to start my show and he wants a picture."

Relenting to my shenanigans, Frank said, "All right." I handed him the camera and said, "Get a picture of me and Frank Junior, will you?"

And I went over and put my arms around Frank Jr. The audience was roaring. Now J. R. rarely smiled and was completely focused during a show. But in that moment, he had the biggest grin on his face, and under his breath he said to me, "He's gonna fucking kill you...."

Frank took the picture, which still hangs on my office wall.

Any other comedian probably would have been fired right after the show, but twelve years in, that was the kind of relationship I had developed with Frank, and it provided one of my favorite memories of my time with his son too.

* * *

As the years progressed and Frank continued to slow, things got to the point where the teleprompters didn't help much. He began regularly forgetting his lyrics, even though they were right in front of him.

One night, we were working in front of another sold-out crowd at The Mark auditorium in the Quad Cities, southwest of Chicago. I told Frank during intermission what a good audience we had that night. Frank went out and did his first three songs flawlessly. However, as he got into to his fourth number, "For Once in My Life," something happened. He totally blanked on the lyrics. The orchestra kept playing, but Frank just stood there. After a few long seconds, he gazed out and whispered into the microphone, "I'm sorry. I'm so sorry."

Finally, the orchestra realized that Frank wasn't singing, and they began to wind down, one instrument at a time until an eerie and unnatural silence covered the auditorium. Frank whispered again into the microphone, "I'm so sorry."

I started walking toward the stage, thinking, "Okay. This is it. He's gonna say, 'Good night, folks,' and we're going home." Suddenly, way up in the top balcony, a guy stood up and yelled as loud as he could, "That's all right, Frank! We love you, Frank!" And he started to applaud, just this one man. And then a second person joined in, then a third, and the applause rippled like a building wave until the whole auditorium was standing and applauding and cheering.

Frank turned his back to the crowd and walked to the piano, and I thought he was going to set the microphone down. He paused for a second, then turned around and went back to the center of the stage. Frank waited until the audience lowered their applause and sat back down. The band fired up as loud as I've ever heard, and Frank went straight into his upbeat rendition of "Come Rain or Come Shine." He hit every note and found every nuance in the lyrics. He simply drilled that song.

When he finished, the audience rose again and cheered for five minutes straight. It was a remarkable thing to witness. Frank finally got the crowd quiet, and just before going into his next song, he stopped and pointed up to the top balcony, his right arm extending so far that his cuff link escaped out of his tuxedo sleeve and caught the glare of the stage lights, casting a bright reflection across the people in the front row. In a strong, booming voice, Frank said, "I love you, too, pal."

Frank continued to perform for almost a year after that night.

36

Anytime I agreed to be interviewed in print or on TV or radio shows during breaks from the tour, I would often be asked, "When is Frank going to quit?"

I always gave a stock answer: "He's not. He's gonna be in the middle of 'My Way' some night, and just fall over."

My prophecy almost came to pass in Richmond, Virginia, on May 5, 1994. We were appearing in a big arena that was incredibly hot and stuffy on an early summer night. Normally, I don't sweat onstage, but I did on this evening. Frank came out for his show, and from the first song, he began to sweat. But he refused to take off his jacket, because that wasn't his style.

I once asked Frank why we wore tuxedos every night. He said, "Tommy, if we were going to go do a command performance for the Queen of England, would we wear tuxedos?"

"Yeah, I'm sure we would," I said.

"Okay," he said, beginning the lesson. "Well, that guy in Detroit who works in a factory, and his wife who busts her ass as a waitress, they worked all year long to save enough money to come and see our show. They are as much royalty as the Queen of England to us, and we should honor that. Every night is a command performance. That, Tommy, is why we wear tuxedos."

If the sun exploded and came hurtling toward the earth at a million miles an hour, incinerating everything in sight, Frank would probably look up, defiantly button his tuxedo jacket, and squint. That's just how he was during a show.

He had one song to go, "My Way," before closing the show with "New York, New York." I was standing in the wings as I normally did, because we usually bolted out of the place straight into the limo to speed to the jet. Sweat was literally pouring off Frank, and lo and behold, the heat overtook him. He passed out. When he fell, his face went down and hit the foot lights.

A collective gasp went through the arena, and several women screamed. Immediately, I ran out onstage and knelt next to him. Frank Jr. hurried over and stood with us, and a doctor in the audience jumped up on the stage to help. At first, I thought Frank had had a heart attack. However, I'd heard that when someone has a heart attack, their lips turn blue, so I thought it was a good sign that his lips were normal in color.

They finally brought Frank around, and he managed to get off-stage under his own power. The local paramedics arrived backstage and offered an early yet encouraging assessment that he was probably just dehydrated from the heat and lack of water. I went out onstage to deliver a stock explanation that I had planned to do if anything ever happened to Frank. I told the audience that "Mr. Sinatra had the intestinal flu and hadn't been feeling well." I said he had been advised not to go on that night, but that he hadn't wanted to disappoint them. I assured them that he was going to be fine.

Meanwhile, the paramedics wanted to take Frank to the hospital to be fully checked out. Frank didn't want to go, but the EMS personnel said it was required by state law that they take him to the hospital before they could release him. Frank snapped, "Just get me to the airplane."

The EMS guys were begging him to listen, and Hank Cattaneo, Frank Jr., and I convinced him to go, assuring him that once the doctors examined him, we'd head right to the airport. The jet would still be ready.

By this time, there was complete chaos outside of the arena. Paparazzi were everywhere, and Hank and I were running between cars to chase them away so the paramedics could get Frank into the ambulance. When we got to the hospital, we had to do the same thing with the news photographers who had been alerted to our destination. I had a leather jacket emblazoned with yellow lettering that said, "Late Night with David Letterman," and I was swinging it around, using it as a shield to block some of the camera shots. I even shoved a big guy out of the way who had a camera on his shoulder and was trying to get footage of Frank coming out of the ambulance. He kind of got shitty with me, but I screamed, "No pictures!"

Once inside the hospital, three doctors came into Frank's room and began to examine him, running every test in the annals of modern medicine. All this time, Frank was alert and wanted nothing more to get out of there right then. The doctors, well-intentioned, said they wanted him to spend the night. Frank dismissed the suggestion out of hand.

Frank Jr. disagreed and was trying to talk his dad into spending the night too. Frank turned to me and said, "Look at this…. My kid is on the other side." And taking J. R.'s side in the matter, I said, "Well, it probably wouldn't hurt if you spent the night, Mr. S."

Frank exclaimed, "You too? No way. I want out of here."

By now, Frank had his clothes back on and was ready to go. The first doctor said, "Mr. Sinatra, may I talk to you? I'm an internist. We did all the tests, and I can't find anything wrong with you, but I would appreciate it if you would spend the night. It's your call, though."

Frank said, "Thank you, doctor."

The second doctor came up and said, "Mr. Sinatra, I'm a neurologist. We did all the necessary scans, and we can't find anything wrong, but I agree with Doctor Williams and would like you to stay the night."

Again, Frank said, "Thank you, doctor."

Then the third doctor approached Frank and gave this big, long speech about how he had graduated with honors from medical school. He then said to Frank, "My esteemed colleagues have requested that you spend the night, and they've made it your call, but I'm not going to do that. I'm going to *demand* that you spend the night," the doctor pompously continued, "...because if anything happened to the great Frank Sinatra on my watch, I could never forgive myself. Therefore, I say to you, Mr. Sinatra, you will spend the night. I hope you understand."

Frank said, "Is that it, doctor?" The doctor nodded yes.

And Frank said, "Good." Then he looked at us and said, "Let's get the fuck outta here." He hopped off the table, and we left as fast as we'd arrived. We got back into the limousine and bolted for the airport. Aboard the jet, Frank let no time pass before delivering his own personal diagnosis. He asked for a glass of Jack Daniel's and lit up an unfiltered Camel cigarette as the plane zoomed for Palm Springs.

37

Time always wins.

The final performance came in February of 1995 at a black-tie affair during the weekend of his golf tournament for the Barbara Sinatra Children's Center. We were doing the show in the main ballroom of the JW Marriott Desert Springs Resort & Spa in Palm Desert. Frank was supposed to do three songs that night, but instead, he did six. He got five standing ovations. The audience couldn't get enough of him that night, and he apparently felt the same way.

When he came offstage, he looked at me and said, "Don't put away that suitcase, Tommy." Before the benefit, he hadn't performed in the past three months, so I thought maybe he was retired once and for all. When he told me that, I said to myself, "Great! We're going on the road again." Sadly, we never did.

On Frank Sinatra's eighty-second and final birthday, I attended a private celebration at his house along with many other friends. He had been very ill for months, and honestly there were times when he seemed to only be physically present. During dinner, as we sat around his magnificent table, Frank was sitting off to the side and being attended to by Vine, his loyal assistant. Frank Sinatra for decades had electrified audiences by merely walking onstage, and to watch that energy dissipate to the point of being a mere spectator at his own party was startling and sad. The dynamic was awkward. After dinner, the guests continued to make small talk while waiting for the birthday cake.

Someone posed a random question, asking about the best place to live. Gregory Peck responded first and said, "I have a villa in France, and I love it there." Then Robert Wagner answered by saying he owned a home in Aspen, and he and his wife liked it very much. Suddenly, with his head still down, Frank summoned his first substantive words of the evening and said, "The best place to live is where your friends are."

There was stunned silence around the table. The poignancy of Frank's timely remark lingered above the hush of his dinner guests. The greatest performer of all time and the recipient of every award and accolade imaginable had floored us once more with a simple reminder: In the end, the only things that matter in life are the relationships with those you love.

In the following months I would often go over to his house to pay him a visit. I missed being around the guy. One night, he wasn't feeling very well, sitting in a chair in his robe, with a large quilted blanket resting across his lap. He looked a little forlorn and lost in his thoughts.

I found it difficult to see him so ill and feeble and alone. I had been with him for so many social events where, no matter where he was standing, the whole room would eventually gravitate to that place. I always chuckled to myself when I watched senators and congressmen, who frequently spoke to audiences about matters of national and global importance, begin to babble nervously when standing before Frank. The nerves would just take over, and they'd have trouble putting two sentences together.

Sometimes it took nerve just to approach Frank. I remember a big party at the Waldorf Astoria when Joe Piscopo came up and said he really wanted to meet Frank. Joe was nervous because he had been doing imitations of Frank on *Saturday Night Live* for years. He asked,

"Tommy, do you think that Frank would be mad at me because of the routines I do?" I said, "Has he called you?"

"No, I'm serious."

I said, "No, *I'm* serious." And then I told Piscopo this story:

Murray Langston, "the Unknown Comic," did a routine one time about Frank on a show called *Make Me Laugh*, and Frank didn't like the routine because his two granddaughters watched that show. Murray did a joke about Frank building a halfway house for girls who don't want to "go all the way."

Frank's two grandchildren called Frank, and not understanding the joke, they just said, "Grandpa, we heard a funny joke on *Make Me Laugh*, one of our favorite shows, and they mentioned your name." When they repeated the joke, they obviously didn't get it, but it really pissed Frank off.

Frank made some inquiries and got the producer's phone number and then got Murray's number and called him at home. Murray thought it was a joke. When Frank said, "This is Frank Sinatra," Murray said, "Oh, really? Doo-be-doo-be-doo." And he started making all these mocking comments. He said, "Are Dean and Sammy with you, Frank?" and started singing "That's Amore."

Frank got even madder. He hung up and got Milton Berle to call Murray. So Milton called and said, "Murray, do you know who I am?" And Murray said, "Yes, of course, Mr. Berle." Milton said, "Well, Frank just called, and he's very upset over the joke you told about him." Realization dawned, and Murray said, "Oh my God. That really was Frank Sinatra."

My point to Piscopo was that if you haven't heard from Frank, then maybe he isn't mad. This story made Piscopo even more nervous, but I calmed him down by saying, "Don't worry. He hasn't punched a comedian in months."

I walked him across the room, but about halfway there, I turned around and Piscopo was gone. I found him and said, "Joe, c'mon." He said, "Tommy, I lost my nerve." I grabbed him by the wrist and we finally got to Frank and I introduced him. I said, "Frank, this is Joe Piscopo, and he wanted to say hello to you."

Frank said, "Hey, Giuseppe, how ya doin'?" Piscopo broke into a big grin and breathed this huge sigh of relief. We had a nice conversation for a few moments, and Joe walked away on cloud nine. About a week later, he was doing *The Arsenio Hall Show*, and Arsenio said, "You really know Frank Sinatra?" And Joe said, "Yeah, he calls me Giuseppe."

Everyone wanted to be around the great Frank Sinatra, to pay tribute and show reverence. Frank didn't demand that, but for some reason, he commanded that respect.

And now here he was, pale and listless. Finally, after a few hours, it was time for me to go, although I didn't really want to say goodnight to him. I knew Frank was never going to sing again, but I didn't know if Frank himself knew he wasn't ever going to sing again.

"I have to go now, Mr. S."

"Why are you leaving so soon, Tommy?"

"I'm having dinner with my kids tonight," I said.

"Oh, give them my love, Tommy." Then he gave me a kiss on the cheek, and said goodnight.

Then he caught me off guard. "You know I love you, Tommy." I was taken aback, because he had never said that to me. He would always, in a fun sort of way, double up his fist and sock me on the jaw and say, "I love ya, pal." But now he said it with a sadness in his voice. Nervously, I said, "Yeah...yeah...uh, Mr. S...I love you too."

And I felt kind of uneasy with the moment, and as I began to babble, I blurted out, "Hey, get well. We'll go back out on the road again." And the moment I said it, I wished I hadn't.

He put his hand softly on my cheek and said, "You're going to have to go on the road by yourself from now on, Tommy." That's when I knew that Frank Sinatra knew he was never going to sing again.

I nervously said goodnight, thinking maybe I was really saying goodbye. I turned and walked to the door with tears in my eyes. As I got to the front door and went outside, Barbara Sinatra followed me.

She asked, "Are you all right?" I said, "Yes...yes, I'm all right, but that was pretty tough."

She said, "1 know...1 know. Please come and see him more, Tommy. He enjoys your visits."

I got in the car that night and drove back home knowing that Frank Sinatra would never, ever sing again. That might have been the saddest show business news I'd ever heard.

The entertainer Glen Campbell was known for his most famous song, "Rhinestone Cowboy," which talks about what a performer will compromise to achieve his destiny. All of us in show business know that song paints an accurate picture. So many times, we compromise and do the proverbial kissing of someone's ass, just to land a job that we were qualified for in the first place.

One of the many things that I loved about Frank Sinatra was that he kissed no man's ass. And as the song goes, Frank never kneeled to anyone; he took the blows, and boy, did he do things his way.

38

Frank Sinatra died on May 14, 1998.

My life was forever changed the day I met him. The fourteen years I toured with him passed by in a beautiful flash, filled with fun, surprises, exciting performances, and the joys of an unexpected friendship. The day he passed away, once again, I knew my life would never be the same.

The phone was ringing off the hook. I had to bring my manager and my daughters, Amy and Jennifer, to my home to help field the calls from media and friends from all over the country. A friend of mine named Carmine, who was a really tough guy, told me, "I don't want to live in a world without Frank Sinatra. I just don't," and broke down weeping.

That afternoon, I went to Frank's house to pay my respects to his family. Of course, paparazzi had set up outside the house, and it was difficult to navigate the throngs of cameras and news trucks and reporters with microphones. When I got inside, I gave my respects to his family and to Barbara, his wife.

To see his friends, mostly famous stars I had seen on film grieving in fictional roles and now inconsolable in real life, was something to behold. Gregory Peck, Kirk Douglas, Jack Lemmon, Robert Wagner, and one of the funniest guys I had ever met, Larry Gelbart, all had tears in their eyes. We took solace in each other, sharing our favorite memories and speaking in clichés: "At least he's not in pain anymore." "The suffering is over." "He's with Dean and Sammy now." And, "Jilly's looking out for him once again."

When Barbara Sinatra asked me to be a pallbearer, I was deeply moved. I considered it an honor and a privilege. The next day at the Church of the Good Shepherd in Beverly Hills, just before Mass, Barbara said to me, "I want you to be the master of ceremonies too, Tommy. Please get up and say something about Frank and then introduce the other speakers."

My daughter Amy had come with me, and we sat in a pew up front and to the left of the altar. Amy is my first child, and Frank and I had talked on several occasions about what a special moment it was to see your daughter for the first time. We both agreed that you're never quite the same man after that. Frank's firstborn, Nancy, and his second daughter, Tina, were sitting across from us, and I know their hearts were aching.

The church was jammed with about six hundred people, so I went to Cardinal Mahoney and asked him when to go up. He whispered in a solemn voice, "After Communion."

Toward the end of Communion, I moved over to the right side of the church, near the lectern, to be ready because I thought they would motion me up immediately. I kept telling myself, "Be funny. Frank wouldn't want you to be serious or sappy. Don't get up there and be emotional. Just be funny."

I felt like I had to set the tone for the other speakers who would follow: Kirk Douglas, then Gregory Peck, then Robert Wagner, then Frank Sinatra Jr., then Bobby Marx, Barbara's son. "Be funny," I kept telling myself.

When Communion finished, I looked for the priest to motion me up, but he signaled for me to stay put. At that moment, the choir began singing "Ave Maria." It was so beautiful and yet so sad that I had to turn my back to the congregation, because I didn't want to get emotional.

An odd thing about attending the funeral of someone you really love is that your subconscious mind reminds you of all the other funerals you've attended for all the other loved ones in your life. I began having flashbacks to the memorial services for my mother, my father, friends from the military, and my sweet sister Darlene. All of this came flooding into my mind and, of course, how much I loved Frank Sinatra. I didn't want to cry. I remembered that Frank once told me, "Sicilians don't cry in public, they cry alone." When I reminded Frank that I was half-Irish, he said "Yeah, well, the Irish cry when they change bus drivers."

I kept biting my lip and distracting myself by looking around, thinking things like, "Gee, there's a crack up in that wall. They really should patch and paint that. We're in Beverly Hills after all." I did everything I could to concentrate on anything but the sad feelings surfacing in my mind and heart.

When the choir concluded, I once again looked at the priest, and he motioned me to be still. It got so quiet that you could hear the crackling of pews when the congregants shifted.

A moment later, out of the speakers came Frank's voice, singing "Put Your Dreams Away." It was his signature sign-off song on his TV show from years earlier. At that moment, I looked out and watched as Vic Damone burst into tears, as Tony Bennett cried along with Quincy Jones, and as James Darren dropped his head into his hands and sobbed. Throughout the church, tears were flowing. After the song was over, the priest motioned me up. And I thought, "That's right, Tommy. Now come up and be funny."

In my mind, as if in prayer, I said to Frank, "Of all the spots you've put me in, and you put me in plenty—like opening for forty thousand people in Hawaii and performing in front of presidents—this is truly the toughest one ever. And I know you're up there saying, 'Be funny, Tommy. Be funny.'"

When I reached the pulpit, a walk that seemed to last a mile, I looked out at the congregation and said, "I toured with Frank Sinatra for fourteen years all over this country. And whether you toured with

Frank or not, you knew one thing: Frank liked to hang out until the sun came up. And not only that—he expected you to hang out with him until the sun came up. If Frank was awake, he wasn't happy if anyone in the whole world was asleep."

People chuckled at that. Then I said, "I'm sure there are many stories about staying up all night with Frank. I'm sure you all have one. But this one comes to my mind: We flew to Florida for several shows, and we got to our first hotel late. I was going to play golf early in the morning, so I decided to sneak up to my room. When Frank went into the lounge to start his evening, I went straight to my room. I was checking messages on the phone when someone pounded on my door. I opened it and there was this big, young bellhop who was about six foot, five inches tall. He looked like a linebacker for the Chicago Bears.

"He said in a Southern drawl, 'Mr. Dreesen, Mr. Sinatra wants you downstairs in the lounge.' I reached in my pocket, took out a twenty-dollar bill, and dangling the crisp bill in front of him, I said, 'Hey, do me a favor. Tell him you couldn't find me.'

He just laughed and said, 'Mr. Dreesen, Mr. Sinatra gave me a hundred dollars to tell you he wants you downstairs in the lounge.'"

The crowd laughed and applauded, because they understood Frank so well. "Now, with my twenty dollars looking slim, almost begging, I said, 'Couldn't you tell him you couldn't find me?' He moved toward me and said, 'Mr. Sinatra said if you resist, he'll give me another hundred when I physically haul your skinny butt downstairs to the lounge.'"

Now the church filled with laughter, which was good, because it changed the tone. I closed by saying, "My mother had a plaque in her kitchen that said, 'The talent you have is God's gift to you, but what you do with that talent is your gift to God.' Frank Sinatra sang his songs all over the world and raised millions of dollars to build Jewish synagogues, and he wasn't Jewish. He sang his songs and raised millions of dollars to build Protestant orphanages, but he wasn't Protestant. He sang his songs and raised millions of dollars so that thousands of African-American children could go to college, and he wasn't African-American."

I continued, "Now if it's true that your talent is God's gift to you and what you do with it is your gift to God, I know of no one who has done more for his God than Frank Sinatra."

The crowd applauded, and I returned to my seat. The procession of other speakers took their turns, sharing stories of laughter and love with all gathered in memory of one special man, before Cardinal Mahoney finished the service. As we carried the coffin up the aisle, I tried to keep my composure. But then came all the distraught faces: Anthony Quinn, Nancy Reagan, Barbara Sinatra, Nancy Sinatra (Frank's first wife), Mia Farrow (his third wife), and other family and friends, all crying and sobbing, some reaching out to touch his coffin. I could barely control my feelings.

As a little boy, I used to carry my shoeshine box into taverns as Frank Sinatra songs played on the jukebox. Now, here I was, carrying Frank's coffin. It all seemed so surreal.

When they opened those big doors and we stepped outside, there were thousands of people in the streets and helicopters overhead and paparazzi snapping pictures. And suddenly, the people began to applaud and cheer, "We love you, Frank." "God bless you, Frank."

When we set his coffin into the hearse, the full sweep of emotions surrounded me, and I lost it. Tears began to flow freely down my face.

It was over. Frank was gone. I thought about all the years that he and I had flown to places, all the fun we'd had and all the laughs. It was time to reflect and thank him for allowing me to share the stage with him. What an honor.

If the whole world of entertainment rejected me now, it meant nothing. I really didn't care. Frank Sinatra had accepted me, allowing me to perform as his opening act on stages across the country. More than that, he was my friend, my mentor, and my father in so many ways. That's all I'll ever need to know.

39

Frank once told me a funny story about when he and Dean Martin did a charity show at the Beverly Wilshire Hotel. After the show, and after a lot to drink, they were driving in Dean's red sports car through Beverly Hills on their way to Frank's place when a police squad car pulled them over.

Frank, in a calm and instructive way, said to Dean, "Okay, when the cop starts talking to you, just talk to the windshield. Don't talk to him directly, because he's gonna smell the booze on your breath. Talk to the windshield."

The cop got out of the car and tapped Dean's window. Dean rolled the window down, and the cop turned on his flashlight and pointed it in Dean's face. Within one inebriated breath, according to Frank, Dean started singing his song, "Welcome to My World." He just started singing to the cop.

Frank mumbled in a giggle, "Dean, what the hell are you doing?" Dean turned to Frank and said loudly, "Hey, Dag, he hit me with a spotlight! I had to do a number."

Frank said the cop had Dean get out of the car and asked him to walk the painted line on the side of the road. Dean said to the cop, "No, I ain't going to do that...not until you put a net underneath that thing. A man could get hurt if he fell off."

Metaphorically speaking, after Frank passed away, I knew how Dean must have felt in that moment. How do you walk a wobbly line in life without the security of a safety net?

For fourteen years, Frank had been my sole landmark by which to view and understand the world. What started out as a steady job turned into a strong and true friendship that opened my eyes to a new way of life, a new way of living. The private jets to every gig, the motorcades that whisked us to and from venues, the sequestered spaces in restaurants after shows where we'd hang out for hours, staying at his compound five or six times a year, the parade of celebrities, CEOs, and heads of state passing before my eyes. There was a rarified air surrounding all of it that is hard to describe and impossible to forget.

In between tours and during breaks, I had done many solo gigs around the country as a stand-up and emcee, and I had been approached with other offers, from hosting my own talk show to regular parts in television and on screen. I willingly chose not to answer frequent knocks at the door of my career, and as I told my agents and managers years earlier when I first started with Frank, I never regretted that decision.

Now I had no other choice, and that reality stood in stark contrast to my privileged experience behind the curtain with a true, global celebrity. I was a civilian once more, with all that entails. Waiting in long security lines at airports. Flight cancellations and delays. Finding my own transportation to gigs. No longer playing to sold-out venues of twenty thousand or more. And, of course, the void created by knowing that Frank would no longer be striding past me onstage after my set to do his own. The excitement of all that was no more.

More than anything, though, I missed my friend. I longed for the time of just being around him, enjoying the special camaraderie we shared as a couple of streetwise wiseacres—the boy from Harvey, Illinois, who found his way into the glorious world occupied by the boy from Hoboken, New Jersey.

As I write this, Frank has been gone for more than twenty-one years. There's not a day that goes by that I don't think about that man and the impact he had on my life. And wherever I go, people still want to ask me about him. People come up to me in restaurants or after a show and simply say, without needing to mention his name, "Tell me, what was it like?"

Not long ago, I was talking to a married couple in their early thirties, and I mentioned Johnny Carson. They just stared at me, blankly. I said to them, "You know who Johnny Carson was, right?" And the guy said, "Wait. Was he the guy before Leno?" I was flabbergasted, but then I realized that Carson went off the air when they were maybe seven or eight years old. How could they possibly remember?

However, that has never happened when I speak of Frank Sinatra. Different generations may know him for different reasons, but his music lives on and on. A singer of love songs is a singer of love songs, no matter the era. And to this day, Frank's music still speaks to lonely souls and euphoric young lovers, just as it did to their parents and grandparents.

After Frank passed away, my manager called to say that a popular disc jockey from a Latino hip-hop radio station wanted to interview me. I couldn't understand why, so I passed. I figured they'd probably get me on there and bust my chops or something. One night, while I was doing some new material at the Laugh Factory in LA, the disc jockey came to my show and waited for me outside. He came up and introduced himself and said, "I want you to do my morning show, man. I have this great following, and I want to interview you." I was still hesitant. Meanwhile, cars passing by were blowing horns, and people were leaning out of windows waving at this guy. A couple of cars even stopped, and kids hopped out to take pictures with him, so I realized he must be a pretty big deal.

I agreed to do the show a week later. During the interview, the switchboard lit up with young kids between the ages of sixteen and twenty calling in, and they all had questions about Frank Sinatra. After we went to commercial break, I said to the deejay, "I don't get it. This is a hip-hop station. These are young kids talking to me about Frank Sinatra. I didn't think there'd be any interest."

He said, "Oh, man, you don't get it. He was a fucking outlaw, man. He did it *his way*." The young kids not only knew of Frank Sinatra, but they often identified with him. I challenge you to name another singer who has that kind of broad and enduring impact more than twenty years after their death.

* * *

I have always been fortunate to have a strong pipeline of opportunities to appear with other artists or for corporate gigs around the country. After Frank died, I began to book more of these dates to fill the extra time in my schedule. There were still plenty of offers to do my own TV series or appear in movies, but having done some of those things before, I realized that at my core, I am happiest being a stand-up comedian—even with some of the craziness that comes with the territory.

Every comedian has horror stories of dealing with strange fans in random places. I'm willing to bet that none of them have one worse than this. My mom passed away on June 18, 1985. The funeral services were held a few days later in Peotone, Illinois, the town where she lived. As we were leaving the funeral home for the memorial service after the final viewing of the casket, a guy walked up to me carrying an 8x10 manila envelope.

He said, "Mr. Dreesen! I read in the newspaper that your mom passed away. I write jokes, and—"

"What?" I interrupted, shocked, as I watched the coffin with my mother in it being carried past us.

"I write jokes, and I wanted to know if—"

"Are you serious? This is my mom's funeral!"

"I know. I'm sorry for your loss. Are you interested in seeing some of my—"

"No, please, this is not the time," and I walked away.

My brother, Glenn, saw this encounter from afar and assumed it was some fan looking for an autograph. When Glenn confronted me, I lied and dismissed the whole thing, too embarrassed to admit how crass this "fan" really was.

Arriving at the church doors before the memorial service, we paused while the coffin was carried up the center aisle of the church. Out of nowhere, the guy reappeared and approached me again. This time, Glenn overheard his whispered pitch selling me jokes and I could see the blood rushing to Glenn's face. Glenn, as you now know, didn't suffer fools, especially at the funeral of our beloved mother.

I looked the guy straight in the eye and said, "Listen, pal, you better get out of here as fast as you can, or there are going to be two funerals today."

If a professional comedian has had a crazier encounter with a fan, I have yet to hear it.

* * *

Doing stand-up comedy is the joy of joys, and I love the economy of it: I write my material, I produce and rehearse it, I walk out, I do my set—bing, bang, boom, boom, goodnight—and I walk off the stage and get paid. When I'm performing in Vegas or Tahoe, showtime isn't until 8:00 p.m., so I go out and play golf during the day, maybe grab lunch or see friends afterward. Then I go back to my room, relax, maybe get a massage, or take a little nap. Then I get ready for the show. About a quarter to eight, I wander downstairs to the dressing room, put on my tuxedo, go out and do my set, walk off, and I'm done.

If you're doing a movie or television show, you show up on set at 5:00 a.m. They put you in your trailer, and you sit around until you do your scene at 4:30 p.m. It's boring as hell. I've appeared in several TV shows, including Columbo, WKRP in Cincinnati, and *Murder, She Wrote*, and movies like *Spaceballs* and *Trouble with the Curve*. And while those were wonderful experiences, I never felt as at home as

I do when I'm on a stage. A lot of people get into stand-up comedy to leapfrog into doing movies or TV, but I just I like being onstage, making people laugh regardless of age, race, or creed. As a comic, there's no describing the joy you feel when something you've written is met with uproarious laughter. It's the highest of highs.

My wallet might be a lot fatter had I fully explored one of those career forks in the road. I can't tell you how many times I turned down the chance to be the host of game shows created around me and my personality. I always shot them down because I didn't want to be pegged as a game-show host.

How stupid I was. Pat Sajak, the longtime host of *Wheel of Fortune* and a friend, works four days every month and makes $15 million. The rest of the month he does what he pleases. I don't know if Pat likes to play golf like I do, but with that kind of salary, I could buy my own golf course.

But I am perfectly content being a stand-up. That's what I prayed for as a young man just breaking into the business. After the first night I got a laugh onstage with Tim Reid with something I wrote, I went to Ascension Church the next morning, which was a Saturday. There were no services, and the church was empty. I got on my hands and knees and prayed. "God, last night I discovered what I want to do in my life. And if you please, let me make my living as a stand-up comedian, I'll never ask for anything else. I'll do charities. I'll take care of people. I promise I'll give back."

That was in September of 1969. Fifty years later, in September of 2019, I returned to that same church to deliver a sermon on the power of prayer, because mine was answered, and I'm forever grateful. I've also worked hard to keep my end of that promise with the man upstairs.

40

My sister Darlene was in her late twenties when she was diagnosed with multiple sclerosis, or MS. She didn't know what it was—none of us did. Sadly, we all witnessed the wretched horrors of that disease as it began to debilitate the life of our beloved Darlene.

Over the next twenty-four years, but also in what seemed like the blink of an eye, Darlene went from leading a perfectly normal and healthy life to requiring a cane to move around. She eventually transitioned to a walker, then to a wheelchair, and finally became bedridden until the day she died. Throughout most of that downward journey, Darlene exhibited strength and grace and was always very positive—just what you would expect from a faithful, churchgoing girl. I'm not sure how she did it. There were certainly times when she was privately struggling and put on a strong front for her friends and family. There were other times when it was impossible to hide her anguish and the loneliness of her disease.

At this point, I had been in show business for several years and had begun doing some motivational speaking to groups, which I still do today. I was in Chicago performing at the Chicago Theatre with Frank Sinatra, and one afternoon I went to visit Darlene in Posen, Illinois, a small suburb next to Harvey, where she lived with her husband and young son, Michael. Darlene had gotten married prior to being diagnosed with MS. A few years after being diagnosed, she found out she was expecting a baby, and for the entire nine months of pregnancy she didn't have any symptoms of the disease at all. It was very strange.

I entered the house to find Darlene in her wheelchair, slumped over, and it was apparent she couldn't right herself. I helped straighten her up, heartbroken at the plight of my sweet sister. Darlene was a person who never said an unkind word to anybody, so I was surprised when she turned around and said, "Don't you come in here talking to me about positive mental attitude—and don't talk to me about God anymore either."

I didn't know what to say. My silence was interrupted when she said, "You've known me all my life. What did I ever do that God would punish me so severely like this? Come on, Tom, you have all those answers. Tell me what I did. Tell me why God punished me like this."

I was dumbfounded. I finally muttered, "I don't know. I don't know." After a few minutes of unburdening herself, Darlene got silent and then looked at me with tears in her eyes. "Tommy, forgive me. I lost my faith. I lost my faith.... I never should have said that."

"Darlene," I said, "if anybody has a right to lose their faith, you do."

* * *

I went home a few days later, still haunted by the sight of my sister in that condition and my inability to say or do anything to make things better. I was on a morning jog in my neighborhood of Sherman Oaks, thinking about Darlene, when I got an idea: What if I start a charity event for her? What if I run the length of a marathon, and people can make donation pledges for every mile, with all the proceeds going to research into multiple sclerosis?

I had never run more than one mile at a time, and I began training for it right then. I wanted to honor her, because to me, people like Darlene are the real stars of our society—not those with a spotlight on them because they're comedians, or singers, or actors, or athletes. In this day, we call people "champions" when they hit baseballs out of ballparks, or shoot three-pointers on a basketball court, or score touchdowns in one of the thousands of football games every year. Society has miscalculated value in this regard. I have witnessed so many men and women in my life who have MS or other life-altering diseases and still face each day with great courage—going to work, maintaining their responsibilities as a wife or husband, as a mother or father. To me, they are the true champions of our communities. I wanted to honor those who bravely face their undeservedly cruel world every day. So many with a smile on their face, never asking for your sympathy.

I returned to Chicago a few months later and met with leaders of the Jaycees, my old organization, and asked them to sponsor my idea for a charitable run, knowing that if the Jaycees got behind it, this might turn into something even bigger. The Jaycees immediately adopted my idea as one of their projects for the year, and my job was to run two miles in every community in that area where the Jaycees had a presence, towns like Harvey, Markham, Homewood, Chicago Heights, Orland Park, and eight other suburbs. I was going to run two miles with the people of a community, and then get on a bus and go to the next community and run again until I finished the trek through thirteen towns for a total of twenty-six miles. The day would be called "26 Miles for Darlene," and came to be known simply as "Day for Darlene."

I asked some of my celebrity friends to join and run with me for as long as they wanted—a mile, a block, or a few feet—whatever they could do. Their notoriety as public figures would help to raise awareness and attract corporate sponsors. I asked all my friends, including Frankie Avalon, Tony Danza, Betty Thomas, Eddie Marinaro, Smokey Robinson, Frankie Valli, Robert Conrad, Dennis Farina, Connie Stevens, Johnny Dark, and Jimmy Aleck. I asked athletes like Rick Sutcliffe and Mark Grace from the Chicago Cubs and Jim McMahon, Tim Wrightman, Tom Thayer, and Jimbo Covert of the

Chicago Bears. All of them graciously agreed, and the Day for Darlene really came to life.

Each year, I would invite a bunch of new celebrities to join us, and many would accept and run a few miles. Smokey Robinson has the distinction of being the only one who ran all twenty-six miles by my side, and my bond with that man only deepened as a result. My mom once told me a friend is someone who, if you asked him to go a mile for you, he would go two. How good a friend, then, do I have in Smokey?

We'd bring Darlene out for a portion of the race so she could watch celebrities run past, followed by a short program to celebrate her and commemorate the day. One time in Park Forest, Illinois, which is not far from Harvey, we had the Illinois Philharmonic Orchestra there. Darlene was sitting in a special van, because she was in a wheelchair, and they opened the sliding door so she could watch the festivities. What she saw when that door opened was a crowd of thirty thousand people. Smokey Robinson and Frankie Avalon got onstage and led all the celebrities in a song written for Darlene by Frankie's conductor, Keith Droste. The song was called "Don't Give Up."

As they sang to her from the stage, the crowd joined in and began singing the refrain, "*Don't give up...don't give up....*"

I went over to the van and sat with her. And I said, "Do you remember that day you asked, 'Why me?' Well, I still don't know 'why you,' but I know that because of you, thirty thousand people today are out here singing to you, including those stars up on stage."

Darlene, shunning the spotlight as always, said, "Tommy, not because of me. Because of you."

I said, "No, Sis, this is because of all the love you gave me when we were growing up. All those things we learned in church. What you sow, you shall reap and cast your bread. All of that love you gave to me and others is coming back to you."

Later that day, a little boy came up to Darlene's wheelchair and said, "Hey! Are you Darlene?" She said yes. The kid said, "Wow! You're famous. Could I have your autograph?"

I know that Darlene was touched by the innocence of that moment, even though it was too difficult for her to undertake even a simple task like signing her name in the autograph book of a little boy. Once again, if anyone ever deserved to sign an autograph, it was Darlene—and people like her, the true champions among us.

We put on the Day for Darlene every year for almost twenty years and raised millions of dollars for the National Multiple Sclerosis Society. It was clear that awareness of the event had begun to spread.

My good friend Sam DiGiovanni introduced me to a guy named Bob Caffarelli, whose wife, Pat, had MS. Bob told me they were high school sweethearts and had been married for many years, and then one day, she was diagnosed with the disease and was confined to a wheelchair. He told me of their struggles, how he had to spoon-feed her and carry her to the bathroom. Whenever they went out to dinner, he'd go to the ladies' room to explain the situation to the women inside and ask them to leave. Then he'd take his wife inside and care for her. Bob was that kind of a husband. Sam and Bob said they wanted to put on a golf tournament. "We're going to raise as much money as we can for research," Bob told me, "because I want to do something to honor my wife, like you did for your sister Darlene."

I immediately understood the potential, because for years, I had been a loyal participant in golf tournaments around the country that excelled in raising money.

In 1986, Jim Karvellas, a Chicago native and a well-known sports broadcaster for professional teams in Baltimore and New York, came up with the idea of creating an invitation golf tournament for celebrities who have a 10 handicap or below. Jim pitched the concept of the tournament to NBC Sports, and they agreed to broadcast the first tournament, which was to take place in Lake Tahoe. He had a tournament planned, bought, and paid for. Now all he needed was a bunch of celebrity golfers.

A friend of mine from Los Angeles, Mike Page, who worked at William Morris, had heard about the tournament and told me about it, thinking that I might want to try out since I was a 5-handicap golfer at the time. We got ahold of Karvellas, who quickly asked me to play in the tournament before enlisting my help to get other celebrities to join up. I recruited friends like Johnny Bench, Frankie Avalon, Smokey Robinson, Eddie Marinaro, Jim McMahon, and a few others. And Karvellas and I became fast friends as a result.

The tournament in Tahoe was a big success for NBC, and so other tournaments were planned in different cities around the country. Eventually, the regular celebrities decided we wanted to run the show, and several of us split off and formed our own group, called the Celebrity Players Tour. Our concept was slightly different than Karvellas's original idea, in that we focused on corporate hospitality and entertainment. This attracted some big companies to underwrite the tournaments because they wanted to entertain their clients and mingle with a bunch of movie stars and professional athletes who weren't snobs just because they had celebrity status. The response from corporate sponsors was tremendous, and anywhere we traveled, the purse would be between $250,000 and $500,000—real money.

We ended up doing up to twelve cities a year, featuring a rotating cast of more than one hundred that included show business celebrities and sports Hall of Famers like John Elway, Mike Schmidt, Mario Lemieux, Dan Marino, Michael Jordan, Rollie Fingers, Jim McMahon, and many others. Rick Rhoden, a former Major League pitcher and a great golfer, won close to two million dollars in those years.

I was the only comedian on that tour. Most folks didn't mind if they played poorly sometimes—that's golf—but absolutely no one wanted to have a score worse than mine, especially the professional athletes. How embarrassing it would be to get beat by a stand-up comic of all people. And the first thing many of my competitors would do upon completing their rounds would be to go to the scorer's tent to ask my score. Whatever I shot became the "Dreesen Line," and if I shot one or more under their score, they knew to expect a message on their hotel room phone saying, "Hi, this is Tom, and I shot seventy-five today. You didn't." It was all in good fun. This was another "pinch me" time in my life. I never imagined as a little boy that one day I would grow up and have the chance to compete with the greatest athletes of my time. But it happened, and I am privileged to say that I've become friends with many of them.

We were serious golfers on the day of the tournament. But in the days prior, we played pro-am rounds with the heads of corporations and their clients. It was a total schmooze-fest, and we had a lot of fun with them, subscribing to the philosophy that the experience should be more about a chance for corporate clients to hang out with their sports or show business idols.

At the end of the pro-am, we'd host a big dinner where the celebrities sat at tables with the people they'd played with that day. We'd have singers like Smokey Robinson, the Gatlin Brothers, Frankie Avalon, and Alfonso Ribeiro perform, and I would do stand-up comedy and emcee. We'd invite several of the celebrities up to talk about the other amateur players they'd met that day, as if they were all friends.

I'd invite Johnny Bench up and say, "John, who did you play with today?" And Bench would report, "I played with Chris Garrett from Maple Lawn, Maryland; Sean Miles from Washington, DC.; and Eric Terrell from Jersey City, New Jersey—great bunch of guys. Not only can they play golf, they are well-respected accountants in their communities...." And those guys would feel like a million bucks.

The *pièce de résistance* of the evening began at the cocktail party when the NBA Hall of Famer Jerry Lucas, who was also a memory expert and wrote books on the subject, would walk around and introduce himself to all the corporate people and their clients, family, and friends and then ask their names. I would call Jerry up onstage after dinner, and he would say to the audience, "Would all of the people I introduced myself to and asked for your names please stand up." The average audience would be 150 to 200 people, and those anointed would stand up. Jerry would say, "Wonderful. As I call out your name, please be seated." And then he would call out names strictly from memory until all those who had stood returned to their seats. Then everyone stood to give him a standing ovation.

Corporate. Hospitality. Entertainment. You see?

So, when Bob Caffarelli and Sam DiGiovanni pitched me on hosting a golf tournament to raise awareness and support research for MS, I immediately agreed, knowing that we could make a lot of money for the cause. We began to work together on the idea and put on a golf tournament, using a framework like the Celebrity Players Tour.

And then, tragically, Bob Caffarelli passed away. I was heartbroken at the news. So many marriages end in divorce when a spouse is diagnosed with MS because the burden on the other spouse is extremely heavy. But until the day he died, Bob had been a selfless caregiver for his sweet wife, and that was something special. Their daughter, Mary Beth, became the primary caregiver after that; Pat passed away eleven years later.

Our charity golf tournament lived on, however, and every year we gave out the Bob Caffarelli Award to honor a spouse who stayed by their husband or wife's side as they faced the plague of MS. I would always say, "We're bringing up this person because when they took their marriage vows, they meant those vows: For richer, for poorer, in sickness and in health, until death do us part."

One of the first recipients was Walter Bethman, Darlene's husband, who stayed lovingly at Darlene's side until the day she passed on.

41

Any book by Tom Dreesen must include a chapter on my beloved Chicago Cubs. Like most sports fans, at a young age I gravitated toward the teams my older relatives followed, and my dad was a Cubs fan. He used to listen to games on WGN Radio. Sometimes, he would plug in a long extension cord and take the radio to the backyard, where he would spend the afternoon sitting on a cheap folding chair with a can of Schlitz beer in hand. I'd listen with him for a bit, in between running around and playing in the yard or going back inside.

In 1945, the Cubs played the Detroit Tigers in the World Series. I was six years old and remember being in Polizzi's Tavern, listening to the first game on the radio along with a bar full of other hopeful patrons. Before the game started, Uncle Frank had issued a decree to those assembled: "We're all Cubs fans in here today." It was a simple statement with a slight edge to it. We lived on the South Side of Chicago, not far from old Comiskey Park, which was home to the rival White Sox of the American League.

I've always joked that I was a Cubs fan before I realized that I was in enemy territory, surrounded by people who were as passionate about the Sox as I was about my North Side heroes. It didn't matter whether you were in the schoolyard or church or a candy shop, baseball was a serious topic, and the North-South divide was not civil. There were taverns on the South Side of Chicago you didn't go into with a Cubs hat on, unless you wanted a beating.

The word "fan" is derived from the word "fanatic," and being a fan in Chicago was all-consuming. When arriving home from school or work, or walking into a bar, the first thing you would do was ask, "How'd the Cubs do today?"

Sadly, the answer was usually the same, causing the fan to say, "Okay, we'll get 'em tomorrow," a refrain often repeated throughout the season until the last game, when the verbiage would become, "Just wait till next year."

In my stand-up routines on television and in clubs during the '70s, '80s, and '90s, I often made jokes about the Cubs. I'd say, "It's easy being a Dodgers or Yankees fan, because you win a World Series now and then. The last time the Cubs won a World Series was 1908. There were forty-five states in the union, Ronald Reagan wasn't born yet, and Haley's Comet had just gone over Chicago. Haley's Comet has returned, and the Cubs still haven't won a World Series." Or I'd joke, "A fan is not someone who goes to the ballpark when the team is in first place. A fan is somebody that goes to Wrigley Field for the last game in September. The Cubs are a hundred and two games out of first place. And you think they still have a chance. You hear the announcer say things like, 'Will the lady with the lost nine children please claim them. They're beating the Cubs, eleven to nothing.'"

Still, we loved our Lovable Losers, and for those of us from working-class, blue-collar neighborhoods, we felt a special identification with the plight and pluck of the Cubbies. When you live in a city like Chicago, with wind-chill factors that can hit forty degrees below zero, you still battle the freeze and go to work every day, trying as hard as you can to make ends meet, and sometimes you just can't. You just don't win all the time. The Cubs represented a summertime version of ourselves. They were doing the same thing, trying their best, but mostly coming up short, hapless.

Now it wasn't like the White Sox were winning championships. For decades, they too struggled mightily season after season. I once received a hundred bucks from a local sports magazine for the Best Sports Joke of the Year: "All my childhood, I used to go to Mass and pray that the Cubs and the White Sox would merge, so that Chicago would only have one bad team."

Most sports fans consider the Yankees and Red Sox to be the top rivalry in baseball. Those people have never lived in Chicago. The Cubs-White Sox rivalry is as ferocious as they come. Many imagine the Cubs' number-one rivalry is with their National League foes the St. Louis Cardinals, given the geographic proximity of the two cities. If distance is a deciding factor in a rivalry, there is but a thirty-minute local train ride between the iron structure of "new" Comiskey Park and the ivy of Wrigley Field.

On occasion, this deep rivalry seeped into families where there were split allegiances. I grew up with Teddy and Bobby Muzanski. Teddy was a devout White Sox fan, and Bobby was a die-hard Cubs fan. And these two Polish kids would argue and physically fight like warriors over the smallest verbal dig toward their preferred team. This was not typical sibling-rivalry stuff either. The rift between the brothers was so bad that when Teddy got engaged, he refused to invite Bobby to the wedding. Their mother, Mrs. Muzanski, cried for days, begging and pleading with Teddy to reconsider and think of the family, not his silly baseball team. Teddy finally relented, but not without reservations. With that settled, Mrs. Muzanski told him that Bobby should also be in the bridal party, since they were brothers after all. Teddy said no way, adding that Bobby could come to the church if he sat in the last row.

The crying and the gnashing of the teeth resumed until finally, Teddy gave in to his mom and allowed Bobby to stand at his side during the ceremony. As Teddy stood with his groomsmen at the front of the church, just before the bride entered for her walk down the aisle, Bobby reached inside the inner pocket of his rented tuxedo and pulled out a Cubs hat, which he donned and wore throughout the service. Miraculously, Teddy kept his cool and focused on the lifelong vows he was committing to in front of his bride and guests. However, it was only minutes into the reception later that night when one of the greatest melees in wedding reception history broke out among the two Polish guys who shared blood, faith, and family— but not the same baseball team allegiance.

Back in the days when my brother Glenn and I were shining shoes and selling newspapers in Harvey, despite the drudgery, there were a few occasional perks. We'd bring home whatever money we had earned and give it to Mom to help pay for groceries or rent. Sometimes, she would put a nickel or a dime aside into a little cracked cup in the kitchen cupboard, which was allocated for us to occasionally do something fun. When we had saved up a couple of dollars, we'd take the Illinois Central train from Harvey to Randolph Street, and then catch the elevated train (known as the "El") over to Wrigley Field on the North Side.

Bleacher tickets cost fifty cents, and we would grab a couple of hot dogs and maybe share a soda as we watched our beloved Cubbies take the field. After the game, the ushers would offer all the kids a free ticket for a future game if we stuck around and helped clean up all the papers and cups and trash, which we did several times.

I also remember attending several games with the nuns from our school, a small perk for those of us serving as altar boys during the year. I came up with this joke years later: "One game while in the company of our nuns, there were two guys sitting behind us who couldn't see the game over the nuns' habits. One guy said loudly enough so the nuns could hear him, 'I'm going to go to Texas. Only fifteen percent of the population there is Catholic.' And the other guy said, 'Yeah, well, I'm going to go to Oklahoma, only ten percent of the population down there is Catholic.' At which point one of the nuns turned around and said sharply, without irony, 'Why don't you go to hell? There are no Catholics down there.'"

Sitting in the bleachers, watching the game unfold from afar, I couldn't help but spot the young boys lingering around the home-team dugout on the third-base side of the field—the Cubs bat-boys. I always used to think how fun that would be to put on a Cubs uniform and be a batboy, but I always assumed that only rich kids from the North Side had that opportunity—not raggedy little kids with holes in our shoes like Glenn and me.

After I had made a name for myself in show business, I came to know Jim Frey, who was the Cubs' manager during the 1980s. Jim once asked how I became a Cubs fan, since the White Sox played so close to Harvey. I told him the story of how Glenn and I would trek to Wrigley on occasion and how I used to fantasize about being a team batboy. Jim's eyes sparkled through his signature dark glasses, and he said, "Well, maybe we'll make that happen one day."

Sure enough, a few months later, he arranged for me to be a celebrity batboy for the Cubs. I was forty-four years old. The only people possibly older than I on the field were Jim and the umpires. And for the next few seasons, Jim would invite me to be a team batboy during a home stand, and my dream was realized in full color.

I would go to Wrigley Field every morning and be escorted to a locker room close to the players where I would suit up in an official Cubs uniform, before taking the field as the team got ready for the game. This was before Wrigley Field had lights, so every game was a day game. The first time I stepped foot onto Wrigley Field in a Cubs uniform was one of the happiest days of my life.

After taking the field, I'd play catch with one of the players to warm up, then run the bases, hit batting practice, and shag fly balls in the outfield—all the while surrounded by players of the day now considered Cubs legends: Sandberg, Bowa, Durham, Dernier, Matthews, Moreland, Cey, Davis, Dawson, Sutcliffe, Maddux, and Moyer.

Could it get any better than this? I had been on *The Tonight Show* numerous times and toured with the biggest entertainers of the day, but I'm not sure I found more personal joy than my time between the lines of the small stadium that sat in a glorious neighborhood at the intersection of Addison and Sheffield Avenues on the North Side of Chicago.

For a kid who had to sacrifice playing Little League baseball in Harvey to shine shoes for dimes on the dollar, this was quite the payoff. During the games, I would perform the traditional duties of a batboy. I'd grab bats after players had their swings at the plate, take the umpire new baseballs, fetch players' gloves to "pick them up" when they made the last out of the home inning. In between, I spent a lot of time with the team in the home dugout.

A Major League dugout is the ultimate foxhole of professional sports. Like a naval ship, these were close quarters where camaraderie was built and nurtured over the course of a long campaign. In baseball, that means six months and the grueling grind of a 162-game season. Baseball can sometimes be a slow and deliberate game, so there is plenty of time for bonding in a dugout setting. I loved the chance just to share the same space with these guys, and considering my outgoing nature, I quickly struck up friendships with most of the players.

I became buddies with Rick Sutcliffe, the team's ace pitcher who was nicknamed "the Red Baron" for his ginger-colored hair and beard. "Sut" was the ultimate game-day professional. He once told me that Sandy Koufax, the Hall of Fame pitcher for the Los Angeles Dodgers, taught him the importance of a game-day routine. Koufax said, "Look, you want to have fun out there. But on days you pitch, you have one objective, and that is to win. So get in your zone. Make sure all the other players know that." Sutcliffe took that advice to heart.

On days when he was starting, he was not to be approached. Sut began to prepare for a start hours before game time, physically and mentally, from the way he dressed himself to his warm-up routine to how he chewed his gum. During the game, he would also sit alone by himself at a certain spot at the far end of the bench, just to find isolation inside the chaos of a dugout. He was no bullshit, and it showed in his results.

Sut was also the team's ultimate jokester, and as our friendship blossomed, I became the unwitting target of some of his more notable pranks on the days he had nothing better to do than sit around in the dugout.

One game, we were sitting next to each other, and he said, "Tommy, I gotta take a leak, hold this," and handed me a Styrofoam cup as he got up from the bench. When he did, neon orange Gatorade came spewing out of a hole he had punched at the side of the cup where he had his finger covering, and my uniform was soaked. I looked like one of the crazy rug patterns I used to walk across in Hugh Heffner's Playboy Clubs.

To kick the joke, Sutcliffe had told the TV camera operators for WGN what he planned to do. They trained their lenses on the prank at hand so that it was aired live and replayed on the evening news across Chicagoland: Tommy Dreesen, the celebrity batboy, taking a Gatorade bath.

Another time, as I was about to run out between innings to deliver balls to the umpire, Sutcliffe managed to blow a huge bubble-gum bubble and stuck it to the back of my helmet when I was looking the other way. Oblivious, I ran up the dugout steps and out onto the field toward home plate with this big pink bubble bobbing in the wind on my headgear. I saw people in the stands pointing at me and laughing, and I thought, "Hey! They recognize me from *The Tonight Show*!" So I smiled and waved like an asshole as I ran back to the dugout, never knowing the pink bubble was the real star.

There was an umpire in those days named Frank Pulli, a street-tough Italian umpire who was working home plate one game. Sutcliffe said to me, "Tommy, I need your help. When you go out to get the last bat of the inning, tell Pulli that I think he's the best umpire in the National League."

I knew that Sutcliffe liked to employ every tactic to help himself when competing on the field, and since Pulli would be calling balls and strikes during one of Sutcliffe's future starts, it all made sense. We're buttering up an ump, I told myself.

I ran out to get the last bat of the inning, and Pulli was dusting off home plate. As I grabbed the bat, I said, "Hey, Mr. Pulli, Rick Sutcliffe said to tell—"

Pulli cut me off, "I don't give a FUCK what Rick Sutcliffe said, and I don't give a fuck what you have to say. You're the fucking BATBOY. Pick up that fucking BAT and get into the fucking DUGOUT!"

I stood at home plate of the hallowed Wrigley Field, completely mortified in front of forty thousand of Cubs Nation's finest.

As I'm skulking back, praying that the WGN cameras had missed the drama, I realized that Sutcliffe had set me up; Pulli had to be in on the gag. When I got back to the dugout, Sut tried to hide a smirk like he disguised curveballs and said, "Tommy, did you tell him? What did he say?"

I looked at him and deadpanned, "He said, 'You tell the Baron I think he's the best goddamn pitcher in all of Major League Baseball.'" Sutcliffe looked deflated, clearly expecting a different reaction. But there was no way I was going to let Sut know he'd gotten me good.

One day, the *Chicago Tribune* wanted to do a story on me fulfilling my childhood dream of being a batboy, so they sent out a reporter and a photographer early in the morning to watch me chasing fly balls in the outfield, running the bases, and taking batting practice. The Cubs' assistant general manager, John Cox, would often pitch batting practice, and he agreed to throw to me. When Sut heard this, he said, "Let me throw to you, Tommy."

"Okay, Sut," I said, "but do me a favor? Groove them to me so I don't look stupid up there." Sutcliffe agreed and threw some nice pitches down the middle. I made enough contact with a few to knock some ground balls, and then I hit one pitch pretty deep to straight-away center field. I was beyond excited and thought I'd have fun with Sut. I hollered out, "Hey, Sut, if I could hit against you, I might be in the Hall of Fame someday." He looked at me with a sly grin on his bearded face, and I never hit another pitch. He threw fastballs, curveballs, sliders, and God knows what else. I was swinging at air for the next ten minutes. My arms hurt from swinging, and my legs were jelly. Satisfied, Sut walked off the mound and said, "When they induct you in the Hall of Fame, Tommy, can I introduce you?"

* * *

During the homestretch in Chicago when I knew I was going to be a batboy, I'd book evening spots at a comedy club called Zanies, not far from the famed Second City club that produced a parade of future *Saturday Night Live* standouts. By that time in my career, I rarely worked comedy clubs because I was appearing in the big rooms in Vegas, Lake Tahoe, Reno, and Atlantic City. But I would work Zanies while in Chicago, because the Cubs players and their wives would come to the show.

What a joy to know that after watching the Cubs play at Wrigley Field that afternoon, those same players had come to my home field to see me perform. Some of the players, including Sutcliffe, would often stay long after the show, and we'd run around downtown Chicago until the wee hours of the morning—quite a tribute, knowing that they'd be back on the field in a few short hours for another day game of Chicago Cubs baseball.

* * *

I still get a thrill walking into Wrigley. And while I gave up being a celebrity batboy many years ago, the team still invites me out every year to throw out the ceremonial first pitch and sing "Take Me Out to the Ball Game," honoring the legacy of Harry Caray, the revered Cubs radio and TV announcer who led the crowd in singing during the seventh-inning stretch at every home game.

Harry was a Hall of Fame baseball broadcaster, a legendary drinker, and a bon vivant. One night, we were out on Division Street at the Hotsie Totsie bar with a group of Harry's friends. The owner, Gary, locked the doors at 2:00 a.m. and let us stay and drink and tell story after story. Around 4:00 a.m., I came up with a trivia question: Name ten players who hit fifty or more home runs in one season. This was in the '80s, so that was quite an accomplishment at the time. It wasn't until a decade or so later when steroids took hold of many clubhouses and swatting fifty-plus homers a season became commonplace. Harry loved baseball trivia and was a real encyclopedia on the game. He quickly and correctly identified nine of the players, but he couldn't come up with the tenth. He started getting pissed and had had quite a bit to drink by that point. He said, "All right, Dreesen, tell me who it was."

I said, "I don't know. I just heard that there were ten players who did it." Harry lived at the Ambassador East Hotel, which was two blocks away, and he said he had a baseball book at home. "I'll be right back," he said. As soon as he left, I told all the guys in the bar the name of the tenth player: Ralph Kiner. Thirty minutes later, Harry walked into the bar with the book in his hand, and all together we shouted, "RALPH KINER!" Now he was really pissed. Harry came over to me and said, "Dreesen, there are a lot of things I could forgive a man for, but I'll never forgive you for costing me half an hour of quality drinking time."

In February of 1987, Harry had a stroke but recovered well enough in three months to return to work in the broadcasting booth. And it wasn't long until he would hit the bars again on Rush Street.

His wife, Dutchie, would remind Harry that the doctor had said he could have one drink a day. So Harry would have one beer, then one glass of wine, then one Brandy Alexander, then one scotch and soda, and on and on. He died eleven years later, and Chicago lost one of its most colorful and beloved characters. I loved the guy, and so did all of Chicago.

* * *

If you're reading this book, you are unquestionably wise and worldly and therefore aware of the fact that in 2016, after 108 long years, the Chicago Cubs won a thrilling seven-game World Series, beating the Cleveland Indians to reign supreme as champions of the baseball world.

I am still basking in the memories of that moment. Several years on, I am still quick to approach any stranger I see wearing Cubs gear in restaurants or airports or on the streets to say, "Hey, how about that? Isn't it great?" And they all know what I'm talking about and say, "Yeah! World Series Champs!"

I had the opportunity to attend the three World Series games played at Wrigley Field, and I've never been to a sporting event with that level of energy, excitement, and anticipation. For Game Three, the first World Series game played at Wrigley in more than seventy-five years, I took my nephew Kerry Polizzi, and even though the Cubs lost in a nail-biter, it was a memorable experience. For Game Four, I went with my road manager Brandon Goehl, and we witnessed another loss that pushed the Cubs to the brink of another disappointing outcome, now down three games to one in a best-of-seven series. And for Game Five, I went with my good buddy, the talented actor Gary Sinise—just one of a number of celebrities from Chicago who, like me, are lifelong Cubs fans, including Jim Belushi, Eddie Vedder, John Cusack, Vince Vaughn, Bonnie Hunt, Nick Offerman, Jeremy Piven, Joe Mantegna, and, of course, Bill Murray, who was captured on camera with tears of joy streaming down his face in Cleveland around the time Rizzo welcomed the winning out into his oversized mitt. There would be no more "Wait till next year" this time.

As much as I wanted to be in Cleveland to witness the decisive Game Seven, I had a previously scheduled corporate gig in Palm Desert at the JW Marriott hotel—the same hotel where Frank Sinatra performed his last song, "The Best Is Yet to Come."

I've done hundreds of corporate gigs in my career, and one thing I never do is perform during dinner, because it's hard for people to eat and pay attention to a headliner at the same time. That's Show Business 101. And that's especially true if you're a comedian counting on the energy of a room. You are guaranteed to bomb.

When explaining this to event planners, I always tell a made-up story about how I was once required to perform during dinner, and I told a joke that made a lady laugh so hard she choked on her filet mignon and nearly died in front of several hundred well-dressed guests. Then she sued the hotel, and...well, that is not a happy out-come for any corporate gathering.

Once I became an established act, my rule for corporate dates is that I take the stage only when dinner is over, dessert is done, and the waitstaff are out of the room—which ensures I have the audience's full attention.

However, that night of Game Seven, I would have gone on as people were entering the room, before even finding their tables, and I wouldn't have cared if eight people choked to death. I wasn't going to miss this game! Fortunately, the timing for the evening worked out perfectly. I did my set and then raced up to my hotel room and watched the game, never bothering to take off my tux and tie.

When the Cubs clinched hours later, I couldn't speak—and that's saying something for me. My daughter Jennifer immediately called me, and upon hearing me choking up in glee, she said, "Uh, Dad, I'll call you back."

Finally, after all those years of falling short and all the harassment and jokes that you took in good nature, all the disappointment was over. We had finally won the World Series! I used to say that among fandom in baseball, Cubs fans had the lowest suicide rate, because we always thought, "Well, maybe next year," and no one wanted to miss that. After the Cubs won, I joked that my biggest fear was that twenty thousand people would leap off the top of the Tribune Tower the day after the celebratory parade, because there wasn't anything left to live for.

My precious Cubs had finally won it all! I experienced emotions that I can't even describe, but I felt the urge to go visit every grave of every Cubs fan that I had ever known in my lifetime, lay some flow-ers on each one, and say, "We did it, man. We finally did it."

Whether it's for a sports team, a chess club, or a company sales prize, there is nothing better than being a true fanatic.

42

On August 22, 1992, I returned to Harvey, Illinois, and found myself on the same street corner where I once stood in awe of the parade celebrating our hometown hero, Lou Boudreau. Only this time, more than forty-five years later, the City of Harvey was honoring me by renaming 155th Street, "Dreesen Street." To make matters more surreal, the man who introduced me to the cheering crowd was none other than Mr. Lou Boudreau.

Do childhood dreams come true? You bet your ass they do.

The story of my life story can be captured in the combination of two quotes. I believe it was Plato, the ancient Athenian philosopher, who first remarked, "The harder you work, the luckier you get."

I've always been a hard worker. As a kid, selling newspapers in the freezing cold, shining shoes in smoky taverns, or setting pins in a rundown bowling alley was required to help care for myself and for my brothers and sisters. That work ethic carried me through the early days of my career, when luck introduced me to Tim Reid, and we found a true calling chasing our dreams in the world of entertainment. I worked long and hard in Los Angeles at The Comedy Store, down but never out, and I rolled a winning seven when I scored on my first *Tonight Show*. At that moment I realized, gratefully, that I would always be able to find steady gigs—touring with the likes of

Sammy Davis Jr., Smokey Robinson, and so many others. And then, of course, Lady Luck found me again; I hit the Powerball when I was asked to go on tour and open for Frank Sinatra.

My life and career since have been a series of glorious "pinch me" moments, some of which I've shared in this book. I know I am beyond fortunate, but I also know how hard I worked to make myself visible to the fates.

Another philosopher by the name of Yogi Berra once said, "You've got to be very careful if you don't know where you are going, because you might not get there."

For the first twenty-seven years of my life, I had no idea why I was put on this earth. My heartstrings and my everyday reality were pulling in opposite directions, and I was left in the center, alone, directionless, and scared. I had no clue where I was going or how I was going to get there. Once I found my way onto the stage, I found my way in life.

As trite and cliché as it sounds, I never really cared much about being rich or famous. If it happened, it happened. What I really wanted to do in life was to influence others in a positive way, to help lighten the load and encourage people to find a path in pursuit of noble endeavors above all else.

My experience with the Harvey Jaycees, when I started a program to help school kids stay away from drugs, gave me a glimpse of how one person can make a difference. To this day, I meet people who'll say, "You don't remember me, but I was in the eighth grade when you and Tim Reid visited my class, and because of your message, I never turned to drugs."

During my time at The Comedy Store, I think some of the younger comics thought of me as an older brother—someone who'd been around and whom they could ask for advice. I was always flattered when this happened, and it got to the point that I decided to host seminars for aspiring young comedians. I'd share my thoughts on how to write a joke and the structure of delivery, but most of all, I wanted to motivate and encourage them not to give up when things looked bleak—not only in their careers, but in life.

Whenever I hear from those comics today, or from those who left comedy to pursue another career, they'll say, "You'll never know how much you helped me when you gave that seminar." This means more to me than anything. Before every Jaycee's meeting, we would recite the Jaycee Creed, and one line always resonated with me: "Service to humanity is the best work of life." There's no greater feeling than knowing that I helped somebody along the way.

That feeling continues to motivate me to give inspirational talks whenever I can to students, corporate leaders, and aspiring comedians across the country—and even in a couple of prisons. And once, I helped motivate a Texas high school football team to overcome the odds and win a state championship, although it was a long time before I heard the tale, and it wasn't because of an inspirational speech.

In 1977, I did an obscure joke on *The Dean Martin Celebrity Roast* about how tough my neighborhood was, and how we'd say things that other people didn't, like "ahmo." As in, "Ahmo kick your butt." It was a silly joke that got a big laugh.

Thirty-eight years later, I received a letter from a woman named Anita Willey Murack from Harvey, who had moved to Wylie, Texas. She was a teacher at Wylie High School and told me that the school's head football coach, Jerry Shaffer, had seen me tell that joke on the show, which happened to air the week before the Wylie Pirates played in the state championship game against Breckenridge, a heavily favored opponent. He decided that "ahmo" was going to be their battle cry.

The next day at practice, Coach Shaffer informed the team about the spirit of Ahmo: "When we break huddle, it's 'ahmo.' When you line up, I want you to growl at the opponent, 'Ahmo kick your butt.'" Sure enough, Wylie High beat Breckenridge with six seconds left and won the state championship, and "Ahmo" became an attitude for the town of Wylie.

The students started putting "AHMO" posters in their car windows. Stores had "AHMO" stickers above the cash registers. The booster club parents began selling "AHMO" t-shirts and hats. The football team had "AHMO" emblazoned across their jerseys. The band would march and form the letters A-H-M-O as their closing act of their halftime performance. The people in the stands chant, "AHMO...AHMO" throughout the game.

I went to Wylie once for their homecoming game to see AHMO-mania for myself. The principal of the school greeted me as if I'd written the Magna Carta, and when others in town learned that I was the originator of AHMO, they all but genuflected. My point is, never underestimate the reach and power of a silly joke.

In my inspirational remarks I always try to deliver a message of hope, determination, and the power of the mind and personal faith to help achieve or overcome, no matter what life throws at you. I try to tailor material for the specific audience, but it normally touches on four topics: perception, visualization, self-talk, and developing a sense of humor. I elaborate on each of these topics with a passion, citing examples from personal experience, and, of course, I throw in a lot of humor. My goal is to elevate them through motivation or laughter, and my audiences have always been receptive to me and my message standing in front of them.

And then, a day arrived that forced me to look in the mirror and heed my own words.

I started getting an annual colonoscopy in 1993, after my friend Robert Wagner threatened to stop speaking to me if I didn't start getting checked—a must for men over fifty. I love "RJ" and our friendship, so I began accepting the medical invasion of my most personal space every couple of years.

After a routine colonoscopy in June 2013, my doctor found a polyp on my appendix that required surgery to be removed. The procedure went well, but the doctor told me the polyp he removed had stage three cancer on it. As a precaution, he removed three inches of my colon on each side of the polyp. He also recommended six

277

months of chemotherapy as insurance, since there was a 40 percent chance that something microscopic may have slipped through.

This was a lot to absorb. "Chemotherapy" is a scary word, and I wasn't fond of the idea of undergoing treatments, so I asked him, "Doctor Headrick, if you had exactly what I have, would you take chemo?" I looked him dead in the eye to see if he would blink. He didn't blink and gave me a resounding, "Yes."

Now I was really shaken. A 40 percent chance? I love Lady Luck, but I also prefer better odds. I told him I needed some time for consideration and soon flew to Chicago to meet with the head of Oncology at Northwestern University. She reviewed my medical records and gave me a tart conclusion: Chemotherapy. That damned word again.

Around the same time, my buddy Clint Eastwood put me in touch with a top pathologist in New York, who agreed to look at my scans. The advice rang familiar. "Take the chemo," he said. "It's like buying fire insurance for your home. You don't expect a fire, but you want the insurance just in case."

Strike three. I agreed to start chemo treatments—and blessedly, I barely had any problems. I never lost my hair, never missed a show, and never missed a round of golf. Only my immediate family knew of my situation, and that's the way I wanted things. Again, in show business circles, if you say, "Did you hear that Joe Jones has a hangnail?" I guarantee that in two days, the story will morph into, "Joe Jones, the poor bastard, he had both arms amputated."

I received chemo treatments while I continued to perform all over the country with my one-man show, emceeing corporate events and playing golf tournaments like the AT&T Pebble Beach Pro-Am and the Frank Sinatra Celebrity Invitational in Palm Springs. I even flew down to Miami, with an online Universalist Church certificate in hand, to perform the wedding ceremony for my good friend Don Soffer and his wife, Michelle, at the Fontainebleau Hotel. During the reception, I performed with Tony Bennett, and everyone had a wonderful time.

After six months of chemo, insurance policy paid for, I returned to normal life, the only lasting reminder being the annual colonoscopy to make sure nothing had resurfaced. Now for an admission: I was diligent about making those appointments the first two years, but then I got lax and began to take things for granted. Ladies and gentlemen, let me be a lesson here.

Three years passed. I was on the golf course and felt some discomfort in my side. I was trying out a new golf swing, so Dr. Dreesen chalked the pain up to that and ignored it. With the pain lingering a few weeks later, I made an appointment with my family physician, Dr. Wulfsberg, who is funnier than his name suggests. He's a great guy who loves to tell jokes and likes it when I try new material on him. Dr. Wulfsberg checked me out and found nothing but encouraged me to see the doctor who performed my polyp surgery five years prior, Dr. Headrick, who also found nothing of alarm.

A week later, on a sunny Friday afternoon, I was playing golf and still feeling the discomfort on my lower right side. I finished the round and went straight to Dr. Wulfsberg's office, without an appointment. He was done seeing patients for the week, and I could tell he was a little pissed when I just barged in and said, "Doc, I know my body. There's something wrong." This wasn't the new comedy material I normally brought him, so he ordered a CT scan for the following week.

Two days after the scan, while I was driving down Ventura Boulevard in Sherman Oaks, Dr. Wulfsberg called my car phone and said, exactly, "This is the part of my job that I hate." Those are not the words you want to hear from a medical professional.

I immediately pulled over to the side of the road. My cancer had returned, the doctor said, confirming my worst fears. I was beyond shaken, as if Ventura Boulevard represented an agitated fault line, the earthquake splitting my car and swallowing the driver's side into a dark abyss.

I managed to complete the short drive home and made an oncologist appointment for the following Monday. My daughter Amy accompanied me to the oncologist in Beverly Hills. With her by my side, I felt reinvigorated to face whatever the road ahead dictated. My bravery was quashed when, in the exam room, after a few minutes of hushed conversation between two doctors reviewing my scans, the oncologist cleared his throat and told me in full color, "Mr. Dreesen, go home and get your affairs in order."

Only the stricken gasp of my Amy punctured the silence. Through my own emotions, I finally asked, "Doc, are you telling me I'm going to die?"

"Yes," he said.

I absorbed that stark conclusion for a few seconds. "How much time do I have?"

"Only God knows," he said, before sharing that I had an incurable form of appendiceal cancer and peritoneal metastasis.

My mind quickly flashed back to a conversation I'd had with myself when Amy sat by my side at Frank Sinatra's funeral. "If I'm forewarned of my demise," I told myself, "I'm going to accept it with a measure of dignity and not go out whining, 'Woe is me.' If that day comes, I want my behavior to provide my children with some sort of road map if they must face this reality on their own." I'd thought about that moment so many times in the time since Frank's death—and now that moment had arrived.

The doctors were silent, respecting my solitude. Finally, I said, "Doc, you don't know me, but I don't give up easily. I've battled my entire life, and I never threw in the towel without one helluva fight."

"Good," the doctor said, "because you're going to need that mentality." Then he said he'd contact me soon with recommendations for eventual hospice care.

43

Amy and I drove home, absorbing the gut punch of news. I've faced plenty of tough circumstances in life. My playbook has always been to accept the reality of the situation, and then come up with a plan to overcome and move on. However, this was a death sentence. Ironically, other than a little discomfort, I felt terrific. I was walking five miles a day, playing golf, exercising, and lifting light weights four times a week. I was arguably in the best shape of my life.

The first call I made was to my dear friend John Romeo, whom my family and his friends affectionately call "Doctor Romeo." He's not a doctor but a comedy writer who wrote for Jay Leno's *Tonight Show* for twenty-four years. If any of his friends have a health problem, they call him because he either knows or will research the right way to combat it. Call it a strange hobby.

John came to my house immediately, and I told him the grim news. He was comforting, and while he didn't know any specifics about my diagnosis, he promised to get right on it. I also called my nephew Kerry Polizzi, who tried to hold his emotions back but then burst into tears. I had loved this kid since he was a little boy, and he later traveled the country with me. After his Dad died, I made it a point to be there for him, and he rewarded me with a fierce loyalty that I've always treasured. Then I called my road manager and good buddy Brandon, who also took the news hard. The funny thing was, I found myself comforting them by offering all the clichés: *"Hey, I've had a great life!" "I did things I never thought I'd do..." "It ain't over yet...."*

These three guys and I have communicated damn near every day for years about every subject in our lives, good or bad. We truly love one another as buddies do, and I am blessed to have them as my kitchen cabinet. I called these close friends first because I didn't want other friends to know just yet. I needed a plan of action first.

Romeo put together a support group that also included Kerry's wife, Jean, and my daughters, Jennifer and Amy, and, of course, Kerry and Brandon. They began to research my diagnosis and reported back on any new tidbit or possible treatment.

The following day, I called two other guys who have been my friends for more than forty years, David Letterman and Clint Eastwood. Because of their enormous celebrity, I felt they might know someone in the medical profession with information on research being done on my condition anywhere in the world.

David put me in touch with a famous nutritionist, who contacted me right away. He also had Tom Brokaw call me, who related how, after his diagnosis of leukemia six years earlier, his doctor had similarly told him to "go home and get your affairs in order." Brokaw, in his best nightly newscaster voice, told me, "I'm still here and fighting, so don't give up." I really appreciated his call.

Clint connected me to his friend Dr. Jonathan Kurie at MD Anderson in Houston, Texas, the world-renowned cancer research and treatment center. We discussed my scenario, and I sent him my scans. He promised to get back to me.

Meanwhile, my support group had tracked down information about a very complicated procedure combining surgery and hyperthermic intraperitoneal chemotherapy (HIPEC) that had been successful in prolonging the lives of those with my specific diagnosis. There were two doctors in the country most associated with the operation, a doctor in Washington, DC, and Dr. Andrew Lowy in San Diego. HIPEC is also known as "hot chemotherapy," because the chemo drugs are heated before being placed directly in your body. I had heard of hot yoga before but never hot chemo. As I came to learn, there are some benefits of HIPEC over regular chemo, including that you only undergo one long, intense treatment, rather than weeks of multiple treatments.

The following day, Kerry called with the name of Dr. Sam Pappas at Rush University Medical Center in Chicago, who had experience with appendiceal cancer and the HIPEC procedure. Within a week, I was in Chicago for a consultation with Dr. Pappas, who affirmed the situation was serious, but in his very warm manner gave me hope and agreed to take over my case. He said it would require two weeks in the hospital and then up to three weeks in a hotel until I would be strong enough to fly home to Los Angeles and continue to recover full strength. He acknowledged I might need follow-up treatment down the line, given the chance for reoccurrence.

I really appreciated his specificity, but I was floored by his optimism. I was ready to go into the operating room with Dr. Pappas that second, but I wanted to do more research to see if anyone in the world knew of a better procedure. Before we left, Dr. Pappas mentioned a surgeon in San Diego to consider, Andrew Lowy, marking the second time I had heard Dr. Lowy's name.

Soon after returning to LA, I was counseled by doctors at USC to start traditional chemo treatments to hopefully slow and shrink the cancer before a likely operation—which I was still hoping to avoid. I wanted to exhaust all research to know if there might be something out there besides surgery. I also knew chemo was no walk in the park.

The problem was, as anyone who has faced cancer knows, that every day your inbox is loaded with "quack cures," trumpeted by polished quotes like, "Lucy C. from Appleton, Wisconsin, had just days to live, and then she took our product. Two months later, she ran twenty-six miles in the Mojave Desert in 104-degree heat." We want so badly to believe these things built on false hope, but practical people demand actual data. And the data for me pointed to chemo as my best shot.

On September 10, 2018, the day before my seventy-ninth birthday, I started chemo for the second time in my life. I finished on November 26th, and like the first round, I tolerated it well; I didn't lose my hair, never missed a round of golf, and I even started to write this book, unsure if I'd see the final product. More importantly, I never missed a show. My love for stand-up comedy has gotten me through some tough times in my life, and going onstage provided a real escape, keeping me focused on something other than my medical situation. It is a proven scientific fact that laughter is healing. I truly believe that making people laugh was why I was put on this planet, but I'm here to tell you that *hearing* the sound of laughter from an audience has always been the best medicine for me.

After the six chemo treatments, I still had to determine if the HIPEC procedure was truly an option to consider, and I was now convinced that there was no magic cure. I was told by several doctors that the HIPEC procedure would be tough on a guy half my age, but Dr. Lowy came up with a plan of action when I flew to San Diego for a consultation. Dr. Lowy said he wouldn't decide on the HIPEC surgery until he did a laparoscopy, a minimally invasive surgical diagnostic procedure used to examine the organs inside the abdomen. As he explained, "I want to see if you're even a likely candidate for HIPEC, because if I open you up and you're not operable, I don't want to leave you in a weakened condition for whatever time you have left."

We scheduled the laparoscopy for a week later. When I came to in the recovery room, the first words I heard were, "You're operable. We can do this."

Showtime! Dr. Lowy wanted to do the HIPEC on February 6, 2019. I said, "Can we do it two weeks later? I'm supposed to play in the AT&T Pebble Beach Pro-Am and perform for all the volunteers." Dr. Lowy laughed and said, "Well, I wouldn't want you to miss that!" This convinced me Lowy was my kind of doctor. The surgery was scheduled for February 28, 2019.

For the next two months, I kept to my normal busy schedule, with an extra dose of praying for grace and guidance. When I was a little boy attending Catholic school, the nuns taught me that God was the Father and Jesus was his Son. Since my earthly father was all but absent in my life, I used to pray to God and talk to him like a son talks to a father, asking him to show me the way. My faith gave me great comfort in my situation, no matter the outcome. God is good and His love for me overcomes everything—even death, when it comes, as it will for everyone.

I played the AT&T Pebble Beach Pro-Am and had a great time. Then I began to really focus on my surgery. I was ready for it and really wanted to get it done, and I prayed for a good outcome.

My daughter Amy and I drove down to San Diego the night before the surgery. During the three-hour car ride, I told Amy I was very optimistic about the surgery outcome, but nevertheless, I wanted to discuss my funeral arrangements. This was a topic we had rarely talked about. As my oldest child and the executor of my estate, these are the decisions she'd face one day on my behalf, and I wanted to equip her with as much information as possible to lessen that burden. While it was an emotional conversation, I'm glad we had it. My other daughter, Jennifer, drove down the next morning from Huntington Beach. They never left my side—and it's impossible to express my feelings of overwhelming love for them. I also knew I was being lifted in prayer by friends and family. In fact, just before I was placed under anesthesia, I joked with Dr. Lowy that, "There are a lot of people praying for you right now." He smiled and said, "Good. That always helps."

I said a few prayers myself and remembered reading a passage that said no matter the situation, "surely the Lord is in this place. Lord give me awareness of your presence." Just before I went under, the light from the medical lamp lasered three beams down on me like a Trinity. I told myself, "Ah, yes. The Father, Son, and Holy Spirit."

The surgery lasted more than six hours. When I revived from the anesthesia, I saw the sweet, smiling faces of my dear Amy and

Jennifer, who reported that the procedure had gone well. Moments later, Dr. Lowy came in and said, "You're disease-free." Glory be!

I was groggy but filled with such gratitude and respect for this gifted man and his incredible skill. "Thank you, Doc, you saved my life. You're a genius."

Dr. Lowy said, "No, I'm not. I'm stubborn."

Later, I found out that he painstakingly had removed more than two hundred minuscule tumors from my abdominal area. My daughters said that when Dr. Lowy called them into his office after surgery, he was sitting at his desk with his head down, rubbing his temples like he had just gone through a war—because he had. I had been led to this amazing surgeon thanks to the research and referral from family and friends around the country. How blessed I am.

44

After seven days' recovery in the hospital, I was released back into the wild of Southern California facing a long recovery. Through it all, my three kids provided enormous strength and support. Amy would sometimes spend the night, caring for my every need while tending to her own family. Jennifer would come down from Huntington Beach and spend weekends with me. My son, Tommy, checked in on me every day. For the next three months, I slowly returned to normal activities, building my physical strength by walking more and more laps around my condo. Finally, I wanted to venture outside, but Amy wouldn't let me go alone. Much like my sweet sister Darlene, Amy would walk by my side, holding my hand, watching out for me.

I was getting stronger by the day and yearned to get back in front of a crowd. I hadn't performed for over two months—by far the longest stretch without being onstage in my fifty-year career. I was concerned about losing my touch but also didn't want anyone in my industry to know what I was going through. To explain my absence from the scene to my friend Jamie Masada, who owns the Laugh Factory in Hollywood, I had told a white lie that I was going out of the country to shoot a film. When I called Jamie to say I was "back from travel," he booked me for the following Saturday. It was one of those memorable nights where the crowd was having a great time and, as we comedians say, "I crushed it."

On the way home riding a jubilant high, I kept thinking of a passage I read many times in the months prior to my surgery from the book *Jesus Calling*: "I will eventually lead you down the mountain, back into the community with others. Let My Light continue to shine as you walk among people again." And He did. Thank you, Jesus.

I'm still standing—doing shows, playing golf, and staying active—and I wouldn't be here without the guiding lights of my children, my friends, and my extended family who supported me through my health journey. Dr. Lowy is keeping a sharp eye on me with constant check-ups; two years ago, he started a research lab for appendiceal cancer. I've helped to raise money for the lab and will continue to do so for as long as I live. Maybe in my lifetime, God willing, the cure will be found.

I'm sure anyone reading this who has endured the same kind of "wake-up call" will agree that your perception of life changes. If it is possible, I now love my family even more deeply, have a far greater appreciation of my friends, and more than ever, I'm humbled to have the chance to do what I love for my career.

No matter what your profession, we all struggle for years as we try to climb the ladder or make it to the big time. As a performer, I realized later in my career that there is no "big time," it's all just show business. If you're a comedian, you know there is no "funniest"; the only rule in comedy is to be funny. By that measure, I hope you'll agree that I've done all right. I've sure had a lot of fun while trying to be funny for you.

The other thing I thought about on the drive home after my triumphant return to the Laugh Factory was a flashback to Caesars Palace and my first performance opening for Sammy Davis Jr. On top of the world that night as I left that stage to applause and adulation, I retreated to my dressing room and wrote down words that captured my feelings of overcoming the odds and finding my way.

I still feel the same, and I'll leave this stage with a small tribute to you.

As far back as I can remember or shortly thereafter
I loved to hear the sound of laughter
Whether grownups or children, it really didn't matter to me
If I could make people laugh, then I was as happy as can be
You see, when you make people laugh, they get such a lift
My mom once told me, "This is a God-given gift"
She said, "Because you'll get so much love and yet, you're still able
*   to give"*
I knew that I wanted to do this for as long as I live
So, I left my home in Harvey, Illinois
To tour around the country and spread some joy
Success was ahead, I just didn't know how far
Soon I was broke and sleeping in a car
But I worked and I prayed and I planned and I dreamed
There were times I was alone, or so it seemed
I begged for jobs everywhere I could
And I bombed a lot of times, but I started getting good
They laughed in Boston one night, I'm proud to say
Soon they were even laughing out in L.A.
Now, if you're a comedian, and you want America to know
Then you've got to get a spot on the Johnny Carson Show
Well that happened one night, and what a break for me
Soon my name was on Caesars Palace marquee
Well, God's been with me now, and I've gone pretty far
Who knows, maybe one day I'll become a big star
But if I don't, it won't matter at all
Believe me when I tell you, "I've had a ball"
So now I wish for everyone what's happened to me
To find the work that you love, because that's really the key
So, when I die and go to the Hereafter
I'll miss all of you, my friends, but most of all,
I'll miss the sound of your laughter

Thank you. You've been a delightful audience.

Author Acknowledgments

Who do you acknowledge after fifty years of being able to make a living doing something you truly love, stand-up comedy?

I must begin by thanking God. I prayed so much during the struggling years and He always saw me through and never let me down. There are brothers and sisters who always supported me and urged me to keep on keeping on. Certainly, I must thank my comedy partner for six years, Tim Reid. I'm convinced that had I never met Tim, I never would have embarked on this journey. Our team split up, but our friendship remains to this day.

Most of all, I thank my children, Amy, Tommy, and Jennifer, who sat at the dinner table many nights while their dad was out on the road, trying to make it in show business. Like so many comedians, I paid the dues necessary to survive in a business that's tough to break into and even tougher to remain successful in. My children paid dues as well: no money for rent or groceries, no family car, Mom and Dad separating on several occasions, and moving them from Illinois to California while leaving family and friends behind. Still, they never stopped saying, "I love you, Dad." They are my greatest blessing in life, and when I now sit at the dinner table with my children, their spouses and my grandchildren, there is no way to describe my joy.

This book is for my family. God knows how much I love them.

Co-Author Acknowledgments

Darren Grubb would like to thank his wife, Lindsay; their children, Cole and Tiller; his parents, Wemus and Cynthia; and sister Danielle. Johnny Russo would like to thank his fiancé, Christine Kenzie; his parents Jerry & Donna; Aunt Barbra; and his puppy bulldog, Suzie-Q. We also owe a debt of gratitude to our researchers, Beth Rose and Savannah Littlefield, for their assistance in bringing this iconic story to life.